EARLY SPANISH AMERICAN NARRATIVE

by
Naomi
Lindstrom

EARLY SPANISH AMERICAN
NARRATIVE

UNIVERSITY OF TEXAS PRESS
Austin

First edition, 2004

Requests for permission to reproduce material from this
work should be sent to Permissions, University of Texas
Press, P.O. Box 7819, Austin, TX 78713-7819.

♾ The paper used in this book meets the minimum
requirements of ANSI/NISO Z39.48-1992 (R1997)
(Permanence of Paper).

LIBRARY OF CONGRESS
CATALOGING-IN-PUBLICATION DATA
Lindstrom, Naomi, 1950–
    Early Spanish American narrative / by Naomi
Lindstrom. — 1st ed.
        p.   cm.
Includes bibliographical references and index.
    ISBN 0-292-74720-9 (cloth : alk. paper) —
ISBN 0-292-70566-2 (pbk. : alk. paper)
    1. Spanish American fiction—History and criticism.
2. Literature and history—Latin America.   3. National
characteristics, Latin American, in literature.   I. Title.
PQ7082.N7L523   2004
863.009′98—dc22   2003023303

To my family

CONTENTS

ACKNOWLEDGMENTS

Special thanks are due to John S. Brushwood, David William Foster, and Raymond L. Williams for reading this work in manuscript and offering extremely useful suggestions. Thanks, as well, to Nancy LaGreca, for her fine work as a research assistant and her conversation. Finally, I would like to thank Theresa J. May, Assistant Director of the University of Texas Press, for her encouragement and wit over the years. Research for this work was supported by a Faculty Research Assignment and a Liberal Arts Dean's Research Excellence Award from the University of Texas at Austin.

INTRODUCTION AND BACKGROUND

The main purpose of the first part of this introduction will be to delimit the coverage of the present overview of early Spanish American narrative and justify inclusions and exclusions. I will also provide a working definition of what I consider, exclusively for the specific purposes of the present book, to constitute *narrative.* The second part of the introduction offers a highly condensed summary of research on Amerindian writing systems and narrative in what are now the Spanish American countries.

THE FRAMEWORK OF THIS STUDY

The time span covered here is, fundamentally, from the Spanish arrival in the Americas until 1900. While the primary works examined are from this relatively early period, the research about them that I cite is, in great part, quite recent. One motive for writing this book has been to show how early Spanish American literature has been reread and reinterpreted during the late twentieth and early twenty-first centuries. In this sense, an important secondary purpose of the volume, besides following the development of early Spanish American narrative, is to show recent and current tendencies in the criticism of this literature.

A glance at the table of contents will show that the bulk of this survey is devoted to nineteenth-century Spanish American narrative, with the period of the Spanish conquest and colonial rule relatively briefly represented. The reason is that narrative fiction as we currently recognize it did not really develop in the Spanish-speaking Americas until the nineteenth century. The delay is the result of factors, such as Spain's attempts to ban novels in its American colonies, which will be explained in the course of this study. The work generally recognized as the first Spanish American novel, *El Periquillo Sarniento* (*The Itching Parrot*) by José Joaquín Fernández de Lizardi of Mexico, appeared in 1816; the text that is often designated as the first Spanish American short story, "El matadero" (The slaughtering grounds), by the Argentine Esteban Echeverría, was composed in the late 1830s. The production of novels increases slowly during the first part of the nineteenth century, accelerates at mid century, and by the late nineteenth century Spanish American writers are producing unprecedented numbers of works in this genre. Short stories also appear in increasing numbers as the century moves toward its close.

In one sense, the section of this study concerned with colonial-era narrative could be seen as little more than background to the lengthier nineteenth-century portions. Yet it should be kept in mind that not only are many of the colonial texts inherently fascinating, but they have marked the imagination of the novelists and short-story writers who appear from the 1800s onward. Some acquaintance with the texts of the conquest and with colonial Spanish American literature is of great value in understanding the ways in which this literature developed in later times. For example, during the early nineteenth century, the independence movement gained enough strength that most Spanish American countries succeeded in breaking away from Spain; after the wars of independence, intellectuals, including creative writers, struggled to strengthen and define the identity of the new nations. During this period of intense literary nationalism, writers frequently revisited the events of the Spanish conquest and the period of colonization in search of national origins. Writers concerned with nation building leaned especially on images of the mighty Amerindian empires and the destruction that the conquistadors wreaked upon them. Accounts of the conquest and of early interactions between Spaniards and native peoples came into vogue.

The colonial period lasted about three hundred years, counting from the conquests of the Aztec and Incan empires (1519–1521 and 1530s, respectively) to the last great battles of the wars of independence (1824). Needless to say, a great deal of writing occurred during such an extended period, and this overview touches upon only a highly selective sample of colonial narrative. This focus here on prose writing rules out discussion of the narrative poetry that abounded in Spanish America from the mid-1500s well into the nineteenth century. Beyond this obvious exclusion, I have made an effort to single out for consideration texts that have received significant critical attention in recent times. Since such an approach to selection could easily yield a highly canonical set of texts, it has been necessary to go beyond the most often-cited works. In particular, I have drawn attention to narratives composed by colonial subjects who are either Native American chroniclers or *mestizo* historians able to tell the story of the conquest and colonial rule from the perspective of the conquered peoples. While these latter texts are not yet as well known as those by historians representing the Spanish outlook, indigenous and *mestizo* accounts have in recent decades assumed a new importance and galvanized researchers eager to see events from an Amerindian standpoint.

Coverage is limited to narrative texts from what are today the Spanish American countries. For reasons of space, and because it involves a different language, Brazilian literature is not within the scope of this survey. Of writing from the Caribbean, only Puerto Rican, Cuban, and Dominican literature comes in for consideration.

In composing any scholarly work that examines the evolution of literature over time, the author must decide how inclusive a coverage he or she hopes to achieve. At one extreme is the attempt to cover, or at least to name, all literary works and writers that achieved any measure of renown. At the other is the selection of only a few works in order to analyze each in almost exhaustive detail. I have sought to discuss a large enough body of works to provide an illustrative sample of the currents, countercurrents, and tensions that came into play in the development of Spanish American narrative. This choice rules out such possibilities as devoting an entire chapter to the examination of a single work. On the other hand, I have included some relatively extensive discussion of certain works. To allow space for this commentary, it has been necessary to choose only a limited set of texts for closer examination. Selectivity was especially called for in the case of the latter decades of the nineteenth century, when an abundance of novels and short stories appeared in Spanish American countries. When making choices between comprehensive coverage and reserving space for analysis of particular texts, I have leaned more toward the latter option. It is inevitable that some readers will feel disappointment that their favorite novels or short stories were not the ones chosen for a closer look. Readers should keep in mind that, if there had been an attempt to mention every worthy narrative text produced in the second half of the nineteenth century, the latter portions of this overview could have consisted almost purely of names of authors and titles of works, with associated factual information.

In selecting the limited number of texts that could receive closer examination, I made a particular effort to choose works that are currently attracting critical study, especially those that are undergoing reappraisal or rereading as critical perspectives shift. In the present era, critics have turned special attention to texts that reveal their era's concepts of gender, sexuality, race, ethnicity, and social class. The current study follows this tendency, looking especially at aspects of narrative texts that give clues to contemporary social beliefs, whether the prevailing ones or those held by reform-minded progressives.

As is often noted, literary histories have frequently included scant coverage of women writers. I have given greater space to the consideration of female authors than has traditionally been the case. Yet, as part of the effort to avoid the "telephone book" approach to literary history, I have not tried to cram into these pages the many names of women writers who have recently been rediscovered, preferring to focus on a representative few. Another area in which the canon of Spanish American literature has expanded and diversified greatly is the writing produced by Amerindian authors and those of African ancestry and cultural heritage. Again I have discussed a limited number of outstanding examples and referred readers to works offering a more inclusive type of coverage.

The early sections of this overview examine many different types of narrative, including the narrative elements found in letters and reports from the era of the Spanish conquest and campaign of colonization. Gradually, more of the texts discussed are specifically literary in nature. After the wars of independence (1810–1824), the majority of the works considered are novels and short stories. From the mid-nineteenth century onward, one genre, that of the novel, receives greatest attention. These shifts reflect the evolution of Spanish American narrative from its nonliterary origins, through the appearance of modern prose fiction, and on to the great flourishing of the Spanish American novel in the latter part of the nineteenth century. After the Spanish American reading public developed a fascination with novels, this genre became the one in which writers of fiction were most able to make their names. Short stories continued to be composed and published, but only a relatively few writers established their reputations primarily through their work in this genre.

On the whole, this survey follows chronological order. Movements and currents come in for consideration in the order in which they developed in Spanish American writing. Individual texts, though, are not invariably discussed in strictly chronological order. The highest priority has been to comment on particular narrative texts within the discussion of the literary tendency that they best represent. Literary movements last for decades and overlap with one another to a considerable extent. For example, a romantic novel can easily be a later work than a predominantly realistic one, even though romanticism appeared in Spanish American writing earlier than realism. In this case, the late-appearing romantic novel would be characterized together with other works composed in the romantic manner rather than with works of the same date.

A special chronological problem is that of novels and short stories that appeared in print long after they were composed, without undergoing any revisions that would bring them up to date. The general rule here has been to discuss these works together with other similar texts composed during roughly the same period. Again the rationale has been to group together texts that illustrate the progression of a particular literary current.

In composing the final chapter, dedicated to naturalism and *modernismo,* it was necessary to decide whether to discuss certain writers whose careers spanned the nineteenth and twentieth centuries. The criterion used in determining whether to include a given writer was whether that individual made his or her greatest impact before or after 1900. For example, Leopoldo Lugones (Argentina, 1874–1938) emerged in the early 1900s as a master of *modernista* short fiction, and Enrique Larreta (Argentina, 1875–1961) wrote one of the best-known *modernista* novels, the 1908 *La gloria de don Ramiro* (The glory of Don Ramiro); the dates of their most significant works place them outside the scope of this overview. In characterizing naturalism and *modernismo,* I stress to readers that these movements were by no means exhausted by the end of the nineteenth century and that their features appear in many twentieth-century works.

Obviously, the cutoff date of 1900 is an arbitrary one, as indeed is any chronological demarcation. In justification of the use of the century mark to delimit coverage, it may be pointed out that many critical histories of Spanish American literature focus exclusively on the twentieth century. This survey seeks to show the processes that led to twentieth-century Spanish American narrative.

The category *narrative* needs to be delimited for the present study. At the risk of stating the obvious, *narrative* refers to texts that have a plot, that is, that relate a sequence of events. Here, only narrative texts composed in prose will come in for consideration. Narrative poetry abounded during the colonial period and continued to be published throughout the nineteenth century. These narratives in verse belong to the field of poetry and are best studied together with other poetic texts. In a few cases, a narrative poem has played such an important part in the evolution of Spanish American literature that I have mentioned it, not as a topic for analysis, but to make readers aware of its significance.

The narratives examined here all contain at least some features that allow them to be analyzed as one would a literary work. Writing, however, does not need to be predominantly literary in nature to come in for discussion here. As is well known, many nonliterary texts exhibit certain features of literature and can be productively subjected to a modified version of literary analysis. Especially in the section dealing with narrative accounts of the Spanish conquest of the Americas, many texts under discussion were not composed to be read as literature. The authors' use of rhetorical strategies is often complex enough that the resulting texts display some elements of a literary or quasi-literary nature. In addition, some of the early writers, such as Hernán Cortés, the conquistador of the Aztec empire, are presenting a highly skewed and partial version of events. In such cases, the authors' creative ingenuity in manipulating and rearranging the facts makes their work resemble that of writers of imaginative literature.

Certain texts contain sections composed in narrative format and others that present arguments in a nonnarrative form. In these cases, the narrative portion will come in for examination. An example is the "Reply to Sor Philotea" by the seventeenth-century nun, poet, playwright, and scholar Sor Juana Inés de la Cruz. This much-noted document is a highly polished and rhetorically sophisticated open letter. While the segments of this lengthy and wide-ranging letter do not all address the same topic, the common thread among them is the author's spirited response to criticism of her intellectual activities. One portion is an account of her life, and it is this autobiography within the letter that is of interest for this study. Though Sor Juana's fame rests on her baroque poetry, her letter of self-defense has recently been drawing attention at an extraordinary rate, attracting scholars, creative writers, and feminists. Because of the exceptional response to this letter, it comes in for extended discussion here.

While any selection necessarily has an arbitrary element, I hope that my choice of works to discuss here will help show a chronological progression as Spanish American narrative develops and changes over time.

All the creative works cited were originally published in Spanish, but the quoted passages appear in English. In those cases where a good English translation exists, I quote from it and credit it in the endnotes. The translations that are not attributed to any translator are my own.

RESEARCH INTO NATIVE AMERICAN WRITING SYSTEMS
AND NARRATIVE

Relatively few specialists are qualified to study in any detail the narratives composed by members of the ancient Amerindian civilizations. A number of indigenous-authored narratives date from after the Spanish conquest and represent the efforts of a culture to preserve its most important information. These narratives often record the history of a given people, for example, an account of the origins of an ethnic community and the succession of its rulers. As is characteristic of pre-modern thought generally, factual material is not kept separate from myth.

The discussion of the narratives of native peoples leads to the topic of the writing and notational systems utilized by Amerindians, although narrative was often transmitted orally even in cultures that possessed writing. The most thoroughly researched is Maya hieroglyphic writing, which includes several hundred glyphs. Maya writing is a condensed form that, even when in widespread use, could be read only by highly trained individuals. It should be noted that the Mayas were not the only Mesoamerican people to use hieroglyphics.

The Mayas used glyphs from the third century CE through the 1600s, but not always for the same purposes. During the Mayas' classical period (fourth to ninth centuries CE), when they constructed great cities, they often carved glyphs into wood or stone. Today examples of these glyphs remain on free-standing slabs (stelae), lintels, portals, roof combs, and other surfaces of monuments. The inscriptions often contain dates. These dates allowed researchers to begin cracking the code. In the 1820s, Constantine Rafinesque deciphered the numbers. By the end of the nineteenth century, scholars had reconstructed the precise Maya calendar. After the classical period, the Mayas no longer carved glyphs in stone, but inscribed them on codices, pleated strips of fibrous material, of which only a few survived.

Some Maya scribes continued to use hieroglyphics for about two hundred years after the Spanish conquest, together with other systems. In Martín Lienhard's words, in many parts of Spanish America "autochthonous systems of notation held on for a more or less extended period of time before they fell out of use and became extinct."[1] Indeed, Spanish missionaries and administrators at times found it expedient to master them. Lienhard cites cases in which Amerindians used their own writing systems to communicate information to the Spanish.[2] Walter Mignolo cites the Franciscan friar Antonio de Ciudad Real reporting that while before the arrival of the Spanish glyphs were only read by Maya priests and a few nobles, after the conquest "our friars understood them, knew how to read them, and even wrote them."[3]

Lienhard observes that native writing vanished when people no longer remembered how to vocalize the material. In his summary, "Orphans without a voice, the autochthonous writing systems (whether traditional or adapted) no longer made sense, literally. This reason, more than the repression of pre-Hispanic cultures, accounts for the gradual extinction of these traditional practices."[4]

Many other ancient Mesoamerican cultures developed graphic writing; for example, written communication was common throughout the Aztec empire. More researchers now study these other Amerindian graphic systems, although Maya glyphs still receive the greatest attention.

There has been an evolution in researchers' approach to Amerindian writing. One major change is in the type of knowledge that students of indigenous writing systems strive to acquire. To take the example of glyphic studies, it is no longer essentially code-cracking. Researchers also seek to visualize the culture.

In earlier decades observers often thought that, of Amerindian systems, only Maya hieroglyphs, which by the 1950s had been determined to utilize some phonetic representation, constituted true writing. This view disadvantaged Amerindian systems that combined pictographic writing, pictorial illustration, and other elements. Researchers were especially reluctant to count as writing systems that were not inscribed. Now many argue that certain nongraphic practices are writing. The best example is the Andean khipu, a device for recording information via knots in a set of cords. The khipu was important in the administration of the Incan empire. Though they are most clearly recognized as a device for recording quantitative information, khipus contained historical accounts such as the dynastic chronicle of the Incan ruling family.

After the conquest, the Spanish learned to read khipus. Lienhard states that in the years following the conquest, "the traditional instrument of notation (khipu) seems to have served above all the purpose . . . of communicating with the Spanish."[5]

In recent times, researchers have paid increased attention to the narrative capabilities of the khipu. Though surviving khipus have not been deciphered, through indirect evidence scholars have come to see them as more than mnemonic devices. For this research, see *Narrative Threads: Accounting and Recounting in Andean Khipu,* edited by Jeffrey Quilter and Gary Urton (2002).[6]

Today the concept of writing as only alphabetic and hieroglyphic systems is being criticized as Eurocentric. Mignolo argues that hesitancy to recognize other notational systems as writing arises from a concept "according to which true writing is alphabetic writing and it is indistinguishable from the book."[7]

Lienhard reflects the broadened definition of writing: "All the known native societies developed, before Europeans burst onto the scene, some graphic or notational system that suited their concrete needs. They were not, contrary to what [El Inca] Garcilaso [de la Vega] and, more recently, [Claude] Lévi-Strauss insinuated through various anecdotes, societies 'without writing.'"[8] Lienhard includes as writing such systems as khipus, body painting, and drum beats. However writing is defined, clearly Amerindians of what would become the Spanish New World had invented many methods of encoding information.

Given the massive upheaval that the Spanish conquest brought to native cultures, it is not surprising that indigenous narratives composed after the takeover are largely a response to the new situation. Many native communities realized that if they did not set down in writing the information central to their cultures, it would be lost as the members of the groups most fully steeped in oral tradition and mnemonic training died out. In many instances, indigenous peoples had recourse to the Roman alphabet, by now widespread in the areas under Spanish rule, even if the material they were preserving was in a native language. In Lienhard's account:

In Mesoamerica (especially in the central *meseta* of Mexico and the Maya areas), the practice of rescuing the indigenous oral tradition is divided between work carried out in the sphere of colonial power and that done by the indigenous communities themselves to fulfill their own objectives: not to allow collective memory, which was now in such danger, to be lost. In the majority of "autonomous" Indian groups there existed a scribe whose job was to transcribe the memory of the community. Here, the alphabet replaces, as a handier technique for writing down continuous discourse, the complicated hieroglyphic writing of the Mayas. With its phonographic rigor, alphabetic transcription probably meant the "petrification" of the traditions that were preserved in this way.[9]

Another reason for indigenous groups to write or paint narratives was the desire to establish what the community was entitled to. In the postconquest era, Mesoamerican peoples used all representational systems they had at hand: pictographs, glyphs, symbols, alphabet, and illustration. Some of these accounts are petitions and claims addressed by Amerindians to Spaniards. A celebrated example is the Lienzo de Tlaxcala (Tlaxcala Textile), which combines images and text. The purpose of this document is to remind Spanish authorities of the assistance that the native community of Tlaxcala provided to the conquistadors.

Indigenous historians were eager to set down in Roman alphabet — which after the conquest was plainly the writing system most likely to endure in the New World — their version of recent events. Miguel León-Portilla and Angel María Garibay increased awareness of these accounts when they published a compilation of Amerindian stories of the end of the Aztec empire. Entitled in English *The Broken Spears: The Aztec Account of the Conquest of Mexico,* this anthology has been a counterweight to the more widely read versions of the same events promulgated by Spaniards.[10] By the late twentieth century, it had become common for researchers into Spanish histories of the conquest to make reference to indigenous accounts. An example is Beatriz Pastor's *The Armature of Conquest: Spanish Accounts of the Discovery of America, 1492 –1589* (first edition, 1983). Although, as its title indicates, the work is a study of writings by Spanish chroniclers, it compares the assertions made by Spaniards to those of indigenous witnesses to the same events.[11]

Among post-conquest efforts to preserve in writing information essential to native communities was the setting down of the Popol Vuh or sacred book of the Quiché branch of the Maya. This important compilation includes an account of the gods' creation of human beings and other divine actions, the origin of the Quiché people and their travels, and the succession of their lordly families. The material existed in some form before the conquest. Between 1554 and 1558 representatives of the Quiché community wrote out the narratives of the Popol Vuh in Quiché Maya, using Roman alphabet. The respected Popol Vuh scholar Dennis Tedlock identifies these scribes as "members of three lordly lineages that had once ruled the Quiché kingdom: the Cauecs, the Greathouses, and the Lord Quichés."[12]

The purpose of writing traditional narratives in alphabetic script was to preserve them for the use of Quiché-speaking Mayas, who were in danger of losing their traditions following the conquest. Over the past three centuries, the Popol Vuh has found its way to a non-Amerindian public. Tedlock explains how this crossover took place: "Between 1701 and 1703, a friar named Francisco Ximénez happened to get a look at this manuscript while he was serving as the parish priest for Chichicastenango [Guatemala]. He made the only surviving copy of the Quiché text of the Popol Vuh and added a Spanish translation."[13] That is to say, the version written out by the Quiché scribe or scribes has been lost, and we now rely on a transcription made by a priest. Father Ximénez's version is in two columns, with his copy of the Quiché-language document on the left and his Spanish translation on the right. Tedlock speculates about what the cleric may have omitted: "The manuscript Ximénez copied . . . may have included a few illustrations and even an occasional hieroglyph, but his version contains nothing but solid columns of alphabetic prose."[14] The manuscript was in Europe for some time but ended up in the Newberry Library in Chicago.

The existing version of the Popol Vuh does not reflect exclusively Maya sources, but controversy rages over the degree of Christian influence. Some researchers view the Popol Vuh as a cultural fusion, while others stress its Mayan character.

These observations on indigenous writing and narrative are intended to make readers aware of these research topics in the hope that they will find occasion to look into them. Nonetheless, the subject of the present overview is Spanish-language narrative, and the next chapter begins with a look at accounts of the arrival of the Spaniards in the Americas and their campaign to claim the land they encountered.

| $\mathcal{N}$ARRATIVE ACCOUNTS
OF THE ENCOUNTER AND CONQUEST

*T*he accounts that Spanish conquistadors, clergy,
and Amerindians composed to tell of the early
years of the conquest, known as *crónicas de Indias* (chronicles of the Indies), today exercise a fascination upon both historians and students of
literature. Apart from their inherent interest, these writings are a point of
reference to which one finds many allusions in literature of later periods.
Christopher Columbus, Admiral of the Ocean Sea (1451?–1506; known
in the Spanish-speaking world as Cristóbal Colón), is in a sense the first
figure in Spanish American writing. While it would seem reasonable to
say that the first examples of Spanish American writing are his work,
there are some issues complicating the attribution of authorship to
Columbus, or at least to Columbus alone. Most probably born in Genoa
into a family of weavers (although alternate accounts of his origins continue to thrive), Columbus learned to write only as an adult. He had little
formal education and grew up speaking the Ligurian dialect, which
would normally exist only in oral form. His Spanish was not that of a native speaker. The gap between Columbus's historical importance and his
shaky grasp of Spanish composition is only one source of the problems
surrounding his writings.

When Columbus's writings came into the possession of others, they
realized that these texts were of considerable significance, yet were not
written the way the recipients would have liked. Here the issue of how
well written Columbus's texts were becomes inextricably entangled with
a second issue: whether he had said exactly what the possessors of his
papers wished he had said. In some cases, the holders of these texts felt
entitled or perhaps compelled to edit and emend them before exposing them to the reading public. (It should be remembered that in the
fifteenth and sixteenth centuries documents were copied by scribes,
who were likely to introduce changes, whether inadvertently or to improve the style.) For example, Columbus's most important single piece
of writing is the ship's log or diary that he maintained to document for

his sovereigns the success of his explorations. Unfortunately, as Margarita Zamora summarizes the situation, "there is no convincing evidence to suggest that anyone since the sixteenth century has seen the complete text of the day-by-day account Columbus himself wrote."[1]

Bartolomé de Las Casas (1474–1566), a Dominican known for his advocacy of the rights of native peoples, used a copy of the diary to produce an abridged, edited, and annotated version. The original has been lost. What researchers of Columbus's diary examine is the abridgement in Las Casas's handwriting. As Zamora reminds readers, "The most complete source we have on the first and third voyages is not a fair copy or even a copy of a copy, but a highly manipulated version of a copy of whatever Columbus may have written."[2] Las Casas's abridgement is supplemented with excerpts from the diary that appear in his *Historia de las Indias* and in a biography of Columbus by the Admiral's son, Ferdinand. In addition to his diaries, Columbus composed other documents, such as dispatches, personal correspondence, and letters that are essentially petitions defending his actions and seeking recompense. As late as 1989, scholars gained access to transcribed letters from Columbus when Antonio Rumeu de Armas published his edition of the rediscovered *Libro Copiador de Cristóbal Colón* (Christopher Columbus's copybook). It is possible that other lost texts by Columbus may come to light.

Some of the documents by or attributed to Columbus overlap considerably with others. The repetition between one text and another is fortunate for scholars, who by comparing versions can in some cases identify what has been excised or added. Even so, the painstaking efforts of researchers have not yet clearly ascertained which texts can reasonably be considered to contain Columbus's own words. In recent times new findings have continued to be published and alter the scholarly outlook upon writings by or attributed to Columbus. Research on the topic is still very active, and scholarly opinion will very likely continue to evolve.

The relation between Las Casas and the diary of Columbus is especially fraught with issues. Las Casas wished to cast Columbus in a favorable light and emphasized that the Admiral's journeys brought Christianity to hitherto pagan peoples. At the same time, this Dominican friar was an opponent of the enslavement of Indians and deplored Columbus's role in establishing this practice. The fact that Las Casas had a polemical axe to grind makes readers approach the currently available version of the diary with even greater suspicion than they already feel toward Columbus, who was constantly eager to defend his project and assert the correctness of his cosmology and calculations.

Needless to say, present-day readers would prefer to have access to Columbus's writing in its original form, however inelegant or incorrect his composition may have been. A considerable amount of research has gone into determining which portions of the writings attributed to Columbus are most likely to offer his actual words. Margarita Zamora's 1993 *Reading Columbus* ably leads readers through the complexities of determining the status of texts attributed to Columbus and reminds them that these documents are very far from being firsthand.

Various contemporary writings are useful supplements to Columbus's texts. For example, on the Admiral's second voyage, other travelers composed letters and dispatches. Not only did Columbus write to his monarchs, as well as to other individuals in court circles, but he also received royal letters, often having to do with the provisions and other entitlements he would receive and what type of information and reporting the king and queen expected from him. Over the years, and with renewed enthusiasm since the 1992 quincentennial of his landing, Columbus has been the object of much research. Information on Columbus has come to light not only through scholarly investigations but also from the enthusiastic amateur efforts of sailors, adventure-seekers, and discovery buffs who have sought to reconstruct the details of Columbus's concepts of world geography, his voyages, and other aspects of his biography. Yet many aspects of the Admiral's life and career remain undetermined. For example, there is no agreement on the exact Caribbean island where Columbus first made landfall, though several islands have been proposed as likely candidates. No one knows for certain whether Columbus ever admitted to himself that instead of discovering a sea route from Europe to Asia, his original goal, he had discovered a vast new land mass. Columbus's origins are another topic of debate; attempts to reveal that he was secretly Jewish have enjoyed a long life. Literary critics tend to be less concerned with specifying Columbus's route, the dimensions of his ships, the rigging of the sails, his physical appearance, or the location of his remains than with scrutinizing his work to identify his outlook on his mission and on the lands and people he encountered.

Columbus's views on geography and on native peoples contain a fair amount of what might be called wishful thinking. The Admiral was a visionary with his mind trained on carrying out a specific mission. He was also an entrepreneur specializing in seafaring ventures, and he had to portray his proposed project in the best possible light. At the end of the fifteenth century, there was a general drive to develop a sea route from Europe to Asia in order to maintain the supply of such items as spices, then needed to preserve food. With overland access to the East blocked by the Ottomans, many Europeans planned routes around Africa. Columbus devised a proposal to reach Asia by sailing westward from Europe, based in part on miscalculations that made the journey seem much shorter than it was. Needless to say, Columbus was also leaving out of account the existence of the then-unknown American continents. Basing his ideas partly on the book of 2 Esdras, 6:42, in which the biblical prophet states that the earth is six-sevenths dry land, Columbus constructed a mental model of the planet that included little open sea. (He represents an era in which it was not considered bizarre to draw directly upon biblical texts for factual information.) In his vision of the earth, the Asian land mass wrapped around the planet, reaching well into the Ocean Sea, a unitary body of water between the Orient and Europe. From the Asian mainland there extended many islands, the most important being Japan, some 1,500 miles offshore. All in all, Columbus underestimated the circumference of the planet by about 25 percent, shrank the distance westward from Europe to Asia drastically, and minimized the distance between landing sites. Columbus found some like-minded supporters, such as a mathematician, geographer, and cosmographer from Florence, Paolo Toscanelli. When contacted by Columbus, Toscanelli encouraged him and sent the admiral his own research on the topic. In addition, Columbus was able to cull from his readings statements that could help buttress his arguments. At least part of the Admiral's personal library survived. Examination of his books, which he annotated, shows that he drew considerably upon, among other readings, two works that were circulating in the late fifteenth century, a Latin edition of *The Travels of Marco Polo* and Pierre d'Ailly's *Imago Mundi*. The celebrated account by the Venetian explorer and merchant, who traveled from Europe to Asia in 1271–1295, was at that time an important source of information about the Orient. Published in the 1480s, the *Imago Mundi* was a compilation by a French cardinal who had combed through both theological and geographical sources in an effort to understand the configuration of the earth. As well as poring over these relatively recent works, Columbus discovered passages in the Bible and in writers of classical antiquity to bolster his cosmological scheme.

Though many contemporaries were reading the same sources as Columbus, on the whole, mainstream fifteenth-century thought about the circumference of the earth and the proportion of land to water was more realistic than the Admiral's vision. Even at the time, he drew criticism for the inaccuracy of his calculations. The oddity of Columbus's original claims, together with his resistance to altering his views in the face of evidence to the contrary, have left later generations to wonder whether Columbus was deluding himself or perhaps practicing deceit. Subsequent readers of Columbus are struck by his wildly erroneous statements about geography and cosmology. A celebrated example is his effort to identify what, in retrospect, seems obviously an island (present-day Cuba) in the Caribbean. In his diary entry for 24 October 1492, written in Cuba, Columbus asserts that he has encountered Japan. On 1 November, apparently noticing that the land does not have the right characteristics for Japan, he changes his analysis and identifies his location as the mainland of China.

At the time Columbus began his explorations, there was a fairly general belief that, if he succeeded in crossing the ocean, he would land in Asia. For example, Columbus's sovereigns, won over by his explanations, had him carry a letter from them to the Great Khan of the Golden Horde, a fabled Oriental ruler. While the new lands were still unknown, it was not extreme to assume that they were the East. More extraordinary than Columbus's early errors is his persistent maintenance of mistaken beliefs even when he had become well oriented in the Caribbean area and had witnessed many phenomena that ran counter to his initial assumptions. In some cases Columbus appears to have placed less stock in firsthand evidence than in the authority of written sources. Pastor tries to reconstruct the Admiral's thinking when he must defend his vision against seemingly contradictory new findings:

The procedure is simple: Columbus is faced with certain unexpected phenomena he cannot ignore, such as the turbulence in the sea caused by the flow of fresh water from the mouth of the Orinoco, the unexpected inhabitability of an area presumed to be largely unfit for human life, the light skin of the natives, the movement of water that appears to be flowing from [the Gulf of] Paria to the Azores. This situation presents him with two possible alternatives: either explore the mouth of the river and the mainland to find out what really is there or resort to some of his literary models for an explanation. He decides on the latter and uses his habitual sources, from the Bible to the *Imago Mundi*, to prove that: (1) the earth is shaped not like a sphere but like a pear or the breast of a woman, (2) the nipple of the breast is in the region of

Paria, and (3) the Terrestrial Paradise is on the nipple, together with the original sources of the Tigris, Euphrates, Ganges, and the Nile. Using the same line of reasoning, he attributes the gentleness of the climate, the kindness of the people, and the lushness of the landscape to the proximity of the mythical garden.[3]

As colonialism has come under fire in recent decades, so has Columbus as the initiator of the Spanish colonization of considerable portions of the Americas. The undeniably Eurocentric Admiral's outlook on the inhabitants of the lands he visited has particularly disturbed later readers. In the years leading up to the five hundredth anniversary of Columbus's arrival, this historical figure came under especially heavy fire. Since then, scholars have on the whole taken a more relativistic view of Columbus, seeing him as neither a hero nor an utter villain. Beatriz Pastor's chapter on Columbus in her *The Armature of Conquest* (original ed., 1983) exemplifies the critical view of the Admiral. She observes how easily Columbus dismissed the information that the local inhabitants offered the Spaniards, especially when it contradicted his own most cherished concepts of world geography. As Pastor notes, "Columbus at times implies not only that the inhabitants of the New World cannot be understood because they speak languages different from those of Europeans, but they are unintelligible because they do not know how to speak their own languages . . . And the step from questioning the natives' ability to speak their own language to questioning their ability to speak at all is, for Columbus, amazingly short and easy. He says in his first journal that he intends to take some Indians back to Spain with him that they may learn to talk. In his 1494 Memorial to the king and queen, he remarks that the natives need to learn Spanish, but he never calls Spanish 'our language' or 'the Spanish language'; rather, he repeats over and over that the natives must learn 'language,' as if they had none of their own."[4]

Margarita Zamora, in an article published in 1999, reexamines Columbus's statements regarding Amerindian speech. There is no denying that as soon as Columbus encounters natives, he begins asserting that they should be taught to speak, as well as seeming to deny that they possess other basic features of human culture. Zamora observes: "It is indeed tempting to deride Columbus for these observations . . . But if one reads beyond the remark in the entry for 12 October to consider the denial of Arawak speech in Columbian discourse as a question not of communication but of agency, what seems like simply a racist remark grows in complexity and significance."[5] By going through the log, Zamora uncovers evidence not only that Columbus was aware of local languages but that the Amerindians were able to exercise considerable agency in their dealings with the new arrivals.[6]

Columbus's mind is riveted on claiming lands and predicting a rosy future for Spain's imperial ventures. Some of his assertions about Amerindian cultures make sense only in light of this concern. An example is his outlook on local religions. Pastor cites as an example of Columbus's ethnocentric vision his statement that the indigenous communities were good prospects for conversion because of "their lack of religion."[7] One can find several such statements in the log. Columbus says of the inhabitants of the Caribbean, whom he has just encountered and whose language he does not know: "I think they can easily be made Christians, for they seem to have no religion" (entry of 12 October 1492),[8] although two days later he claims to have heard them "shouting and praising God."[9] On 11 November he states, "I see and know that these people have no religion,"[10] and on 27 November, ". . . one will labor to make all these people Christian, since it can easily be done. They have no sect nor are they idolaters."[11] In none of these cases is he offering an ethnographic account. Rather, each time he is arguing that the natives do not possess any religion that would pose a serious obstacle to an evangelical campaign, whose easy success he is predicting. He was accustomed to the situation in the Mediterranean. There Christianity had made arduous headway by wresting believers and sometimes land away from entrenched rival faiths, Islam and Judaism. Columbus, with his customary wishful thinking, was foretelling that the spread of Christianity would be simpler in the new lands, an untouched pagan realm beyond the grip of these well-recognized systems. Roman Catholicism was the only religion allowed in Spain, and as a representative of King Ferdinand and Queen Isabella, known as the Catholic Monarchs, Columbus was required to regard all non-Christians as either obdurate infidels spurning the true faith or else heathens not yet exposed to the Word.

Whatever Columbus may have meant in 1492 by "no sect," he cannot be said to have persistently overlooked native beliefs and practices. As Martín Lienhard summarizes it, "Toward the end of the fifteenth century, Admiral Columbus charged the Catalonian Ramón Pané, a 'poor hermit of the Order of St. Jerome,' with the writing of a treatise on the 'beliefs and idolatries' of the Taíno Indians of Hispaniola."[12] In Columbus's view, the only reason for obtaining information on native beliefs is to expedite the implantation of Christianity among these new Spanish subjects. The Admiral could see the point of Spaniards acquiring strictly a working knowledge of native languages, beliefs, and social organization.

More worrisome than Columbus's faulty appreciation of indigenous language and religion is his eagerness to enslave the native peoples. While later readers are often uncertain how to interpret Columbus's statements, his desire to put the natives to work is unambiguous. Indeed, in his journal entry for 12 October 1492, Columbus is already observing of the inhabitants of the just-sighted islands, "They ought to make good and skilled servants, for they repeat very quickly whatever we say to them."[13] In the entry for 14 October, he offers to send the king and queen captives who could carry out orders of all types. While the captives that Columbus offered to the monarchs would clearly have been gifts, he also embraced the concept that the local people and their work could be sold. There is no doubt that he intended to use the peoples he encountered as forced laborers, both in Europe and in the Americas. He brought seven indigenous captives to court along with parrots, spices, gold, and other trophies that he had acquired on his first voyage, hoping to make a convincing display of the wealth that would come from the lands he had claimed for Spain. (There were numerous precedents for bringing captives back from voyages outside Europe.) As Columbus's original mission of discovery evolved into a program of settlement, the practice of forcing native peoples to perform labor for Spaniards became common. Columbus and his brothers Bartholomew and Diego were all eager to put the indigenous people to work in the Caribbean as well as sending them to Spain. There was enthusiasm for the idea that the original inhabitants of the islands could reveal the location of gold and then extract it.

The use of native peoples as forced labor had already begun to pose legal and ethical problems in the Spanish colonies. Although slavery was still legal under certain circumstances, the practice made a number of contemporary observers uneasy, leading to considerable discussion. Soon there were several ways of looking at the relation between colonization and slavery. At the time of Columbus's journeys, Spaniards were not allowed by law to enslave fellow subjects of the Spanish crown. However, enemies of Spain who became prisoners of war could be used as slave labor. This distinction might be applied to the Indians: if they accepted Spanish Christian rule, they became subjects, and if they resisted, they were enemies. The concept of a just war was at times invoked as a rationale for violence against Amerindians. Juan Ginés de Sepúlveda, a philosopher most clearly remembered for his arguments in favor of the conquest, developed a just-war rationale in his 1547 *Tratado sobre las justas causas de la guerra contra los indios* (Treatise on the just causes of the war against the Indians). This line of argument could be adapted to support various types of aggression against the existing population, up to and including their enslavement. Columbus approached the problem from a less legalistic perspective when he argued that captive Indians, under direct Spanish supervision, would quickly become Christians. A similar argument was that Indians should be deprived of their liberty if they were exercising it to commit sodomy or practice cannibalism, demonic rites, or witchcraft. In addition, de facto slavery occurred through the system known as the *encomienda*. The *encomienda* was a land grant, often to someone who had served well in the conquest. The people who had been living on these holdings were in effect given away as well, with the idea that the *encomendero* would convert the inhabitants to Christianity. The situation of the Indians on these lands was legally analogous to that of European and Russian serfs, who were adscript to the soil and therefore had to obey the lord of the estate. However, while European or Russian landowners generally held fellow Christians of similar ethnicity in thrall, in the New World colonies the *encomenderos* were distanced from their workers by their Caucasian ancestry and Christian upbringing.

The manner in which Columbus referred to native peoples is not merely considered incorrect in the present era, in which slavery is generally banned. In the sixteenth century, Columbus's editor Fray Bartolomé de Las Casas was already made uncomfortable by the ways in which the Admiral spoke of native peoples. In a turn of phrase that has since made many readers wince, when giving a count of the number of indigenous women captives taken on board, Columbus says that "they brought seven head of women" (entry for 12 November 1492). Zamora notes that, while Fray Bartolomé nearly copies Columbus's diary entry as a quotation in the friar's *History of the Indies*, "noteworthy is the excision from this passage, otherwise a close paraphrase of the diary, of the offensive term *cabezas* (heads, as of livestock), which Columbus used to refer to the women captives. It would seem that some of the Admiral's words were so offensive to Las Casas that his criticism of them could take no form other than tacit suppression."[14] More recent readers are also likely to be disturbed by Columbus's habit of speaking of Indians as if they were chattel or merchandise.[15] Of course, slavery actually does confer on human beings the status of possessions; slaves are, by definition, owned, and can be sold.

Columbus's texts reveal one of the most questionable aspects of the Spanish campaigns in the Americas. Religious fervor and the profit motive are thoroughly commingled in his thought and writing. The Admiral pored over biblical and theological texts, although often he seems to have read them in a single-minded search for support for his beliefs. The more mystical side of Catholicism seems to have fascinated him, especially in the later years of his life when he grew more eccentric. He began compiling a book of prophecies, took to referring to himself as "Christbearer," and added a mystical graphic sign to his signature. At the same time, though, Columbus was an entrepreneur who had to produce, if not an actual profit, at least the confidence that gains would later materialize from his undertakings. The justification for the conquest was formalized in elevated terms, as an effort to spread the true faith and bring infidels under Spanish rule, where they would acquire a European language and cultural knowledge. Yet the desire for personal enrichment, especially in the form of gold, was unmistakably a driving force.

Hernán Cortés (1485–1547), who for his leading role in the conquest of Mexico was made Marquis of the Valley of Oaxaca, is like Columbus in having left his mark on Spanish America and having composed accounts in which his decisions and actions appear in the best light. Also like Columbus, Cortés directed his most important writing to a royal audience. Cortés's often-studied letters, known in Spanish as *Cartas de Relación* and in English as *Letters from Mexico,* are addressed to Emperor Charles V (who was also King Charles I of Spain).

Cortés was a well-educated individual who had pursued legal studies. He wrote proficiently, but of course he was a military commander rather than a writer devoted to cultivating a pleasing style. He is known above all as the leader of a campaign that greatly expanded Spain's overseas possessions. Cortés brought down the Aztec empire, which occupied the central and south-central part of Mexico, by defeating the Aztecs in their elaborately constructed capital, Tenochtitlan. After the fall of Tenochtitlan in 1521, the lands controlled by the Aztecs became part of the Spanish empire. Cortés, who had ordered the destruction of the existing capital, had a Mediterranean-style city built on the site. Essential elements of the old imperial center, including the Templo Mayor (Main Temple), were buried under similarly key features of the new Spanish city in what is now the historical downtown of the Mexican capital. Over the course of the twentieth century, excavations started by construction crews revealed that some elements of Tenochtitlan remained in good enough condition to be useful to archeologists. The most important of these finds resulted in the excavation of considerable portions of the Main Temple, which was the focus of intense archeological scrutiny during the late 1970s and early 1980s.

Cortés is a controversial figure who has often been reviled for the tactics he used in the capture of Tenochtitlan and, even more, for the damage inflicted upon indigenous peoples after Aztec imperial rule was replaced by that of Spain. Although Cortés's invasion of Mexico turned out enormously to Spain's benefit, the expedition began as a rogue operation and only received royal authorization after it was well under way. In October 1518, Diego Velásquez, governor of Cuba, named Cortés as captain of a new foray into the mainland, that is, into what is now Mexico. At the time, Cortés was a rising young figure of leadership in Cuba. It appears that his success in winning support and participants for his expedition worried Velásquez, who sought to relieve the ambitious Cortés of his post. Before he could be replaced, though, Cortés had already embarked, first stopping along the Cuban coast, then sailing for the Yucatan peninsula. Cortés's unauthorized departure and the resulting enmity between him and Velásquez color not only later events but also many of the assertions in his letters.

While Cortés's first letter to the emperor has been lost, other accounts make it possible to reconstruct his activities around the time he left Cuba. Cortés initially took with him some five hundred men, to which he would later add reinforcements. The number five hundred is often cited, rather misleadingly, because of the disparity between the size of the invading army and that of the defending forces. Cortés made a gradual and deliberate approach to central Mexico, starting in the Yucatan peninsula. On the island of Cozumel, he encountered a Spanish cleric living as the sole European in a Maya community. This individual, Jerónimo de Aguilar, who had grown proficient in Maya, became one of the interpreters for the expedition. From the Yucatan, Cortés worked his way along the southeastern coast of Mexico. His account of his actions in his second letter refers back as far as his travels in the Yucatan. One of his goals is to cull from the local native communities information that could prove useful in defeating the Aztecs. The letters relate the hearsay that Cortés acquired about the Aztecs, their wealthy imperial capital, and their relations with their non-Aztec subjects, many of whom chafed under the rule of the tribute-demanding rulers. The Spanish commander expresses particular interest in schisms and tensions within the empire and the existence of communities that the Aztecs have never been able to annex. His plan, which he states plainly in the letters, is to recruit the assistance of both the Aztecs' declared enemies and others who, while apparently vassals of the Aztec emperor, harbor enough resentment to wish for the defeat of the ruling people.

Before marching inland, Cortés spent some time in Tabasco. Among the gifts he received there was a woman of royal lineage who stood out for her abilities as an interpreter and her knowledge of various indigenous peoples. Known variously as Doña Marina, Malintzín, and La Malinche, this displaced princess became Cortés's mistress and was invaluable to him during his conquest of Mexico. The figure of La Malinche has long gripped the popular imagination. In recent decades, motivated by the increased awareness of women's role in history and new concepts of race and nation, scholars and essayists have reexamined her importance. As Sandra Messinger Cypess asserts in her *La Malinche in Mexican Literature: From History to Myth* (1991), this interpreter has become an important point of reference in Mexican literature.[16]

Readers who are aware of La Malinche's crucial role in the success of this campaign will be struck by the meager attention that Cortés accords her in his letters. For example, he refers to her in passing as "my interpreter, who is an Indian woman,"[17] principally to establish that information she supplied justified the destruction that the Spanish wrought in Cholula. If it were not for other accounts of the conquest, both Spanish and indigenous, La Malinche would remain a shadowy participant. Cortés was probably reluctant to admit his dependence on an Amerindian woman, with whom he moreover became sexually involved. But apart from these specifics, a general unwillingness to recognize the contributions of others is a hallmark of Cortés's writing. In some cases he trains attention so exclusively on his own deeds as to give the impression that he has been warring single-handedly against hosts of Aztec warriors: "And so I proceeded through the city [Tenochtitlan] fighting for five hours or more."[18]

Cortés began to gather lore about Quetzalcoatl, a divinity who might also be characterized as a hero. Quetzalcoatl was often said to have left for the east after suffering unjust defeat, and the Aztecs were dreading his imminent return to settle scores and reclaim his rightful place. His arrival was expected to bring about such catastrophes as earthquakes. Apprehension over the coming of this aggrieved deity and the cataclysmic events to accompany it was spreading apocalyptic panic in Tenochtitlan, whose inhabitants were reporting various ominously unnatural events. Quetzalcoatl was expected to return from the east during a particular type of calendar year. The year Cortés appeared on the coast, 1519, was such a year. One of the forms this returning divinity could assume was that of a bearded man with pale coloring, and in this respect as well Cortés appears to have met the criteria.

While on the coast, Cortés founded the city of La Rica Villa de la Vera Cruz, today the Mexican seaport of Veracruz. With the establishment of a city, Cortés's men became the local citizenry and in this capacity formed a municipal council that chose their commander as captain general of their campaign, the leadership post he had hitherto been lacking, as well as chief justice. The town council sent a petition asking the emperor to confirm their appointment. The petition, which was preserved, sometimes appears in editions of Cortés's letters. This editorial practice reflects a widespread suspicion that the commander was heavily involved in drafting it. After his time spent gathering information and organizing his invading army, Cortés set out for Tenochtitlan.

In a much-noted move to prevent defections, Cortés had his ships run aground. This bold step has left a mark on the popular imagination, giving rise to a widespread belief that Cortés had burned his ships, although such a measure is not specifically mentioned. The passage in which Cortés explains his actions is characteristic of his portrayal of his extreme or reckless behavior as perfectly rational. Leaving aside the issue of his destruction of naval property, he emphasizes instead his sangfroid and astute calculations: "Believing, therefore, that if the ships remained there would be a rebellion, and once all those who had resolved to go had gone I would be left almost alone, whereby all that in the name of God and of Your Highness had been accomplished in this land would have been prevented, I devised a plan, according to which I declared the ships unfit to sail and grounded them; thus they lost all hope of escape and I proceeded in greater safety and with no fear that once my back was turned the people I had left in the town would betray me." [19]

Between the Gulf Coast and the capital, Cortés spends time in the indigenous community of Tlaxcala, known for its warfare with the Aztecs. Once their initial resistance was subdued, the people of Tlaxcala made common cause with the Spanish and contributed troops to the assault on their enemies' capital. Cortés then narrates the Spanish encounter with the community of Cholula, and here his evasive strategies are fully on display. Sixteenth-century accounts vary widely as to what happened in Cholula, although all agree that the Spanish destroyed a good deal of the city. Las Casas characterizes the incident as a massacre, as do accounts based on Amerindian sources. Cortés, though, states that he discovered that the Cholulans were planning a sneak attack on the Spanish. He reports that he lured the local chieftains into a room, "left them bound up and rode away,"[20] and then waged a defensive battle.

During the march inland to the imperial capital, Cortés was in communication via messengers with the king of Tenochtitlan and ninth Aztec emperor. This ruler, who lived from 1466 to 1520 and whose original Nahuatl-language name is rendered as Moctezuma II in Spanish and in English as Montezuma II, is one of the most enigmatic figures in Mexican history. He apparently made a decision not to oppose the intruders by force and instead tried to dissuade the Spaniards from their mission of conquest by sending them gifts. Later observers have often tried to reconstruct Moctezuma's thoughts during this time of crisis, at times characterizing him as superstitious or weak. While judgments on Moctezuma vary widely, it is likely that he was understandably hesitant to use military force against an invader to whom divinity was attributed.

The second of Cortés's extant letters narrates his 1519 arrival in the center of Mexico. He approaches the capital and is met by Moctezuma and other members of the ruling family, who host him in lavish style. This letter holds special interest for its description of Tenochtitlan. Although Cortés would eventually have the native capital destroyed to quell the resistance to Spanish rule, he expresses his admiration for its size (later estimated at perhaps 200,000 inhabitants), the ingenuity with which it is constructed, and the Aztecs' evident prosperity. In his description of the city, Cortés manifests little interest in recording the religious and philosophical thought of the Aztecs, the aspect that has especially fascinated later researchers, although he is impressed by the number and magnificence of the temples constructed in Tenochtitlan. Nor can the second letter be said to contain a wealth of ethnographic detail. Consistent with his mission of conquering the city and gaining its treasures, Cortés focuses on items that will be useful in formulating strategy. He notes that Tenochtitlan has been constructed in a salt lake. Access is by means of causeways, which have gaps spanned by removable bridges. Cortés describes the causeways and bridges carefully, noting that if the bridges were not in place, the Spanish could not escape the city. The system of causeways gives the Aztecs an advantage that Cortés begins to counter by constructing brigantines. According to Cortés's account, he realized instantly that the Aztecs could gain the upper hand through their mastery of these intricately constructed foot passages; later events confirmed his astute foresight. In his analysis, the Spanish, coming from a great sea power, would be better equipped to wage war in ships. In line with his mission of taking the capital, his account of his entry into the city includes such features as a "very strong fortification with two towers ringed by a wall four yards wide with merloned battlements all around commanding both causeways."[21]

Cortés's narration of his encounter with Moctezuma has riveted the attention of later readers, who hope to find in it clues to the Aztecs' initial decision to admit the invaders into their capital. In his letter to his monarch, Charles V, Cortés recalls that Moctezuma ushered him into a magnificent room, had both of them sit on elaborate thrones, and explained to him the religious background to the events that were unfolding. In Cortés's recollection, Moctezuma said:

> For a long time we have known from the writings of our ancestors that neither I, nor any of those who dwell in this land, are natives of it, but foreigners who came from very distant parts; and likewise we know that a chieftain, of whom they were all vassals, brought our people to this region. And he returned to his native land and after many years came again, by which time all those who had remained were married to native women and had built villages and raised children. And when he wished to lead them away again they would not go or even admit him as their chief; and so he departed. And we have always held that those who descended from him would come and conquer this land and take us as their vassals. So because of the place from which you claim to come, namely, from where the sun rises, and the things you tell us of the great lord or king who sent you here, we believe and are certain that he is our natural lord, especially as you say that he has known of us for some time. So be assured that we shall obey you and hold you as our lord. . . .[22]

Cortés reassures his monarch that he told Moctezuma that the great lord or king returning to claim the Aztec lands was not the person with whom he was speaking, but the distant Charles V: "I replied to all he said as I thought most fitting, especially in making him believe that Your Majesty was whom they were expecting."[23]

After his formal meeting with the Aztec emperor, Cortés is lodged in one of the many palaces of the ruling family and witnesses at first hand the lavish manner in which the Aztec nobles live. He describes his tour of the emperor's quarters, which include not only palaces but an aviary, a menagerie, and a collection of human freaks. Cortés is especially prolix in his description of the principal marketplace. He has been emphasizing all along the wealth of the Aztecs, and his account of the market, which appears as a gigantic cornucopia, affords him an opportunity to inventory the valuable goods to be had in the New World. Items that the Europeans especially needed or desired, such as precious metals, spices and herbs, and a wide variety of both familiar and novel edibles, figure prominently in the description of the market. Throughout his letters, Cortés continues to characterize himself as acting just as would any right-thinking, cool-headed commander and loyal subject of the king. His unemphatic manner is evident in his justification of his unprovoked imprisonment of Moctezuma, who had been showing him such magnanimity. While later readers may well perceive Cortés as an ungrateful guest and the capture of Moctezuma as an arbitrary action, Cortés assumes that his behavior will make complete and obvious sense once he has had a chance to explain it: "Most Invincible Lord, six days having passed since we first entered this great city of Temixtitan [Tenochtitlan], during which time I had seen something of it, though little compared with how much there is to see and record, I decided from what I had seen that it would benefit Your Royal service and our safety if Mutezuma were in my power and not in complete liberty, in order that he might not retreat from the willingness he showed to serve Your Majesty; but chiefly because we Spaniards are rather obstinate and persistent, and should we annoy him he might, as he is so powerful, obliterate all memory of us." [24]

Cortés had earned the lasting enmity of Velásquez. The governor of Cuba sent a force, headed by Pánfilo de Narváez, to Mexico to remove Cortés as commanding officer. This counterexpedition backfired when Cortés not only defeated Narváez but won over and recruited his men. In Cortés's account, the men went over to his side when they realized that he was the legitimate commander of the Mexican campaign. It seems likely that his talent for evoking the immense wealth of the Aztecs was also useful on this occasion. Velásquez also sought to make trouble for Cortés in high circles in Spain, and the repercussions of their feud continued to bedevil Cortés's career. One of Cortés's chief motives in composing his letters was to counter the idea that he was running out of control and to repair his image in his monarch's mind as a loyal subject. He addressed his correspondence to his king in line with his claim to be directly under royal command, and not required to obey the governor of Cuba.

While Cortés was dealing with matters on the Gulf Coast, the already somewhat tenuous Spanish hold on Tenochtitlan grew weaker. In retrospect, it seems clear that Cortés's naming of Pedro de Alvarado to control the imperial capital in his absence was ill advised. Alvarado massacred many members of the ruling families during a religious celebration. Reaction was so intense that, by the time Cortés returned, the Spanish were plainly losing the city. However, Cortés, with his extreme reluctance to admit to any errors on his part or that of his troops, omits mention of the Spanish aggression against the city's native dwellers during his absence. Recalling a speech to his assembled soldiers, Cortés says, "Likewise I reminded them how, for no good reason, all the natives of Culua, that is, those from the great city of Temixtitan [Tenochtitlan], and those from all the other provinces which are subject thereto, had not only rebelled against your majesty, but moreover had killed many men who were our friends and kinsmen and had driven us from their land."[25]

Cortés's account is the story of how, through his astute decisions and bold actions, the painful defeat that his soldiers had suffered was transformed into a triumph for the Spanish colonial enterprise. First Cortés summarizes the hopeless situation that he found upon his return, with the Spanish soldiers trapped in their quarters. Although the Spanish still held Moctezuma, his value had diminished. The Aztecs no longer looked to him for leadership and had acclaimed his brother Cuitláhuac as chief of the resistance.

In subsequent centuries readers have scrutinized Cortés's account to see how he explains the death of Moctezuma, an event charged with controversy. All accounts of this episode, whether originating from Spanish or Amerindian sources, coincide in stating that the Aztec ruler died a violent death while in Spanish custody. Each side blames the other for his death, and there are many versions of how it occurred. Cortés asserts that Moctezuma "asked to be taken out onto the roof of the fortress where he might speak to the captains of his people and tell them to end the fighting."[26] Moctezuma appeared on an elevated breastwork, standing behind a parapet. Before he could speak, his estranged subjects, enraged by Moctezuma's acquiescence to the Spanish invasion, fatally wounded him with well-aimed stones. This account is internally consistent and realistic, since it is generally agreed that many Aztecs were angry that Tenochtitlan, an imperial capital containing sacred sites, had not been aggressively defended. However, a number of Aztecs maintained that, even if stones were hurled at Moctezuma, they were not the cause of his death. Rather, the Spanish killed the Aztec ruler and sought to transfer the blame to the Amerindians. *The Broken Spears: The Aztec Account of the Conquest of Mexico,* a mosaic of narratives that Miguel León-Portilla assembled from a variety of Amerindian sources, shows how little the Aztecs believed the Spanish account of Moctezuma's death. One example is the report of Fernando de Alva Ixtlilxochitl. As a bicultural historian with a Spanish education but descended from the ruling house of Texcoco, he was able to utilize old Nahuatl sources. He offers this account, in which both sides' competing explanations are given: "On the third day, Motecuhzoma climbed onto the rooftop and tried to admonish his people, but they cursed him and shouted that he was a coward and a traitor to his country. They even threatened him with their weapons. It is said that an Indian killed him with a stone from his sling, but the palace servants declared that the Spaniards put him to death by stabbing him in the abdomen with their swords."[27]

There are other variants, such as that Moctezuma was already dead when he appeared before the crowd (as recounted in the Codex Ramírez).[28] The Franciscan friar Bernardino de Sahagún, who gathered information about the fall of Tenochtitlan from Amerindian informants, records a slightly different version: the appeal that Moctezuma and other nobles made to the Aztecs backfired: "not only did they not wish to be pacified, but also their ire and anger grew."[29] Frustrated by the failure of persuasive tactics, the Spanish vowed to use brute force. Their first measure was "to strangle all the nobles [i.e., including the emperor] whom they held prisoner, and throw them dead outside the fort."[30]

However Moctezuma died, it is unquestionable that his public appearance, intended to quell the rebellion, was a fiasco. Cortés, who often narrates dramatic events without editorializing or expressing emotion, merely notes that the Aztecs fought harder after the incident. He then tells of his decision to retreat under cover of darkness and the chaotic withdrawal. As he had imagined in his first survey of Tenochtitlan, the causeways are an impediment to the retreat, and many Spaniards either fall or are pulled into the lake by Amerindians skilled at fighting in canoes. The Spaniards' loss of Tenochtitlan, which occurred on 30 June 1520, has become known as the Sad Night of Hernán Cortés. Indeed Cortés narrates the retreat as a pitiful tale, in a woeful manner unlike the self-confident, unemotional tone of earlier episodes. The soldiers are injured and exhausted. Cortés describes his own wounds, which include serious head and hand injuries and result in the loss of two fingers.

The evocation of the miserable retreat helps emphasize Cortés's achievement in recapturing the city. His account stresses the good use he was able to make of the native peoples whose resentment of the Aztecs and desire to cooperate with the new invaders he had been assiduously cultivating ever since he arrived on the mainland. The military strategy used to regain the capital city comes in for detailed description. Again, the commander's decision-making skills are a prominent theme; Cortés is given to observing that the Spanish troops would not have known how to proceed had he not appeared on the scene to guide them. This time the plan of attack takes more fully into account the fact that Tenochtitlan is built on a wide lake and that access to the city normally depends on narrow causeways. Cortés orders the construction of brigantines for a new assault designed along the familiar lines of an invasion by sea and land. The Spanish, who during their retreat had been thrown into disarray by their inability to negotiate the city's causeways, under Cortés's leadership turn these constructions to their advantage. Gaps in the causeways and canals in the city are filled in with rubble, ruining one of the Aztecs' best defenses.

Pastor analyzes the letters of Cortés with special emphasis on a process she calls *fictionalization*. She notes that Cortés possesses the ability to narrate events with seeming objectivity and a high degree of internal consistency. While the resulting narrative appears to be a realistically probable version of what transpired, Cortés has omitted key pieces of information. Pastor points out that, while Cortés was writing the first three letters, he was still proceeding without authorization; only subsequently did his king name him to the captaincy that he had already been occupying de facto.[31] She cites a passage in which Cortés narrates the capture of two men who, under orders from Velásquez, had sought to intercept a ship that Cortés was sending to the king. The two men appear as miscreants who confess and receive punishment from Cortés, who describes himself explicitly as acting in the service of his monarch.[32] Pastor notes that Cortés has produced a coherent and logical story to explain what transpired, but it leaves out real-world facts: "outside this context [of Cortés's logic] and the general consistency of his letters, it is Cortés who is delinquent and a traitor, and the 'justice' he claims to be administering is a seditious act against 'delinquents and traitors' who are in fact the representatives of legal authority."[33]

T he conquest of the Incan empire occurred in the 1530s, a decade after the fall of Tenochtitlan. While a number of accounts of the Incan state and empire and their collapse exist, the narratives of greatest interest to literary scholars were composed in the seventeenth century. For this reason, the Spanish conquest of Incan lands and its aftermath will be discussed in the following chapter. It should be noted, though, that there are accounts written closer to the time of the events. The most frequently cited example is the history composed by Pedro Cieza de León. Cieza de León, who died in 1560, was born sometime around 1520 and sailed to the colonies as a young teenager. He first arrived in what is now Colombia, traveled extensively through the northern part of South America, and made his way to the Andean region. Cieza de León was not actually an eyewitness to the collapse of the Incan empire and state. However, he appeared on the scene soon enough afterward to collect fresh firsthand accounts. He became involved in the aftermath of the Spanish conquest, when the conquistadors divided into factions and fought civil wars. During the 1540s, this chronicler undertook the writing of a history of Peru. It was eventually declared an officially authorized project, so many sources were available to the author. Cieza de León enjoyed access to documents, but he is most noted for his accomplishments as a conscientious interviewer. He not only surveyed both Spaniards and native Andeans, but questioned informants from diverse factions within both groups and used only material that seemed reliable. His *Parte primera de la Crónica del Perú* (First part of the chronicle of Peru) appeared in 1553 and *Del señorío de los Incas* (Of the realm of the Incas) not until 1880. Apparently the author envisioned a seven-volume work but did not complete the project.

Other Spanish historians who focused on the Andes include Agustín de Zárate (who died sometime after 1560) and Pedro Sarmiento de Gamboa (1530–1592), known for his unfavorable history of the Incas. On the whole, though, sixteenth-century Andean accounts of the conquest have attracted less attention than those concerned with the Caribbean and Mexico. Certainly the Andean histories do not offer the feature that fascinates readers of accounts of the Mexican conquest, that is, the proliferation of competing versions of the same highly charged events.

Fray Bartolomé de Las Casas, already mentioned for his abridged transcriptions of Columbus's shipboard diaries, earned a great deal of attention during the sixteenth century with his polemical campaign against the use of native peoples as forced labor and in favor of their humane treatment. His admirers gave him the unofficial title of "The Apostle of the Indians."

Las Casas had an extremely variegated career, including participation in both the military and the church, agricultural and mining enterprises, preaching and evangelization, considerable travel, public debate, and unusually prolific writing. He arrived in the Caribbean as a soldier in armed expeditions, although he appears to have already begun the studies that would lead to his second, more notable career in the clergy. It was as the lord of an *encomienda* that he grew concerned over the European practice of depriving native peoples of their liberty. This preoccupation grew at the same time that Las Casas was abandoning his military career for an ecclesiastical one. He became a catechist, then was ordained as a priest and, later in his long life, entered the Dominican order, eventually being named Bishop of Chiapas.

In the course of evangelizing the Indians on his estate, Las Casas became uneasy over holding fellow human beings in peonage. In a much-noted sermon of 15 August 1514, Las Casas stated that he was renouncing the use of Indian serfs and returning his to the governor of Cuba. This speech marked the beginning of a long career dedicated to combating the enslavement of Indians and promoting peaceful evangelization.

In casual references Las Casas is occasionally singled out as if he were virtually the sole Spanish defender of Indian rights in the Spanish colonies. Supporters of Spanish American independence, including Simón Bolívar, tended to refer to Las Casas as the only worthy Spaniard in the early colonial era. However, colonization was scarcely under way before a number of Spaniards began expressing unease over the treatment of native peoples. Members of the Dominican order, in the course of proselytizing, often had extensive contact with the Amerindians and came to sympathize with their plight. Fray Antonio de Montesinos is an important early figure in the reaction against the enslavement of Indians. During Las Casas's career, he was by no means an isolated figure, but was successful in rallying other clergy to his cause and winning support in court circles and in the ecclesiastical hierarchy. For example, in 1526 he and other Dominican friars engaged in a successful petition-writing campaign to Pope Paul III, requesting a bull recognizing Amerindians as beings endowed with reason. While Las Casas was not the only or even the first Spaniard to draw attention to the deteriorating situation of the Amerindians, it is fair to say that he was the most visible. Moreover, Las Casas composed memorable narratives to illustrate his ideas.

Columbus and Cortés addressed their best-known writings to their respective monarchs, but Las Casas sought a broader audience; he was eager to take his case to the court of public opinion as well as convince influential persons of the need for reform. Of course, he addressed his letters of petition to particular authorities, whether at court or in the ecclesiastical hierarchy. In his lengthier writings, though, he calls out to anyone concerned with social justice. He seeks to instill in Spanish readers a sympathetic outlook toward native peoples and to produce general revulsion toward the ill treatment these communities have suffered. Las Casas often underlines the similarities between the indigenous groups of the New World and Spanish Christians. In his idealized portrayals the Indians are far from being hardened infidels and idolaters whom the Spaniards must bring under control. While Las Casas goes into little detail about Amerindian religions, he suggests that they are not fundamentally so different from Christianity. In his vision, Amerindians can shift easily to Catholicism once peaceful evangelists have exposed them to the new faith.

Las Casas's vigorous campaigns produced some reform measures, though of course he was unable to prevent Indians from becoming forced labor. He was a major force behind the New Laws that King Charles promulgated in 1542. This legislation weakened the *encomienda* by forbidding recipients of such land grants to will their Indian serfs to their heirs. Las Casas immediately realized that the regulations would not completely abolish involuntary servitude. In 1545, as Bishop of Chiapas, he prohibited confessors from granting absolution to landowners who held their Indian workers in thrall under the *encomienda* system.

As well as composing numerous petitions, proposals, treatises, memoranda, and letters, Fray Bartolomé was the author of historical narratives designed to promote his outlook on Spanish-indigenous relations. The most significant of these is the *Historia de las Indias* (History of the Indies), a polemical account of the Spanish conquest and colonization of the New World from 1492 to 1520. Las Casas stipulated that this three-volume work be withheld from publication until forty years after his death, and indeed it was not printed until 1875. With the polemical fire that typifies all his efforts, Las Casas explains his rationale for delaying publication. As Zamora quotes and translates the relevant passage from his testament of 17 March 1564, "Because if God should decide to destroy Spain, it may be seen that it is because of the destruction we have wrought upon the Indies and the reason for his justice be made evident."[34] At a more pragmatic level, it is also likely that Las Casas believed that the forty-year delay would improve his work's chances of reaching the public uncensored. Once the people whose careers and fortunes were most apt to be damaged by the *History* were dead, there would be less motivation to tamper with the manuscript.

While the classificatory term *history* is the one most easily applied to the *History of the Indies,* the narration and interpretation of past events are not the sole purposes of the work. As noted, it is also a prophetic work showing how the Spanish will have brought ruin upon their own nation through their collective sins in the colonies. Las Casas was a dedicated propagandist, regardless of the genre in which he was composing. Polemical assertions appear frequently in the *History;* at times argumentation seems to dominate over the narration of events. In some passages the *History* resembles a wide-ranging, encyclopedic reference work; it offers information that does not move the story forward.

One of Fray Bartolomé's many adversaries, and a figure particularly illustrative of the opposing school of thought, is Gonzalo Fernández de Oviedo y Valdés (1478–1557). Appointed Chronicler of the Indies by Emperor Carlos V, Fernández de Oviedo composed his *Historia general y natural de las Indias* (General and natural history of the Indies), published in 1535 and 1851–1855, to support Spanish imperial policy. In Fernández de Oviedo's outlook, as agents of Catholicism, the Spanish are entitled to conquer any and all other lands in order to spread the one true faith. He does not deny that this religiously justified imperialism in practice deprives Amerindians of their liberty and occasions suffering. He argues, though, that the native peoples of the Americas deserve their current misery to atone for the idolatry, sorcery, sodomy, and other diabolical practices in which they engaged before the arrival of Christians. Fernández de Oviedo attributes numerous failings of character to the native peoples of the Americas, concluding that they are unworthy of living as free beings. While finding few redeeming features in Amerindians as they currently exist, Fernández de Oviedo does not see them as beyond Christian redemption. He leaves open the possibility that, once they are Christians, they will improve in both character and physical appearance.

As one might expect, there were points of view between those of Fray Bartolomé, with his open advocacy of the rights of native peoples, and Fernández de Oviedo, who stressed the unworthiness of the Amerindians. A well-known example of a writer sympathetic to native Americans, yet eager to replace their ways with those of Christian Europeans, is Motolinía (real name Fray Toribio de Benavente; d. 1569), author of *Historia de los indios de la Nueva España* (History of the Indians of New Spain). Motolinía's position is that, before the Spanish showed them the error of their ways, the inhabitants of the Americas were inadvertently plunged in sin, cultivating idolatry and sorcery. At the same time, the author was a dedicated ethnographer, and the material he collected from his informants has proven enormously useful to later students of Amerindian cultures.

Álvar Núñez Cabeza de Vaca (1490?–1559?), of all the conquistadors whose accounts of the New World are known today, is the one who entered into closest contact with indigenous communities. Cabeza de Vaca was one of a handful of surviving castaways from an ill-fated expedition to Florida. He ended up wandering for eight years through what is today Florida, Texas, the U.S. Southwest, most likely Kansas, and northern Mexico. His band of shipwrecked conquistadors, which dwindled to three Spaniards and a Moroccan taken along as a slave, had no contact with other speakers of Spanish and no word of Europe during much of this time. The resulting experience of immersion in indigenous American cultures is in great measure what motivates the present-day fascination with Cabeza de Vaca. When he was first stranded, Cabeza de Vaca was unequipped to make his way in the Americas and relied on the altruism of native communities to survive. He acknowledges openly that he would have perished without the aid of the Amerindians who sheltered and fed him.

Cabeza de Vaca is best known for a first-person account of his travels in North America, which appears in Spanish-language editions either as *Naufragios* or as *Relación* (usually published in the same volume with a later work relating the author's subsequent activities in South America). It has been translated into English as *Castaways: The Narrative of Alvar Núñez Cabeza de Vaca*. The author's original motive for composing this narrative was to document to his sovereign the extent of his efforts and suffering in the employ of the crown; like many returning conquistadors, Cabeza de Vaca was seeking recompense. However, *Castaways* goes well beyond a statement of services rendered, and its digressive passages are perhaps the most attractive to current-day readers. A sharp-eyed participant-observer of the Amerindian communities that hosted and in some cases enslaved him, Cabeza de Vaca included a good deal of ethnographic detail.

Once published in 1542 and in a second edition of 1555, *Castaways* attracted a readership beyond court circles. An increasing number of Spanish readers, including historians who were competing with one another to make their versions of the conquest prevail, had developed an interest in New World matters. Over the centuries, the narrative has drawn a variegated audience, including readers who enjoy its literary qualities, historians, and anthropologists; these last value *Castaways* as the first document to describe native communities of what is today the U.S. Southwest and northern Mexico. Cabeza de Vaca's hosts include such still-extant tribes as the Pima and Zuñi. The author provides considerable detail about these peoples' way of life prior to contact with Europeans. Readers with a literary education are likely to appreciate Cabeza de Vaca's sparingly embellished manner of narration. Like other early accounts of New World undertakings, especially those directed to the authors' respective monarchs, *Castaways* contains standard boilerplate offering praise to the royal reader, expressing humility, and acknowledging debts to divine providence. Though some conventions are inescapable, Cabeza de Vaca relies fairly lightly on rhetorical adornments and instead focuses upon his experiences and observations.

Cabeza de Vaca's misadventures begin in 1527, when he signs on as treasurer of an expedition to Florida headed by Pánfilo de Narváez. *Castaways* portrays Narváez in a negative light. This commander repeatedly gives ill-considered orders whose disastrous results Cabeza de Vaca foresees. At the outset of the journey, Narváez commands a crew of some six or seven hundred men on five ships. The expedition spends some time in the Caribbean, where the Spanish presence is well established, before sailing to Florida, an area still largely unknown to Europeans. In April 1528 the ships land near Tampa Bay. Cabeza de Vaca reports that the attempt to explore Florida is fraught with quarreling, confusion, incompetence, and errors in judgment, especially poor decisions on the part of the commanding officer. Narváez sets out with about three hundred men to explore on foot. The idea is for the ships to trail along the coastline and eventually reunite with the foot soldiers.

Cabeza de Vaca claims to have realized immediately the dangers of this plan and to have tried in vain to dissuade Narváez, pointing out that "the pilots were not sure of themselves, nor did they agree with each other, nor did they know where they were."[35] He ends up joining the land exploration crew against his better judgment, so as to avoid the appearance of cowardice. The tracking ships soon lose contact with the explorers on land and sail away. In his account of the land expedition, Cabeza de Vaca seeks to elicit sympathy for the hardships endured by the men abandoned in the swampy northern regions of Florida. Their concern shifts from exploring new lands and claiming them for Spain to the immediate requirements for survival. *Castaways* emphasizes the horror of contending with an inhospitable environment, including days of swamp-wading, poisonous snakes, disorientation, and the hostility of the communities whose lands the Spanish soldiers have entered. Cabeza de Vaca portrays the Spanish, unacquainted with the dangers and diseases of the New World, as bewildered and pathetic. Describing an all-day march, he says, "The journey was extremely laborious, for there were not enough horses to carry the men who were sick, nor did we know what cure to apply, for they grew worse every day; and it was a very pitiable and painful thing to see the deprivation and hardship we were undergoing."[36]

Cabeza de Vaca and other survivors of his expedition attempt to sail westward from Florida, following the shore of the Gulf Coast, with the intention of reaching New Spain (Mexico), where there are many Spaniards. Instead they drift in the Gulf of Mexico until they wash up that autumn on the shore of what is now East Texas, quite likely on Galveston Island. The Spaniards, weakened by hunger and exhaustion and disoriented in the unfamiliar landscape, are already barely managing when they capsize a boat containing their personal belongings. Naked and cold, "in such a plight that one could have counted our bones without difficulty,"[37] they receive help from communities of Karankawas. Though Cabeza de Vaca recognizes the generosity of various groups of Amerindians, he does not idealize native communities as unfailingly kind. Some of his hosts are fundamentally captors, and he spends time as a slave. Cabeza de Vaca observes that his status in Amerindian communities at first tends to be low, since he appears as an inept stranger. Over the years, Cabeza de Vaca develops skills as a trader and healer that allow him to win respect and grow relatively prosperous.

Eventually, Cabeza de Vaca becomes celebrated among the Amerindian communities for his ability to restore health. To acquire this fame, Cabeza de Vaca has to gain considerable knowledge of tribal cultures and adopt a number of indigenous folkways in such matters as dress and personal adornment. In the *Naufragios,* Cabeza de Vaca takes pains to attribute a Christian character to his career as a healer, which could easily be perceived as a foray into paganism and witchcraft. He states that the Gulf Coast Amerindians "tried to make us into medicine men"; the shipwreck survivors resisted the idea, but their hosts "withheld our food until we did as they had told us."[38] The healing practices that Cabeza de Vaca recalls using to cure sick and wounded Amerindians were, according to his account, first and foremost appeals for divine assistance rather than displays of his own restorative powers. (However, he does express approval of some Amerindian practices, such as the cauterization of wounds.)[39] While the cures may be attributed to the providential actions of God, Cabeza de Vaca adopted some practices that he had observed among indigenous healers, such as blowing upon the patient. The episode in which Cabeza de Vaca has success in treating an apparently dead patient displays this mix of Christian piety and folk healing:

> And when I came near to their settlements I saw the sick man whom we were going to heal, who was dead, for many people were around him weeping and his house had been pulled down, which is a sign that its owner has died. And so when I got there I found the Indian with

his eyes rolled up and without any pulse and with all the signs of being dead, as it seemed to me, and Dorantes said the same. I took off a
reed mat with which he was covered and as best I could I implored
Our Lord to be pleased to give health to that man and all others who
had need of it. And after I had made the sign of the cross and blown
on him many times, they brought me his bow and gave it to me . . . And
that night they returned to their homes and said that the man who was
dead and whom I had healed had stood up in their presence entirely
well and had walked and eaten and spoken with them. . . .[40]

Readers from later centuries have been anxious to determine the answer
to a question that Cabeza de Vaca never directly formulates in the course
of narrating his travels and sufferings and that would be unlikely to have
occurred to him: to what degree did he enter into Indian cultures? While
Cabeza de Vaca does not speak of his own view of his identity, he tells of
the perception of others. When Spanish soldiers encounter Cabeza de
Vaca after his eight-year absence, they are "thunderstruck to see me so
strangely dressed and in the company of Indians. They went on staring
at me for a long time, so astonished that they could neither speak to me
nor manage to ask me anything."[41] The Amerindians who accompany
Cabeza de Vaca and his companions when they return to the Spanish
forces also find it difficult to believe that the stranded men could belong
to the same community as Christian Spaniards.

Since the twentieth century, there has been a widespread fascination
with the dynamics of cultures in contact, especially when features of
two or more cultures become commingled and fused to create a new cultural blend. *Castaways* is a story whose narrator-protagonist is required
by circumstances to adopt and transform for his own use many traits of
another culture, and this interactive union of cultures appeals to readers now.

From the time of the first Spanish incursion into
the Aztec empire in 1519, this particular campaign
of conquest began to be exceptionally well represented in documents
and historical accounts. It should be remembered that Mesoamerican
peoples had a long-established tradition of chronicling what befell their
communities and especially their monarchs. The Amerindians who witnessed the conquest recorded their accounts by various methods, including oral transmission, pictorial representation, and pictographic,
glyphic, and alphabetic forms of writing in various combinations. Natu-

rally, Spanish historians were drawn to the subject of their nation's rapid overseas expansion and vied with one another to establish their accounts as the definitive ones.

In 1552 Francisco López de Gómara published in Zaragosa the second part of his *Historia general de Las Indias* (General history of the Indies), which tells the story of the conquest of Mexico. Sometimes referred to as the *Crónica de la Nueva España* (literally, Chronicle of New Spain, the term for colonial Mexico) and sometimes as the *Istoria de la conquista de México,* this history appeared in English in 1578 as *The Conquest of the Weast India.* (In the sixteenth century the standardization of spelling did not hold the importance that it does today.) This work presented an authorized version of the conquest of the Aztecs, and the author obtained a good deal of his information from Hernán Cortés. Readers of Cortés's letters are often struck by this commander's reluctance to share credit with those who accompanied him on his campaign of conquest. The same tight focus on the accomplishments of the expedition leader typifies Gómara's history. Lesley Byrd Simpson, the translator who published a modern English version in 1964, aptly entitled it *Cortés: The Life of the Conqueror by His Secretary.*

This Cortés-centered history is most often mentioned today in relation to a competing, and more complex, account of the Spanish campaign against the Aztec empire. The latter work is the *Verdadera historia de la conquista de la Nueva España* (*Discovery and Conquest of Mexico*) by Bernal Díaz del Castillo (1490s–1584). Bernal, who is generally referred to by his first name, was an old soldier (over eighty-four, according to one of the prefaces to his *Discovery*) who had accompanied Cortés. Between the mid-1540s and about 1575, Bernal composed his own account, which was not published until 1632. He often invokes his authority as an eyewitness and participant. While Bernal appears to have begun his history before he read Gómara's, he became incensed by the latter's sight-unseen account of the conquest and excitably contradicts and inveighs against the historian.

Bernal Díaz's account is likely to strike current-day readers as one of the more believable Spanish versions of the conquest. One factor is his direct manner of narration, especially in comparison with the deliberate and elegant style of writers like Gómara, trained in rhetoric; less elaborate writing today produces an effect of sincerity. Bernal goes into extensive detail. As authors of realist fiction know well, specific details tend to make a narrative more convincing. Moreover, Bernal appears less self-seeking than many chroniclers. In reading Cortés's letters, readers quickly note a salesman's tendentious insistence and perceive that the mission commander is justifying his course of action. Of course, the letters and reports that subjects address to their monarchs are inherently somewhat suspect. Bernal was no doubt hoping that, by displaying the services he had rendered, he might enrich the estate that he would leave to his descendants. Yet his history is not first and foremost a bid for recompense. He appears more bent on changing the general public's understanding of how the conquest transpired. The old soldier has some scores to settle and, like many participants in the conquest, is aggrieved over the meager reward he received for his service. Although he can hardly be called neutral, he is not as openly opportunistic as Columbus or Cortés. His writing of history appears directed primarily toward his announced goal: to set the facts straight. In addition, while Cortés's letters display a persistent strain of self-aggrandizement, Bernal states that he is old, infirm, impoverished, and "no Latin scholar,"[42] most likely meaning that he had no secondary or higher education.[43] (In comparison, Cortés had studied law for a time, and even his detractors admit that he possessed a good education.)

Bernal is eager for greater recognition of the part played in the campaign by persons other than Cortés, especially by other Spanish soldiers such as himself. It is important to him that his own efforts come in for acknowledgment. Although he sometimes emphasizes his humble status, he can be irritatingly vain. He also brings out the assistance the commander received from Amerindians. For example, in Cortés's own account of his first meeting with the Aztec emperor Moctezuma II, he makes no mention of the help the two principals received from interpreters. The Aztec ruler and the Spanish conqueror appear to be addressing one another in a common language. Bernal, in describing the same encounter, emphasizes that the exchange was mediated by two interpreters, La Malinche and the Maya-speaking Spaniard Jerónimo de Aguilar. This historian often draws attention to the Spanish soldiers' dependence on the interpreters "Doña Marina and Aguilar, who always went with us on every expedition—even when it took place at night."[44]

Readers often turn to Bernal for further information on matters about which Cortés is reticent. Bernal supplies much of what is generally known about La Malinche. As noted, Cortés has little to say about her, whether out of a desire to keep his Amerindian mistress in the shadows or out of his pervasive habit of maintaining the spotlight on his own accomplishments. Amerindian observers were vividly aware of La Malinche, who often appears in their accounts and representations. Bernal views her from a perspective that is clearly pro-conquest and Christian. Even so, he recognizes that she is a significant person in her own right as well as for the aid she rendered to the Spanish: "Doña Marina was a person of the greatest importance and was obeyed without question by the Indians throughout New Spain."[45] All of Chapter 37 is dedicated to La Malinche, and she makes many other appearances in the history. Bernal treats La Malinche respectfully, praising her intelligence, interpretive talent, high birth, good character, and devout Christianity. In an homage that is enthusiastic, even if today it would appear sexist, Bernal says, "Let us leave this and say how Doña Marina who, although a native woman, possessed such manly valour that, although she had heard every day how the Indians were going to kill us and eat our flesh with chili, and had seen us surrounded in the late battles, and knew that all of us were wounded and sick, yet never allowed us to see any sign of fear in her, only a courage passing that of woman."[46]

To some extent Bernal's history is a revisionist one, but it still represents the Spanish outlook on the conquest; it is not as radically divergent as Las Casas's denunciations or the accounts of indigenous chroniclers. For example, Bernal is like Cortés in justifying the Spanish actions at Cholula as a justified response to a treacherous attack being planned by the local people in collusion with those in the Aztec capital. As does Cortés, Bernal cites La Malinche as the source of information about the alleged conspiracy. As evidence of the Cholulans' evil designs, he adds a colorful detail: "So in return for our having come to treat them like brothers and to tell them what Our Lord God and the King have ordained, they wished to kill us and eat our flesh, and had already prepared the pots with salt and peppers and tomatoes."[47]

On the whole, Bernal is franker than Cortés in admitting that the Spanish troops used a good deal of violence in taking Mexico. In his account of the incident at Cholula, Bernal notes that the Spanish were the first to strike: "a blow was given to [the Cholulans] which they will remember for ever, for we killed many of them, so that they gained nothing from the promises of their false idols."[48] Concerning another massacre, the one in Tenochtitlan under Pedro de Alvarado's command while Cortés was away on the Gulf Coast, Bernal provides an Amerindian perspective and again draws attention to Spanish violence. In his account, "There arrived four chieftains sent to Cortés by the great Moctezuma to complain to him of Pedro de Alvarado, and what they said, with tears streaming from their eyes, was that Pedro de Alvarado sallied out from his quarters with all the soldiers that Cortés had left with him, and, for no reason at all, fell on their chieftains and Caciques who were dancing and celebrating a feast in honour of their Idols Huichilobos and Tezcate-puca, Pedro de Alvarado having given them leave to do so. He killed and wounded many of them."[49] On another disputed point, the death of Moctezuma, Bernal's account is quite close to that of Cortés. He adheres to the official Spanish version by assigning blame to the Aztecs.[50]

The accounts composed during the sixteenth century cover many events that are considered today, as they were then, indisputably major historical events, especially the Spanish invasion and defeat of the Aztec and Incan empires and the European exploration of the Americas. In addition, contemporary narratives touch upon some aspects of the New World explorations and campaigns that by now seem merely fabulous embellishments, such as the persistent idea that seven cities of gold existed somewhere in the north of Mexico or what is today the southwestern United States. One should keep in mind that some legendary beliefs motivated real-world expeditions. An example is the search through the Florida peninsula for waters capable of bringing back youthful vigor. Juan Ponce de León is most clearly associated in most people's minds with the quest for the Fountain of Youth. Many other seekers, both Spaniards and Amerindians, persevered in the search of the restorative waters. It is not uncommon to find in otherwise realistic accounts a few features that by today's standards are irrational and fantastic. A celebrated instance is Cabeza de Vaca's statement, at the end of *Castaways*, that after his return to Spanish society he realized that the misadventures that befell his expedition had been foretold by a Moorish woman: "the whole voyage had happened just as she had told us."[51] These and other similar references, fascinating to come across, are reminders that in the sixteenth century there was not as great an effort as today to distinguish reasoned from supernatural explanations. It was not considered bizarre for a well-educated person to express a belief that astral, demonic, or oracular forces, as well as the divine providence to which the conquistadors frequently express thanks, had influenced or determined the outcome of a given sequence of events.

After the fall and destruction of Tenochtitlan, there were still some Aztecs who had fought in or observed the defense of the imperial capital and lived to tell the tale. Testimony from these witnesses and participants may be found in, among other sources, the material gathered and edited by the Franciscan Bernardino de Sahagún. Sahagún arrived in New Spain in 1529, not so long after the 1521 conquest, and learned Nahuatl, the language of the Aztec empire. Around mid-century, he began systematically collecting data about many aspects of Aztec life, the rationale being that knowledge of the language and customs would further the conversion of the Amerindians. This information, together with some additions that are clearly pro-conquest, went into a twelve-volume compendium entitled *Historia general de las cosas de Nueva España* (General history of the things of New Spain). This work exists in several versions. Especially valued is an unusually complete 1576–1577 version that, housed in Florence, is known as the Florentine Codex. (Scholars sometimes prefer to consult an even earlier, though incomplete, manuscript in Madrid.) However, even after Sahagún had finished this version and sent it to Europe, he continued to revise his encyclopedic manuscript and produced a second version in 1585. In the reworked manuscript, the Franciscan's outlook, favorable to Cortés's expedition, is more in evidence.

Sahagún meant for his compilation to teach the Nahuatl language to clergy who would be working with Amerindian communities. The Florentine Codex is in two columns. One is in the Nahuatl of Sahagún's informants. The other is his Spanish version, a free translation, perhaps better called a paraphrase, with some additions and emendations of his own. Sahagún, who after all assembled the work as an aid to conversion, identifies the Aztec gods as "idols" and inserts other signs of his disapproval of non-Christian beliefs and practices. Although the 1585 version was bilingual at one time, to the frustration of researchers only the Spanish version is extant.

The *Historia general* has many themes, including religion, the calendar, festivals, divination, medicine, topics in natural history, and the social and economic organization of the Aztec empire. The final volume is the only one that takes the form of a narrative. It splices together various informants' accounts of the Spanish conquest of Aztec-ruled central Mexico. Fortunately for subsequent generations, Sahagún appears to have recognized the importance of pictorial representation as a means of narration among Mesoamerican communities. He solicited, preserved, and included drawings by Amerindian scribes. The vivid graphics of the Florentine Codex are frequently reproduced to illustrate such events as the catastrophic Spanish retreat from Tenochtitlan.

Like other accounts of the conquest that were either composed by Amerindians or based on their information, Sahagún's work tells of unnerving events that were occurring in the Aztec capital during the year before word of the approaching Spaniards reached central Mexico. The Aztecs witnessed, suspended in the night sky, "a tongue of fire of notable size and brilliance."[52] Then the temple of Huitzilopochtli, the sun and war god closely associated with the destiny of the Aztec people, inexplicably burst into flames that intensified when water was thrown on them. Other ill omens included a comet, bizarre disturbances in the lake upon which the city was built, and the appearance of monstrous beings.

This and other information from Sahagún's informants helps explain the apparent lack of resistance the Spanish troops encountered when they first entered Tenochtitlan. The Aztecs had apparently been living in a state of apocalyptic dread. Moctezuma is reported to have been in despair. The general sense of imminent catastrophe was heightened by the reports of the messengers that Moctezuma sent to negotiate with the Spanish as they came nearer to his capital. Unacquainted with firearms, the Amerindian ambassadors collapsed when the Spanish fettered them and detonated a cannon in their presence.[53] Sahagún's informants also point out that the Aztec ruler, distraught as he was, continued to consult with his advisors, some of whom were wizards rather than strategists, and to plan a defense: "Moctezuma resorted to all the ancient measures used by the Indians in their warfare, except the peremptory one, which was to come to blows with the Spaniards."[54]

A number of other sources give an indigenous perspective on the conquest. As the events of 1519–1521 receded in time, though, survivors who could provide information died. It should be remembered that Aztec society included learned scribes and chroniclers who maintained a record of everything considered important to the Aztec people and state. For some time after the conquest, this native writing activity continued. Almost immediately after the fall of the empire, missionary friars taught already-literate Aztecs to write Spanish and Nahuatl in the Roman alphabet, hoping that they would use this skill to spread Christianity. Some of their students quickly used alphabetic writing to set down, in either Nahuatl or Spanish, information important to their own communities. The subject matter could come either from ancient manuscripts or from post-conquest developments. The survival of Amerindian chronicling and scribal practices after the conquest is a fascinating and complex phenomenon, though it lies outside the scope of this survey.

Unfortunately, the accounts that the Aztecs kept did not survive as well as those written by priests and historians who were either Spaniards or had a Spanish education. Only a limited number of books actually by the Aztecs or other peoples of central Mexico are extant even in fragmentary form today, and there are not many people who can interpret them. However, information derived from Aztec books appears in Spanish compilations, such as the three-part *Historia de las Indias de la Nueva España e Islas de Tierra Firme* (most of which was published in English as *The Aztecs: The History of the Indies of New Spain*), composed sometime around 1580 by the Dominican Diego Durán. Another author who draws on native sources is the historian Fernando de Alva Ixtlilxochitl (c. 1568 – c. 1648). Spanish-educated but a direct descendant of Ixtlilxochitl II, the Aztec ruler of Texcoco who allied himself with Cortés, Alva Ixtlilxochitl enjoyed access to Amerindian records. His "Relación de la venida de los españoles y principio de la ley evangélica" (Account of the arrival of the Spaniards and beginning of evangelical law [i.e., Christianity]) focuses attention on the role that Ixtlilxochitl II and the people of Texcoco played in the conquest.

Even if the chronicles were not of such absorbing interest, one would want to have an acquaintance with them in order to recognize their reflections in later works, whether in the form of overt allusions or of a more general revisiting of the same themes. These early writings represent a period in which the Spanish New World settlements were still by and large a wild frontier society. As the Spanish succeeded in claiming the bulk of the Amerindian lands, the active phase of the conquest came to an end, though uprisings and border skirmishes would continue for some time. By the late sixteenth century, life in Spain's American colonies became more settled.

As the next chapter shows, the establishment of stable cities and towns brought on the development of literary life. Most of the early writers were men of action who, even if they possessed good writing skills, were composing documents for specific, pragmatic purposes and had no time or motive to polish their style. After the main campaign of conquest ended, the New World came to include more people with the education and free time to devote to literature as an art. While official letters, reports, and histories continued to be written, so were texts in less immediately useful genres, such as epic and lyrical poetry and various types of more artistically composed and stylistically polished narratives.

Chapter Two	$\mathcal{T}$HE SEVENTEENTH AND
	EIGHTEENTH CENTURIES

Literary Life in the Colonies

$\mathcal{I}$t was in the seventeenth century that Spain's New World cities clearly emerged as centers of literary life, and narrative prose was cultivated with artistry by writers based in the Spanish American colonies. Before looking at the relatively settled seventeenth and eighteenth centuries, I review quickly the events of the more tumultuous century that preceded it, often alluded to in later literary works.

The great conquests occurred early in the sixteenth century. Tenochtitlan fell in 1521. The Spanish conquest of the Inca empire, begun at the outset of the 1530s, was basically achieved by 1533, although resistance to Spanish rule would still flare up. By the end of the sixteenth century, Spanish forces controlled most, though not all, of the lands Spain claimed. As strife diminished, existence in the New World lost its frontier character.

The establishment of the vice-regal capitals stimulated the growth of intellectual activity in the colonies. As noted in the previous chapter, after defeating the Aztecs in November 1521 and wreaking destruction on their imperial capital, Hernán Cortés had the city rebuilt in Spanish style. Francisco Pizarro, commanding officer of the campaign against the Inca empire, sacked the capital of Cuzco. The Spanish established a government center in Cuzco, but their South American capital was Lima, which Pizarro founded in 1535.

The vice-regal capitals had as their main purpose the administration of the colonies, but they served other functions. Court life included poetry, song, and theater. Monasteries, convents, and educational institutions also provided places for intellectual and creative activity. In the seventeenth century, religious houses at times attracted intellectuals seeking a place to write. In 1539 Mexico City came to house the first press in the New World, and Lima acquired a press in 1584, although there were tight restrictions on what could be printed. Universities were chartered in both capitals.

The more refined narrative works that appear after the conquest era reflect this less rough-and-ready environment. Beyond doubt, a number of the narratives generated during and immediately after the conquest exhibit near-literary qualities in the sense of being especially imaginative, involving, or well executed. Cortés, who possessed an unusually advanced education for a man of arms, composed his letters with a good mastery of contemporary rhetoric and style. Alvar Núñez Cabeza de Vaca, not as accomplished a stylist as Cortés, was a spellbinding storyteller. Yet the chroniclers did not set out to write belles lettres. The literary qualities that readers ascribe to their works are secondary to pragmatic purposes.

Poets came to abound in Spain's American possessions. A lengthy heroic poem, *La Araucana* by Alonso de Ercilla y Zúñiga (1533–1594), appeared in installments in 1569, 1578, and 1589. It is an account of the Spanish attempt to wrest Chile from the Araucanian people, who proved impossible to defeat militarily. As well as being an important Renaissance heroic poem, *La Araucana* fascinates researchers with its characterization of the Araucanians. While Ercilla had fought against the Araucanians, his poem shows unusual admiration for them. Not only do the bravery, strength, and tenacity of Araucanians come in for praise, but at times the poem appears to suggest that their resistance was justified. The celebration of the Araucanians' virtues goes beyond establishing that these Amerindian people were worthy adversaries. Absorbing as these issues are, *La Araucana* lies outside the scope of this study because it is in verse.

A more sophisticated and cultivated style of writing began to appear in narrative prose as well. Garcilaso Inca de la Vega (often called the Inca or the Inca Garcilaso; originally named Gómez Suárez de Figueroa, 1539–1616) exemplifies this change. The Inca Garcilaso, whose major works appeared in the seventeenth century, is often referred to as a historian, although this term does not cover all aspects of his work. His most important writings are primarily histories, but he should also be considered a literary writer. He acquired a humanistic education and was a careful stylist. This figure was the son of an aristocratic conquistador, Sebastián Garcilaso de la Vega, and an Inca princess from Cuzco. At the time of his birth, Amerindian-Spanish mestizos were still a recent phenomenon in Peru. The Inca Garcilaso feels the need to explain to his Spanish readers what a mestizo is.

The Inca Garcilaso's father did not marry his mother, but he had their child baptized. Eventually the father was pressured into taking a young

Spanish bride; his concubine was married off to a lowlier Spaniard. These events are never mentioned in the author's works. The father gave his mestizo child a Spanish, Christian, and militaristic upbringing. When he became a colonial administrator (*corregidor,* or magistrate, of the city of Cuzco), the son accompanied him as his secretary.

Once the Spanish had conquered a people with a nobility, they often cultivated the existing elite to help win the population over to Christianity and acceptance of Spanish rule. In line with this policy, the Inca Garcilaso's father invited into his home selected Inca nobles, including his son's maternal relatives. The adult Inca Garcilaso would later relate that as a child he seized this opportunity to learn everything he could about the days of the Inca rulers. He also learned Quechua, the language of the Inca empire. As a historian, he often reminds his readers of his knowledge of Quechua, which gives him greater authority than monolingual Spanish competitors. In the "Preface to the Reader" of his *Comentarios reales de los Incas* (*Royal Commentaries of the Incas;* 1609, 1616–1617) he states: "In the course of my history I shall . . . set down no important circumstances without quoting the authority of Spanish historians who may have touched on it in part or as a whole. For my purpose is not to gainsay them, but to furnish a commentary and gloss, and to interpret many Indian expressions which they, as strangers to that tongue, have rendered inappropriately."[1]

The Inca's situation was complex, to say the least. In some respects he was a figure of high prestige. In his *Royal Commentaries* the Inca Garcilaso brings to the fore those elements of his identity that confer status. He was of noble blood and the descendant of an imperial line, with both a ruling-class European background and a privileged knowledge of elite Inca culture. During his early years, owing to his father's administrative position, he associated with a number of distinguished people, a fact to which he often draws attention. The title "Inca" appears in the author's name, and has proven useful in distinguishing him from the renowned (and related) Spanish poet Garcilaso de la Vega. The Inca Garcilaso appears to have used this title primarily as a reminder of his royal lineage. While *Inca* in general usage now refers to the entire people, the Inca Garcilaso stresses that within the Inca empire "To begin with the name *Inca,* it must be realized that it means 'king' or 'emperor,' referring to the royal person; but when applied to those of his lineage it means 'a man of royal blood'."[2] These men, of which he is one, are regarded as descendants of the sun and divinely endowed with special entitlements. Moreover, the Inca was from Cuzco, "imperial and sacred city," as he calls it. The references to Cuzco bring to the fore the city's exceptional significance. Cuzco is associated with the line of the Inca emperors and the destiny of the Inca state; it holds a central place in the cosmos as well as in the Inca empire; before the conquest, it was admired for its architectural splendor. The Inca is given to comparing Cuzco, the empire it governed, and the Quechua language to Rome, the Roman empire, and Latin.

As an independent adult, the Inca Garcilaso staked a further claim on readers' respect by obtaining and displaying a formidable education. Beyond the relatively practical career skills that his father had him master, he acquired on his own an impressive grasp of contemporary humanistic thought and letters. For all his prestigious attributes, though, he was illegitimate. The Inca Garcilaso frequently drew attention to his Amerindian background to demonstrate his authority concerning Peru. Yet mixed ancestry could not reasonably be called an advantage in a society where purity of blood was the ideal.

Adding a further complication to his identity is the question of his residence. The Inca Garcilaso is best known for his accounts of New World matters, and especially of the Inca empire and its conquest, but from the age of twenty one he resided in Europe and never returned to Peru. Based in Spain, he first pursued a military career, in which he attained the rank of Captain of His Majesty. In later life he followed instead a clerical and literary vocation, taking minor orders and dedicating himself to his manuscripts. Part of the fascination that the Inca's writing exerts lies in his struggle to reconcile the competing factors in his identity.

The Inca's earliest major writing project was a translation, published in 1590, of *Los diálogos de amor*. (The English translation of the same work bears a somewhat different title, *The Philosophy of Love*.) This treatise by the neo-Platonic humanist León Hebreo or Leo Hebreus (also known as Judah Abrabanel), originally written in Italian, was admired by many contemporary thinkers, but was under suspicion because of its author's Jewish background and the questions raised about his adherence to doctrine. It was written in an elaborately artificial dialogue format, and the Inca Garcilaso's version is regarded as solving difficult problems in translation while actually refining the work's style. This project gives evidence of the Inca Garcilaso's thorough involvement with the humanistic culture of contemporary Europe. The lengthy original Spanish title of this work begins *La traduzión del Indio de los tres diálogos de amor de León Hebreo* (The translation by the Indian of the three dialogues of love of León Hebreo). The striking inclusion of a reference to the translator's ethnic identity early in the title, well before his name appears, is an indication of the widespread preoccupation with the Inca Garcilaso's origin.

Later the Inca Garcilaso specialized in histories of Spanish America. In 1605 he published an account of the ill-fated Spanish exploration that Hernando de Soto led in what is now the southeastern United States. This work is *La Florida del Ynca o Historia del Adelantado Hernando de Soto* (*The Florida of the Inca*). Over time, the author's distinctive outlook on the Spanish in the New World and his approach to writing have come to be valued more than any factual light *The Florida* might shed on De Soto's expedition. The Inca had never been in Florida and had to rely on second-hand sources.

Of most enduring interest is his historical and ethnographic account of the Inca empire and the Spanish colonization of Peru. Like many contemporary works, it bears a title so long-winded that it cannot be used to refer to the work. Instead, it is known by the handle *Los comentarios reales de los Incas* (*Royal Commentaries of the Incas*). The first part, concerned with the Inca people, state, and empire, appeared in 1609. The second was a volume that came out over the period 1616–1617 under the title *Historia general del Perú* (General history of Peru). This installment centered attention on the activities of the Spanish in Peru, both their conquest of the existing empire and conflicts between the conquistadors. The author had already delivered the final manuscript at the time of his death, but the actual publication was posthumous. In both parts of the *Royal Commentaries* the Inca is uninhibited in showing his personal involvement with the subject matter. As the title indicates, the Inca Garcilaso's survey of Inca history, society, and culture focuses on one sector, the elite from which he descends. When he refers to the civil wars that wracked the Inca empire shortly before the Spanish invasion, he is openly partisan to the royal house of Cuzco, that is, to his mother's family. In the second part, the Inca Garcilaso is concerned with defending his father's reputation.

The Inca emphasizes that his account of the Inca empire is based on privileged sources to which few had access. He places considerable importance on his knowledge of Quechua, the language of the empire, and on his childhood experience of listening to the Inca nobles speak of their lost glories. Even as a child, the Inca reports drawing information from his relatives and others:

I was brought up among these Indians, and as I frequented their society until I was twenty I was able to learn during that time something of all the subjects I am writing about, for in my childhood they used to account their histories, just as stories are told to children. Later, as I grew up, they talked to me at length about their laws and government, and compared the new rule of the Spaniards with that of the Incas . . . they told me, as if I were their own son, all about their idolatry, their rites, ceremonies, and sacrifices, the greater and lesser festivals, and how they were celebrated . . . Apart from what the Indians told me, I experienced and saw with my own eyes a great deal of their idolatry, festivals, and superstitions, which had still not altogether disappeared in my own time, when I was twelve or thirteen.[3]

As an adult researcher, he becomes more systematic in canvassing the descendants of Inca nobles: "I wrote to my old schoolmates at my primary school and grammar school, and urged each of them to help me with accounts they might have of the particular conquests the Incas made in the provinces their mothers came from, for each province has its accounts and knots to record its annals and traditions, and thus preserves its history much better than that of its neighbors. My schoolfellows earnestly complied with my request, and each reported my intention to his mother and relatives, and they, on hearing that an Indian, a son of their own country, intended to write its history, brought from their archives the records they had of their histories and sent me them."[4]

The Inca is extremely aware that Inca culture included no system that European readers would recognize as writing and that his readers might consider the Incas less advanced for this reason. The *Royal Commentaries* contain many allusions to issues of writing. At no point does the author claim that the Incas possessed writing, which he considers the best method of preserving information. The author's chief criticism of the oral transmission used by the Incas is that it is too fragile. He laments that much of the cultural knowledge of the Incas is already lost because it was not written down before the conquest. On the other hand, he emphasizes that the Incas developed practices that served some of the same functions as writing and worked so long as society remained stable. For example, the Incas systematically strengthened their memories to retain the information that most needed to be passed along. Oral transmission using a trained, focused memory was more accurate and sophisticated than it might seem to European readers, who had been taught to rely on writing.

The khipu (discussed in the introduction to this work), which records information in knots, also comes in for discussion. Since the khipu was still in use when the Inca was a child, his discussion of this medium of communication is of great interest. The Inca indeed provides information about the khipu, but his statements deepen rather than solve the mystery of its function. He states that the khipu encoded numbers, not words: "In short they may be said to have recorded on their knots everything that could be counted, even mentioning battles and fights, and all the embassies that had come to visit the Inca [emperor], and all the speeches and arguments the king had uttered. But the purpose of the embassies or the contents of the speeches, or any other descriptive matter could not be recorded on the knots, consisting as it did of continuous spoken or written prose, which cannot be expressed by means of knots, since these can only give numbers and not words."[5] Other statements in the *Royal Commentaries* might seem to contradict this characterization of the khipu. As noted, the Inca asserts that "knots" record "annals" and help to preserve the history of the Inca empire. The use of khipus to record or reconstruct history suggests that this device could preserve information in narrative form. A contemporary historian, Father Blas Valera, whose *Historia del Perú* the Inca consulted, apparently believed that folktales and poetry could be retrieved from khipus. The Inca's ambiguous remarks suggest that, as early as the seventeenth century, there was already uncertainty over how to describe the khipu, especially when explaining it to people accustomed to alphabetic writing.

Many more reflections on linguistic issues appear in the course of the *Royal Commentaries*. Alberto Escobar, the scholar most closely associated with the campaign for a national bilingual policy in twentieth-century Peru, has examined the *Royal Commentaries* to identify the general outlines of the Inca's linguistic thought. Escobar finds in the Inca's work a coherent set of ideas about the relations between society and language. The Inca's thought resembles contemporary European ideas about such issues as the need to preserve an international language in an era when vernaculars were in the ascendant. At the same time, the Inca's discussion of the maintenance of Quechua exhibits parallelisms with twentieth-century ideals of bilingualism and biculturalism.[6]

The *Royal Commentaries,* according to their author, draw information from the author's childhood recollections, from oral sources that he encountered later in life, and from khipus. The Inca acknowledges as well his consultation of writings by other historians. Earlier studies on the Inca Garcilaso often emphasize the links between his work and the European humanistic tradition and historiography. In recent times researchers have been particularly drawn to those aspects of the Inca's work that utilize memory and Andean oral sources. Given the current in-tense concern with hybrid cultural forms, it is not surprising that schol-ars seek to understand the ways in which the Inca Garcilaso blended to-gether his oral background and his mastery, in his mature years, of a highly literate European humanistic culture.[7]

The term *history* does not quite cover all that the Inca Garcilaso does in his summary of Inca civilization. He is a cultural historian, but he is also attempting an ethnographic reconstruction of imperial Inca life and, to some extent, writing elements of an autobiography. He includes a great deal of material concerning intellectual life and the cultivation of the arts in the Inca empire.

In the *Royal Commentaries* the author makes an attempt to relate the history of the Inca people as they themselves viewed it, that is, including elements that are more legendary than factual. A number of narratives centering on Inca emperors are reproduced in the volume; they include such supernatural elements as ill omens, premonitory dreams, and com-munications from the dead.

The author demonstrates his Christian outlook by occasionally dis-paraging the supernatural beliefs of the Incas as superstitions. But, within the narratives, the information that the Incas obtain through div-ination, augury, and revelation is accurate and dangerous to disregard. For example, Huayna Cápac, the last emperor to rule the undivided Inca empire, witnesses a number of ominous portents. These signs include the violent death of an imperial eagle during the Festival of the Sun, "many fearful and horrifying comets," and a night on which "the moon was surrounded by three large rings, the first the color of blood; the second, farther out, greenish-black, and the third smoky-looking."[8] A "soothsayer or magician, called by the Indians *llaica*," correctly predicts the Spanish conquest and the dissolution of the Inca state, religion, and empire.[9] The story of the seventh king, the Inca "Weeping-Blood," also supports the value of omens. In "a warning given by an apparition to the prince to be conveyed to his father," "Weeping-Blood" reluctantly hears out his son's account of a visionary warning of a threat against the impe-rial capital.[10] Though the king rejects the message as the "nonsense" of an "arrogant madman," it proves to be true, and the son who experi-enced and believed in his vision saves the day.[11]

Religion, whether pre-Inca, Inca, or Christian, is a major topic in the *Royal Commentaries.* In the seventeenth century even highly educated Spanish readers were often quite devout, and both the reading public and authorities were concerned that Christian doctrine be upheld at all times. Having no special royal warrant or commission ahead of time to write his histories, the Inca Garcilaso had to be particularly cautious not to offend the censors. In reading the *Royal Commentaries,* one sees immediately what care the author takes to maintain the fundamental principle that Christianity is the one true faith. At the same time, he is eager to cast Inca culture in the best light, so it must not appear as paganism without redeeming features.

The Inca's solution is to emphasize the parallels between Inca religion and Christianity. Though the Incas were obviously not Christians before the conquest, according to the Inca Garcilaso, "The Incas glimpsed the true God, our Lord." [12] The author does not attempt to deny that the Incas recognized many divinities. Instead, he argues that, despite their outwardly polytheistic religion, in their heart of hearts they had already made the transition to monotheism. According to his account, they held various specific phenomena to be divine but gave central importance to Pachacámac, an invisible god considered to be the creator of all things. According to the author, "They held the name in such veneration that they dared not utter it except when they must, and then only with signs and demonstrations of great respect . . . If asked who was the Pachacámac, they would say 'he who gave life to the universe and sustained it,' but they did not know him and had never seen him, so they did not make temples to him or offer him sacrifices, but adored him in their hearts — that is, mentally — and held him to be the unknown god." [13] In essence, they were worshipping the Christian God without possessing the proper nomenclature to identify the truths they had discovered. The Inca Garcilaso states that the Incas had managed to develop on their own a prototype or forerunner of Christianity, using their natural intelligence to compensate for a lack of Christian education.

This argument not only places the Incas close to Christians but also distances them from the Andean cultures that they conquered. In the Inca Garcilaso's version, prior to the establishment of the Inca empire the human being in the Andean region possessed nothing that could be called civilization or religion. The Inca Garcilaso impresses on readers that "It must therefore be realized that in the first age of primitive heathendom there were Indians who were little better than tame beasts and others much worse than wild beasts. To begin with their gods, we may say that they were of a piece with the simplicity and stupidity of the times, as regards the multiplicity of gods and the vileness and cruelty of the things the people worshipped." [14] While the author recognizes that pre-Inca religions at times grew more complicated, he views them as all irrational and paganistic.

According to this account, it was the Incas who brought, along with

agriculture and other technical advancements, reforms in sexual morality. Such concepts as chastity and marital fidelity—in fact, marriage itself—are seen as Inca impositions. The Inca Garcilaso states that the Incas brought modest dress to lands in which, when they were not simply
nude, "the Indians were so simple and stupid in their way of dressing
and covering their bodies that their attempts at dress were laughable" [15]
and "their dress was so indecent that it is more a subject for silence and
secrecy than for discussion and description." [16] But, most importantly,
the Incas established a religion that was virtually Christian in all but
name. In this way, they laid the groundwork for the conversion of Andean peoples to Christianity as such. The Inca's version does not do justice to non-Inca Andean cultures and omits certain aspects of Inca religion. While it may not be literally accurate, his explanation is certainly
an ingenious solution to one of the problems he faced: how to praise Inca
religious culture without seeming less than faithful to the Christianity
that had replaced it.

As the Inca Garcilaso portrays Inca religion, he attempts to eliminate
those features that would arouse the disgust of European readers. His
discussion of offerings to the gods consists largely of an energetic denial
of the existence of human sacrifice among the Incas: "I can bear witness
to having heard my father and his contemporaries many times compare
the two states of Mexico and Peru, with particular reference to the question of human sacrifice and the eating of human flesh. They praised the
Incas of Peru for not indulging in or permitting these two practices, and
equally abominated the Mexicans who performed both of them." [17] The
topic of sacrifice provides another opportunity to distinguish the Incas
from the "Indians of the first age," that is, Andean Amerindian peoples
prior to the Inca influence, to whom he attributes the practice of offering
up human lives. [18]

The Inca's flattering, nostalgic portrait of the Inca empire did not occasion him serious difficulties with the authorities, though it had the potential to generate anxiety. After the anti-colonial Tupac Amaru rebellion
(1780) in Peru, the *Royal Commentaries* were banned there lest they
strengthen the desire to return to home rule.

In many respects, the Inca Garcilaso unites the elements of his identity and loyalties, but his work reveals inconsistencies and ambivalence.
The author often refers to himself as an *indio* while in other passages he
situates himself, with greater precision, in the category of *mestizo*. His
self-identification as an *indio* is emphasized with particular frequency in
the first part of his history, dealing with the Inca imperial period. It gen-

erally demonstrates his inside knowledge of the Inca state, empire, religion, and, above all, language. For example, to settle a linguistic issue he will say, "The Indians had not the word in their language, to which I, as an Inca, can testify."[19] Even in this part of his history, his recollections reveal that he was not raised as a member of any Amerindian community. His peer group consisted of other first-generation mestizos. He was schooled among other offspring of conquistadors and Amerindian women.

Toward the end of the first part of his history, the Inca dedicates a chapter (Chapter 31) to explaining the racial categories that have been created in colonial Peru. Here he unmistakably identifies himself as a mestizo and proclaims that membership in this category should be a source of pride: "The children of Spaniards by Indians are called mestizos, meaning that we are a mixture of the two races. The word was applied by the first Spaniards who had children by Indian women, and because it was used by our fathers, as well as on account of its meaning, I call myself by it in public and am proud of it, though in the Indies, if a person is told: 'You're a mestizo' or 'He's a mestizo,' it is taken as an insult."[20]

In the second part, where he tells the history of the Spanish in Peru, the Inca Garcilaso emphasizes that he is well qualified to be even-handed in his treatment of Amerindians and Spaniards. For this purpose, he calls attention to his dual background. The "Prologue" is addressed "To the Indians, mestizos, and *criollos* of the kingdoms and provinces of the great and very rich empire of Peru, from the Inca Garcilaso de la Vega." He hails the inherent talents of the major groups in Peru, but his praise is less than equitable: "ability is not in short supply among the natural Indians; and there is ability to spare among the Mestizos, the offspring of children of Indian women and Spanish men, or of Spanish women and Indian men. And among the criollos born here, and naturalized there." He then appeals to all three groups as "brothers and friends, relatives, Sires," and pleads for a unified effort to advance Peru.[21] In his dedication, addressed to the king, he names his illustrious forebears on both the maternal and paternal sides. In the latter case, he emphasizes his relatives' service to the crown and empire. In a postscript to the dedication, he states, "And the goal I most seek and hope for, is for everybody in that Empire [i.e., Peru under Spanish rule], Indians and Spaniards alike . . . to enjoy it together with me . . . because I have features that connect me to both peoples."[22] At the same time, in the front matter to this volume the author still refers to himself as an Indian when it suits the point he is seeking to establish. The instability of the Inca Garcilaso's identity, and his tortuous efforts to cast the best light on his ethnic makeup, today exercise a strong appeal upon readers of the *Royal Commentaries.*

Amerindian accounts of the conquest and its aftermath continue to become more available, fascinating both scholars and general readers. Felipe Guaman Poma de Ayala, an Andean author of indigenous ancestry, has been the object of increasing critical scrutiny since his work came to light in 1908. Guaman Poma's writing is not the only text left by Amerindians from the now-colonialized Andean region. The somewhat earlier Tito Cusi Yupanqui, who wrote in approximately 1570, and Guaman Poma's contemporary Santa Cruz Pachacuti, also set down in writing the information and principles that they considered most important. However, Guaman Poma's written testimony is the most wide-ranging and, simply, the largest. It also contains the greatest store of information about the life of Andeans (i.e., the various native peoples of the Andean region) under Spanish rule. Rolena Adorno summarizes the exceptional importance of the document: "Guaman Poma stands out as being one of the few Andeans who took part in the debate over the Conquest and colonization, and who left written testimony to it." [23] Andean oral history and genealogy were important sources for Guaman Poma, but he was also acquainted with European debates over colonization and the rights of native peoples under natural law. As he argues for the recognition of Amerindian rights and entitlements, Guaman Poma relies on the authority of both European and Andean predecessors.

The biography of this figure has proven difficult for researchers to reconstruct with certainty. Adorno, the most recognized authority on Guaman Poma, does not venture to give his birth and death dates. From what this author says about himself, it is fair to place his date of birth sometime after the Spanish conquest of the Inca empire in the early 1530s. He completed the work for which he is known, *Nueva corónica y buen gobierno,* sometime in the early to mid-1610s. After finishing the *Nueva corónica,* Guaman Poma brought it to Lima, meaning for it to be delivered to the Spanish king, Philip III. Guaman Poma's death date is unknown, although he was clearly still alive when he composed a separate letter in 1615.

Little is known about the document's fate between 1615 and the 1900s. It was in the antiquities collections of the Royal Library of Copenhagen in the mid-nineteenth century, when it was bound and stamped with the royal seal of the then-ruling Danish king. It would appear that the document was filed and forgotten. In 1908 the German researcher Richard Pietschmann came across the *Nueva corónica y buen gobierno* in the Royal Library. Now the document's value began to be recognized, but for years only a few researchers were able to view the manuscript. It was often in the hands of scholars attempting a transcription. In 1936 Paul Rivet, the director of the Ethnological Institute of Paris, resolved the problem of access by publishing a facsimile edition.[24] This edition became the basis of much research on Guaman Poma. Even though the facsimile reproduces the original quite clearly, reading it is an arduous task. Guaman Poma, whose mastery of Spanish was uncertain, tended to fill in the gaps with Quechua words. In composition and lettering, he had many idiosyncrasies, including a tendency to run words together, to form letters oddly, and to use cryptic abbreviations. In 1944 the first typeset edition appeared. Arthur Posnansky, in preparing this edition, had to make many judgment calls concerning the exact nature of the author's annotations. Although probably very few people have come to know this difficult document at first hand, information about it has become more and more widespread and has affected the way scholars view Andean culture under Spanish rule.

This manuscript, 1,179 pages in length and containing 397 drawings, could be characterized in various ways. It contains sections on history, genealogy, geography, and religion. The author describes his own efforts in the "extirpation of idolatries," or campaign to eliminate native religions, a form of service to the king for which he hopes to receive due recognition.

In some of the most-quoted passages, Guaman Poma evokes the suffering of the Amerindians under Spanish rule and proposes remedies. He calls for the return of Peru to the native peoples of the Andes, although the Spanish king would still enjoy global dominion as Monarch of the World. Since the *Nueva corónica* was intended to be sent to Philip III, and since it includes petitions and claims, it is fair to describe it as an undelivered letter to the king. Yet it is not intended for a single reader. Guaman Poma also hoped to take his case to the court of public opinion. Adorno points out that Guaman Poma referred to his document as a "book and chronicle" and that he "requested that it be published."[25] In her analysis, Guaman Poma would especially desire his document to be read as a history book, because histories were "the most authentic forum of debate about the practical and philosophical problems arising from the discovery and colonization of the New World."[26]

In serving as an advocate for the Andean peoples, Guaman Poma devotes considerable space to his own distinctive attributes and personal history. This is never more the case than in his extensive discussions of religious matters. Guaman Poma includes many reminders that he is a Christian. The author's mestizo half brother, Martín de Ayala, is a priest; in his letter, Guaman Poma speaks respectfully of Martín, to whom he owes his literacy. The *Nueva corónica* contains some positive comments on the work of religious orders. The Dominicans, a number of whom argued in defense of the rights of indigenous peoples, come in for praise for their education and religious devotion. At the same time, Guaman Poma is quick to criticize the cruel and corrupt practices of members of the clergy, especially those who venture out, virtually unsupervised, into Andean communities. As a participant in the extirpation effort, Guaman Poma observed many violations of the native Andeans' human rights, and he is eager to apprise the king of these abuses. The extirpation campaign at times took on the character of an inquisition, including the use of torture to produce false confessions of idolatrous practices.

Although Guaman Poma objects to the methods used by the clergy, he favors the establishment of Christianity. In his proposed plan, the Andean region would form part of a vast Christian empire in which all other forms of worship would be supplanted by Christian beliefs and practices. According to Guaman Poma, the ancient peoples of the Andean region were essentially Christian. They worshipped the same god as Jews and Christians and pursued an ideal of moral conduct identical to the Christian virtues. Guaman Poma is only one of many defenders of native peoples who claim that the Amerindians had absorbed the tenets of Christianity even before being introduced to its formal terms. According to Guaman Poma, idolatry was a misguided deviation from this natural Christianity; the dynasty of Inca emperors receives the blame for this misstep. Moreover, Christianity as such arrived in Peru in the early Christian era. The *Nueva corónica* asserts the then-popular belief that St. Bartholomew was in the Andean region and planted a cross.[27]

Guaman Poma is eager to affirm his identity as a prince. In his terms, he is one of the *principales,* that is, princes or high nobles, among the Andean peoples. He details his own genealogy, which includes both Inca and non-Inca noble families. His father was a descendant of the dynasty that ruled before the rise of Inca power. His mother was descended from the tenth Inca emperor, Tupac Inca Yupanqui. In this respect, his concern goes beyond affirming his own elite status. He argues that the

Spanish should respect the systems of royalty and high nobility that were already in place before the conquest.

A s the seventeenth century moves along, a number of texts exhibit a tendency to satirize human nature and society. The authors, many of whom were born in the Americas, ridicule humankind, especially those who are high on the social hierarchy. Among these is the work known as *El carnero,* translated into English as *The Conquest of New Granada,* by Juan Rodríguez Freyle. (There are variant spellings of his name.) Rodríguez Freyle was the son of a conquistador who was born in Sante Fe de Bogotá, today's Bogotá, in 1566 and died sometime around 1640. The *Carnero* gives 1638 as its date of completion. It circulated only in manuscript copies until it was printed in 1859. The original is lost.

While he spent six years in the colonial service in Spain, Rodríguez Freyle has a more American identity than most early New World writers of Spanish ancestry. The *Carnero* is considered an early manifestation of the Spanish American colonies' growing disaffection with Spain, which would eventually lead to the independence movement. The meaning of the word *carnero* has been much discussed. *Common grave,* perhaps a reference to the miscellaneous character of the text, is an often-proposed interpretation, but other possibilities remain open.[28] The full title of the work occupies most of the title page but does not help define *carnero.*

The *Carnero* is a hybrid text that draws upon both oral and erudite tradition, weaving tales and anecdotes together with literary allusions in a highly inventive exploration of history and human nature. The work presents itself as a chronicle of the period 1538–1638, the first hundred years of Nueva Granada (with some changes in borders, current-day Colombia), focusing on Santa Fe de Bogotá. Some portions are dry lists of information, but other passages veer off into gossip, folktales, and myth.

Readers with a literary bent have paid the greatest attention to those sections of the work that most closely resemble imaginative writing and tended to skip the portions heavy on names, titles, and dates. As David William Foster observes, numerous anthologies of Spanish American literature feature excerpts from the more fictionlike parts of the *Carnero.* In Foster's judgment, "By isolating these segments from the overall text, anthologies give the illusion that *El carnero* is a history punctuated by parenthetical segments that may be read as autonomous short stories or narrative sketches."[29] Foster argues against the habit of culling out and focusing upon those sections that most readily lend themselves to a literary type of reading. In this critic's view, it is the narrator's ability to integrate such diverse elements into the *Carnero* that "gives the text its peculiar literary quality," an achievement that readers should not try to undo.[30]

In his "Notes Toward Reading Juan Rodríguez Freyle's *El carnero:* The Image of the Narrator," Foster proposes a reading strategy that would respect "the necessary structural integrity of a text."[31] In search of a way to read the text as a unity, Foster concentrates on the role of the narrator of the *Carnero.* The speaker in the *Carnero* frequently justifies his activities as a chronicler and makes a number of appeals to the reader. In Foster's analysis, a common feature of all portions of the text is the narrator's effort "to demonstrate that, in fact, the history of the Nuevo Reino de Granada is worth telling about." Reciprocally, the narrator calls for a reader who possesses "the quality of curiosity" about the information revealed.[32]

In the more narrative sections, Rodríguez Freyle enjoys withholding secrets and delaying revelations. He has a special predilection for stories in which troves of valuables are buried, sunken, or otherwise concealed; in real life, the author was a persistent, though not very successful, treasure hunter. Secret passageways, encoded communications, and hidden identities also figure in his tales. Rodríguez Freyle favors lurid subject matter including witchcraft, adultery, and murder. As a literary moralist, he condemns such practices yet describes them with many lively details and rhetorical flourishes. In some instances, the author claims to be relating events that he witnessed at first hand. In others, he asserts that he worked with knowledgeable informants. He presents himself as a dedicated interviewer who takes care to obtain the indigenous perspective on local history as well as the Spanish viewpoint.

Many of Rodríguez Freyle's strategies for holding the reader's attention come from the repertory of oral storytellers, whose techniques the author has clearly studied closely and creatively reworked for his own needs. Rodríguez Freyle today is especially admired for his successful transformation of the methods of tellers of tales to suit the demands of written narrative exposition.

In the twentieth century another Colombian writer, Gabriel García Márquez (b. 1928), earned high critical praise for his adaptation of oral tradition to the genre of the novel. The *Carnero* can be seen as one of the sources or pre-texts for García Márquez's most celebrated novel, the

1967 *Cien años de soledad* (*One Hundred Years of Solitude*). One parallel is particularly striking: the *Carnero* is the chronicle of one hundred years of Colombian history, while *One Hundred Years of Solitude* tells the story of a fictional town over a like period. (Actually, the events of the novel cover somewhat more than one hundred years.) Rodríguez Freyle purports to tell the history of real-world Nueva Granada, and García Márquez presents his story as the plot of a novel. Rodríguez Freyle starts from Bogotá's beginnings and leaves the city still bustling in 1638; García Márquez takes his fictional town from its founding to its cataclysmic destruction.

Beyond pointing out links between the *Carnero* and *One Hundred Years of Solitude,* Foster observes more subtle and pervasive similarities between Rodríguez Freyle's chronicle and Spanish American fiction of the latter part of the twentieth century. For example, the narrator's preoccupation with the misdeeds and pettiness of figures of authority "foreshadows the demythificational thrust of so much modern Latin American literature."[33]

There was a widespread fascination during this period with narratives of Spaniards or American-born *criollos* living for extended periods in alien milieux. The protagonists, who may be captives or stranded castaways, become the sole representatives of Western Christian society, surrounded either by members of radically different cultures or by deviant Europeans, such as cannibalistic pirates, who have abandoned civilized ways. An outstanding example of these narratives of immersion in exotic cultures is a Chilean work (manuscript of 1673, printed version 1863), *El cautiverio feliz y razón individual de las guerras dilatadas del Reino de Chile* (Happy captivity and the reason for the protracted wars in Chile). It is the only work that Francisco Núñez de Pineda y Bascuñán (1607?–early 1680s) is known to have written. In 1629 this Chilean-born soldier was wounded and captured while fighting against the Araucanians, the same indomitable indigenous people that Alonso de Ercilla depicted favorably in his above-mentioned *La Araucana.* During the more than six months that Pineda spent as a prisoner of war, he developed an admiration for the Araucanians and a respect for their struggle to resist conquest and maintain self-rule.

In the first half of the work, Pineda offers an adventure-filled narrative of his time in the custody of a benevolent, honorable Araucanian chieftain, Maulicán. The narrative is crammed with dramatic episodes, ethnographic detail, and various literary embellishments. In the section relating the author's captivity, the main plot centers on the efforts of the noble Maulicán, who has vowed to return Pineda to his father, to protect the white man from other Araucanian chieftains who would like to kill him. To keep Pineda alive, Maulicán must keep him continually on the move, so the narration is also a traveler's account of Araucanian territory. Several episodes focus attention on the prisoner's relations with Araucanian women, whom he praises for their cleanliness, grace, and beauty. Araucanian men, as a sign of hospitality, invite Pineda to enjoy the favors of female tribe members, and the women themselves make very frank overtures to him. These episodes, which at times include erotic descriptions of the women, invariably end with the Spaniard resisting temptation and maintaining his chastity.

The second half is an essay on Spanish-Araucanian relations. Pineda is in the line of Spanish commentators who sympathize with native peoples and draw attention to the cruelty with which the Spanish have often treated the Amerindians. In this author's analysis, the Araucanians continue their resistance because the Spanish have antagonized them with needlessly harsh treatment.

*T*he seventeenth century also saw the most distinguished intellectual figure of the colonial era, Sor Juana Inés de la Cruz. This Mexican Hieronymite nun, whose original name was Juana Ramírez de Asbaje or Asuaje, was probably born in 1648, though earlier her birth date was believed to be 1651, and died in 1695. Sor Juana was the most accomplished of the numerous Spanish American baroque poets. She composed a good deal of poetry, both pious and worldly, secular and sacramental plays, devotional works, carols, letters, and various treatises, critiques, and statements.

While women wrote in the Spanish colonies, they generally chose religiously approved topics or discreetly concealed their identities. Sor Juana was in the spotlight as an intellectual and a poet on secular themes. Georgina Sabat-Rivers points out the public recognition that distinguished Sor Juana from her often pseudonymous and little-known predecessors and contemporaries: "Sor Juana, even though her literary reputation has suffered from the critical ups and downs of *culteranismo* [a form of baroque], never had to conceal her own name and has always been fully recognized as a major figure in Mexican and Hispanic letters." [34]

The defense of women's rights, especially the right to education and intellectual activity, is one of Sor Juana's great themes. She is often called a feminist, though of course the term was not in circulation in her time, for her promotion of educational equality. Seventeenth-century New Spanish society stressed the education of girls in Catholic doctrine, devotions, and morality, along with household management. But it was not considered necessary to add academic subjects. Literate women were the exception even in the upper classes. Public intellectual life, such as lectures and polemics, was a flourishing but all-male activity.

Although Sor Juana was not primarily a writer of narrative prose, her most widely read and quoted work, an extensive letter of 1 March 1691 justifying her much-criticized dedication to intellectual endeavors and secular verse, contains an account of her life. Sor Juana included the autobiographical narrative in her own defense to demonstrate that her devotion to learning and the arts was a God-given, irresistible "inclination" and not a quest for personal glory. This rhetorically intricate and sometimes bitterly sarcastic document, enjoyed by non-specialists and continually debated among scholars, is known in Spanish as the "Respuesta a Sor Filotea de la Cruz" or variants on this title. International readers' discovery of Sor Juana starting in the 1970s has resulted in several English translations with various titles. One of the first English versions, by the noted translator Margaret Sayers Peden, is "A Woman of Genius."[35] Alan Trueblood entitles his translation the "Reply to Sor Philotea"; it is the version that will be cited here.[36] Electa Arenal and Amanda Powell produced a bilingual critical edition entitled "The Poet's Answer to the Most Illustrious Sor Filotea de la Cruz."[37]

Sor Juana composed the "Respuesta" at a moment when she was under fire. By the late 1680s, she had earned a great deal of esteem as a writer and intellectual. She benefited especially from her friendship with two wives of viceroys. The first of these was Leonor Carreto, the Marquise of Mancera, who favored Juana when the latter served as a maid-in-waiting in her court.

Later, when Sor Juana was already established as a Hieronymite nun and respected poet, she enjoyed an affectionate relationship with María Luisa, the Countess of Paredes, who held an important title of her own as well as sharing the influence of her husband. Some believe that the two may have been in love with one another. Since the 1980s, in a phenomenon reaching well beyond academic studies, Sor Juana has become an emblematic figure of the cultural expression of lesbians. The 1990 film biography of Sor Juana, *Yo la peor de todas* (*I, the Worst of All*), directed by María Luisa Bemberg, upset some viewers and appealed to others by showing the relation as one of lesbian desire. Whatever the nature of this attachment, both the viceroy and his wife were powerful protectors for a nun pursuing a public writing career.

After María Luisa and her husband were recalled to Spain, Sor Juana's critics increased their objections to her worldly contacts and preoccupation with secular learning and arts. The Countess of Paredes oversaw and most likely underwrote the 1691 publication, in Madrid, of the first volume of Sor Juana's work, *Inundación Castálida* (Inundation from the Muses' spring).

The publication of Sor Juana's book made it clear how daring her activity was becoming. It was not uncommon for contemporary nuns to write, but for spiritual perfection. Asunción Lavrín summarizes:

> Writing was a common enough activity within the cloisters. However, prior to Sor Juana, none of the works of these women seems to have been published or to have received much attention . . . Some of these works were written at the instigation of the nuns' confessors, and this confessional character has apparently condemned them to oblivion. In their times they were regarded as a means of refining the self and ultimately achieving its perfection, but not as literary pieces. Nuns were not supposed to write for pleasure. Even so, the variety of these works is surprising: autobiographies, biographies, histories of convents, plays, poetry, and personal letters. Most remain in manuscript in the archives of Mexico and Spain; others have been lost forever and are known only through excerpts or references in other works.[38]

Writing by colonial-era nuns is today being rediscovered and published. Indeed, fascination with this previously little-known body of early women's writing has spread to an international readership, as witness the success of Electa Arenal and Stacey Schlau's English-language anthology *Untold Sisters: Hispanic Nuns in Their Own Works* (1989) and Elisa Sampson Vera Tudela's *Colonial Angels: Narratives of Gender and Spirituality in Mexico, 1580 –1750* (2000).[39]

Jean Franco's highly influential *Plotting Women: Gender and Representation in Mexico* (1989) increased awareness of the expression of colonial Mexican women as a "struggle for interpretive power."[40] Franco begins by analyzing the writing that mystical nuns carried out under the supervision of the priests who were their confessors.[41] Female mystics at moments appear to elude ecclesiastical restraint; their "rough vernacular language that often rips through the sanitized prose of hagiography opens up a space beyond the boundaries of the rational, a space of potentially transgressive female desire."[42] Yet the confessors' supervision and editing contain the nuns' expression within norms, and their "religious experiences were caught up in the dominant discourse."[43]

In contrast, Sor Juana appears disinclined to mysticism; instead, she pushed the boundaries of the acceptable by writing on worldly themes. She composed many poems with amorous subject matter. Some are clearly not allegories of divine love but secular love poems. Readers have been especially taken aback by the poems of loving friendship that Sor Juana addressed to the Countess of Paredes. Octavio Paz observes that the fervid poems directed to the countess are not merely surprising to us today but also seemed unusual to Sor Juana's contemporaries: "Their perplexity is similar to our own; they asked the same questions we ask ourselves: how to interpret them?"[44] It was Sor Juana's worldliness that would bring her trouble.

For a cloistered nun, Sor Juana was certainly in the limelight, especially during the 1680s. She was able to maintain outside friendships in part because her rise to fame coincided with a period of relaxed rule in convents. Another factor was the just-noted favor she enjoyed in court circles. Visitors were allowed to come to the convent for intellectual discussions with Sor Juana, and devotees sent her gifts and letters. She was sought after to compose verses celebrating highly placed persons and official events. Her celebrity frequently gave rise to apprehension and resentment. Sor Juana's confessor was urging her to be less of a worldly, public poet and more of a seeker of spiritual perfection. It should be remembered that humility, and even self-humiliation, were regarded as great virtues for devout women.

The tensions that had been building around Sor Juana brought open conflict when, sometime in the late 1680s, she began to take issue with a published sermon by Antônio Vieyra, a Portuguese Jesuit with admirers in New Spain. He was very much identified with the Jesuit order, which was flourishing in the colonies but, then as always, a lightning rod for controversy. Sor Juana first formulated her critique in oral form. Contemporaries were fascinated by the fact that Sor Juana had boldly raised objections to Vieyra's sermon, and second-hand reports of her arguments began to circulate. The critique caused a notable stir, not just for the sharpness of the reasoning but for the author's daring in questioning the logic of such an authoritative churchman. Some observers surmised that Sor Juana was finding weaknesses in Vieyra's thought as an attack either on the Society of Jesus generally or on local church officials, up to and including the Archbishop of Mexico, who belonged to the order. Sor Juana eventually wrote her ideas up at the request of a person (most likely the Bishop of Puebla, Manuel Fernández de Santa Cruz) whom she does not name. Though Vieyra is not identified by name either, it was common knowledge among Mexico City intellectuals that he was the individual whose ideas were under attack.

Finally, the Bishop of Puebla had this controversial critique published in November 1690 under the title *Carta atenagórica* (Letter worthy of Athena). The critique was later published in the second volume (1692) of Sor Juana's collected *Obras* (*Works*) under a lengthy title beginning *Crisis sobre un sermon . . .* (Crisis over a sermon . . .). Though it has always been easy to obtain access to the critique, over the years this text has lost much of its interest. Considerable stretches of its detailed argumentation now strike readers as, to use Paz's term, "vain subtlety and empty ingenuity." [45] Even if the theological arguments no longer grip the imagination, today's readers must be struck by the daring directness with which Sor Juana assailed the logic of such a distinguished ecclesiastical official. In the assessment of Georgina Sabat-Rivers, the *Carta atenagórica* "represents a landmark in the relations, on an intellectual level, of woman with the authorities." [46]

A subject of endless discussion and conjecture is the way that the critique was printed and presented and the consequences of its publication. The bishop added as a foreword an open letter addressed to Sor Juana and signed with the conventional pseudonym Sor Filotea de la Cruz. [47] The bishop's letter is available in English as "Admonishment: The Letter of Sor Philotea de la Cruz." It was clear to the many contemporaries following this conflict-fraught affair that the bishop had composed the letter. Yet both the pseudonym and the text maintain the fiction of female authorship. Sor Filotea refers to "our sex, inclined as it is to vanity." [48] Possibly the feminine persona was meant to soften the criticism by giving the effect of an affectionate but rule-enforcing mother superior offering guidance to a nun who was straying too far into the world. In his letter the bishop recognizes Sor Juana's exceptional talents and recommends that she continue to study and write, but always with sacred content. He singles out her secular poetry, which appears to have been disturbing to a number of her critics, as her most objectionable undertaking.

The motive for publishing the critique and writing the pseudonymous letter has long aroused curiosity, with many Sor Juana aficionados seeking to second-guess the bishop. Georgina Sabat-Rivers, greatly respected for her research on Sor Juana, asserts that the bishop's intention was to help Sor Juana. As Sabat-Rivers points out, by the time that the *Carta atenagórica* appeared in print Sor Juana was already under fire, and the publication cannot be considered the cause of her difficulties. Sabat-Rivers summarizes the situation of 1690: "Battle lines were drawn up, and Sor Juana found herself in great difficulties she had not foreseen ... The bishop of Puebla, Manuel Fernández de Santa Cruz, a friend and defender of Sor Juana, intervened on her behalf by publishing in Puebla, in 1690, her critical essay with the admiring title of *Carta atenagórica* ... He appended a letter of his own, with the pseudonymous feminine signature 'Sor Filotea de la Cruz,' in which he praised her and urged her to stop writing profane works in order to concentrate on theology." [49] This expert's analysis is consistent with the longstanding intellectual friendship between the relatively liberal bishop and Sor Juana.

Another view is that the bishop intended both the *Carta atenagórica* and the foreword as a potshot at the Archbishop of Mexico, Francisco Aguiar y Seijas, who besides being the bishop's rival was a Jesuit, an admirer of Vieyra, a misogynist, and a hard-liner about discipline in religious houses. If this is true, Sor Juana's activities, controversial as they were, did not constitute the principal issue; rather, the publication was another episode in the rancorous relations between two powerful ecclesiastical authorities.

The attempt to guess the real story behind the *Carta atenagórica* has long been a pastime of Sor Juana researchers. The 1982 publication of *Sor Juana Inés de la Cruz, o las trampas de la fe (Sor Juana or, the Traps of Faith,* 1988) by the renowned Mexican poet-essayist Octavio Paz, set off a proliferation of sometimes arcane speculation. As a Nobel-winning poet and public intellectual, Paz enjoys greater freedom to speculate than do academic researchers, who must support all their claims with evidence. His book provides both facts and well-informed guesses about the hidden agendas underlying Sor Juana's critique of Vieyra and the letter from "Sor Filotea" that prefaced it.[50] His reconstruction of the behind-the-scenes motives gained wide exposure after his book reached a readership well beyond academic circles. The earlier-noted film biography by Bemberg draws to a great extent on Paz's book. The movie offers its own speculative reconstruction of the hidden circumstances surrounding the publication of Sor Juana's critique, which is not identical to that presented by the Mexican essayist. Paz's analysis supports the idea that "the *Carta atenagórica* is a polemical text in which criticism of Vieyra veils criticism of Aguiar." [51] The publication, the foreword, and even the bishop's female pseudonym were all part of a thinly disguised campaign to insult the archbishop.[52] In composing the critique, Sor Juana was willingly, if not very wisely, involved in the veiled attack on Aguiar y Seijas: "Sor Juana was not the instrument of the Bishop of Puebla. She was his ally."[53] Paz concludes that "Sor Juana intervened in the quarrel between two powerful Princes of the Roman Church and was destroyed in the process."[54]

However benign the bishop may have meant his letter to Sor Juana to be, the recipient clearly did not appreciate it as constructive criticism. Her "Respuesta a Sor Filotea" ("Reply to Sor Philotea") is written in rebuttal of the letter and in self-defense. Like the original letter from Sor Filotea, Sor Juana's "Reply" is an open letter; she would have expected it to be read by a number of people who had been following with rapt attention the conflicts surrounding her. The "Reply" has come in for repeated scrutiny both for its content and for its indirect and even devious rhetoric. The letter begins and ends in what is on the surface an unctuously eager-to-please tone. Sor Juana continues the fiction that Sor Filotea is another nun. Presenting a display of submissive groveling, Sor Juana apologizes for not having replied sooner and explains that "in reality I know nothing worthy of you."[55] In the same apparently servile vein, she asks: "Am I, perchance, anything but a poor nun, the least of all the world's creatures, and the most unworthy of engaging your attention?"[56] Readers of the text soon begin to encounter signs that indicate that the superficially abject letter-writer has not been in the least humbled by the reproof. Josefina Ludmer, in a much-cited analysis entitled "Tricks of the Weak," views the "Reply" as a text designed to compensate for Sor Juana's lack of power. In particular, Sor Juana possesses much less strength than the authorities with whom she has engaged in conflict and cannot face her accusers head on. With directly confrontational strategies ruled out, Sor Juana develops an ingenious set of devices for stating her case. As Ludmer puts it, "We shall read in Sor Juana's letter tricks of the weak, of one in a position of subordination and marginality."[57]

It soon becomes clear that Sor Juana is eager to express, usually between the lines, her anger at male domination. Her discontent becomes increasingly evident as the letter proceeds. Finally she brings into the open her belief that her criticism of Vieyra was considered out of line because it came from a woman. Late in the letter, she enters into a debate about the interpretation of St. Paul's words "Women should be silent in church," arguing that the intention was simply to diminish extraneous noise during services, not to forbid women from speaking on important religious matters.

Viewed in its totality, the "Reply" is not a narrative as such but rather a defense and justification of her intellectual activity. However, the central portion of the "Reply" is an autobiographical account. This much-studied document is not one unitary statement; rather, Sor Juana repeatedly changes the type of writing task that she is carrying out. In Josefina Ludmer's summary: "Juana's letter contains at least three texts: (1) the text written directly to the bishop; (2) what has been read as her intellectual autobiography; and (3) the polemic regarding St. Paul's statement that women remain silent in church." [58] Ludmer further comments: "We also note the insertion of one lesser genre, autobiography, within another, the letter." [59] The implication is that, seeing the main avenues of literature and philosophy dominated by more powerful men, Sor Juana took the side roads. The narrative portion of the "Reply," in which Sor Juana tells the story of her life, is clearly the section that has galvanized readers over the centuries.

Sor Juana's defense of her devotion to learning rests in great part on the principle that God endowed or afflicted her with an irresistible natural bent. As corroboration, she relates anecdotes in which she acted in the grip of this tendency. She learned to read at three by following her sister to school and telling the teacher that her mother had sent her. Later she begged her mother to dress her in male attire and send her to the university in Mexico City. As a child, Sor Juana developed rituals to make herself learn; she would cut off some portion of her hair and only allow it to grow out if she had mastered a given lesson by a deadline. Although she liked cheese, she stopped eating it after hearing that it diminished intelligence. Sor Juana emphasizes that, because she was a female child, she had little opportunity for formal instruction and taught herself, for the most part, through readings in her grandfather's library. On most occasions, she had "no other teacher than books themselves. One can readily imagine how hard it is to study from those lifeless letters, lacking a teacher's voice and explanations. Still I happily put up with all those drawbacks, for the sheer love of learning." [60]

After this account of her childhood, single-mindedly focused on her relentless studies, Sor Juana skips over her years at court; throughout the "Reply," the author downplays the more glamorous aspects of her life. Leaping from childhood to her later teen years, she attempts to answer a question that was evidently raised by some contemporaries as well as by many curious observers in later centuries: why did she become a nun?

One may certainly wonder, since Sor Juana, although she was a good enough Catholic, gives no sign of being especially pious. Her primary devotion was evidently to learning and intellectual activities, not to worship. The explanation of her decision that Sor Juana offers in the "Reply" has been reread and reexamined obsessively. Sor Juana admits that she was not particularly attracted to convent life: "I knew that that way of life involved much that was repellent to my nature." She worried that religious observances would interfere with her studies, although she also appears to have hoped for an opportunity to read and write. Her rationale for the decision is that she had few alternatives in life and a religious order seemed to offer the safest haven, "given my total disinclination to marriage."[61]

Dorothy Schons, in "Some Obscure Points in the Life of Sor Juana Inés de la Cruz," points out that many commentators "have examined this point in her life with the eyes of the present instead of with the eyes of the past."[62] In Schons's analysis, Sor Juana, had she remained at court as a mature woman, would have feared the loss of her virginity in this at times dissolute environment.[63] While Sor Juana does not allude openly to her chastity in the "Reply," she refers to convent life as "the least unreasonable and most becoming choice I could make to assure my ardently desired salvation."[64] Schons reminds readers that the role of the maiden aunt did not yet exist.[65] The expectation was that a respectable woman would either marry or take the veil. Schons's explanation is realistically likely, especially given the contemporary preoccupation with female chastity.

In her account, Sor Juana says little of the glittering success that she enjoyed during the 1680s or the distinguished and influential friends who paid her visits. Downplaying her secular contacts is consistent with her outwardly humble characterization of herself as "a poor nun" rather than a celebrity.[66] Sor Juana tells her story as that of a plucky, tenacious scholar driven to learn in the face of adversity. She says that her true wish was "to live alone"[67] and that convent life was the next best thing to this unattainable ideal. Once in the convent, the studious nun suffers constant disruptions, "such as when I am reading, those in a neighboring cell take it upon themselves to play music and sing. Or when I am studying and two maids quarrel and come to me to settle their dispute. Or when I am writing and a friend comes to visit . . . This goes on all the time."[68]

Beyond the inconveniences of communal living, Sor Juana complains of persecution. As a result of her poetic talent, "what nastiness have I not been subjected to, what unpleasantness has not come my way!"[69] In an argument not completely consistent with her earlier protestations of humility, she asserts that the hostility toward her is motivated by envy of her accomplishments. Here Sor Juana mentions "the encomiums of general acclaim" that her work has brought her, yet the mention of her fame is part of her self-characterization as a beleaguered seeker after truth: "amidst the bouquets of that very acclaim, such asps of invidiousness as I could never describe have stirred and reared up."[70]

In 1981 Sor Juana students were astonished by the discovery of a previously unknown letter from her, written around 1681 or 1682, that seems to be the forerunner of the "Reply." Aureliano Tapia Méndez found the letter in a seminary library and published an annotated facsimile edition.[71] Despite initial skepticism, experts came to regard the letter as genuine. Paz included it in the third edition of his *Sor Juana,* and it is in the English version.[72] Often called the *Carta de Monterrey,* this document is not an open letter like the "Reply" but a private message to Sor Juana's confessor, Antonio Núñez de Miranda. According to the letter, Núñez de Miranda had been complaining about his headstrong protegee. His comments came back to Sor Juana, provoking her to write the letter. The letter found in Monterrey is shorter and less literary than the "Reply." Its arresting feature is the vehemence of Sor Juana's reproof to her confessor. Stephanie Merrim summarizes the relation between the letters: "Though in many ways a blueprint for the *Respuesta,* and touching on several of the same topics, the language and argumentation of the *Autodefensa* are shockingly different. Rather than the unctuous rhetoric of subordination, here we find assertive and biting rhetoric with no subterfuges; these few pages effectively deflate the many concerted efforts on the part of exegetes to render Sor Juana a saintly servile nun."[73] In this letter, Sor Juana appears ready to dismiss Núñez de Miranda as her confessor, saying, "What obligation is there that my salvation be effected through Y. R. [Your Reverence]? Can it not be through another? Is God's mercy restricted and limited to one man?"[74]

Since the emergence of feminist literary criticism in the 1970s, Sor Juana's writings have been reread in search of their insights into issues of gender. Of course, this theme is most evident in her reply to Sor Filotea, where she complains of male domination of intellectual endeavors. Other of Sor Juana's works, such as a much-cited poem beginning "Foolish men . . . ," also criticize men's outlook on and behavior toward women. However, the feminist study of Sor Juana's writings has expanded to texts in which gender is not an overt theme. An outstanding example is Sabat-Rivers's "A Feminist Rereading of Sor Juana's *Dream.*"[75] Sabat-Rivers finds in Sor Juana's great baroque poem, the *Primero Sueño* or *Sueño* (translated into English as *El sueño* and *The Dream*), a number of "emphases and characteristics that give evidence of the woman behind the pen that did the writing."[76]

While Sor Juana was the outstanding baroque poet in the Americas, there were many practitioners of this style. Sabat-Rivers in her 1992 *Estudios de literatura hispanoamericana: Sor Juana Inés de la Cruz y otros poetas barrocos de la colonia* (Studies in Spanish American literature: Sor Juana Inés de la Cruz and other baroque poets of the colonial era) offers analyses of baroque poetry by both female and male poets living geographically dispersed in the Spanish American colonies.[77]

It would be possible to generate a long list of names of Spanish American baroque writers, but just one other will be mentioned here. Among the most significant scholars of the colonial period was a Mexico City–based professor and poet who moved in the same circles as Sor Juana and supported her participation in intellectual life. Carlos de Sigüenza y Góngora (1645–1700) was a scholar skilled in mathematics and cosmography as well as a creative writer. His penchant for independent critical reasoning came to the fore during a controversy over comets, provoked by the appearance of one of these celestial bodies over Mexico City (1680–1681). The preponderant ecclesiastical outlook was that comets heralded catastrophe, while Sigüenza y Góngora recognized them as naturally occurring phenomena. His baroque poetry is not easily appreciated today, but there is still interest in his narrative of 1690, *Infortunios de Alonso Ramírez* (*Misfortunes of Alonso Ramírez*). *Misfortunes* is Sigüenza y Góngora's reconstruction, in the first person, of the experiences of an informant who has endured imprisonment by pirates, shipwreck, and other unusual experiences in exotic locales.

On the whole, it is fair to say that eighteenth-century Spanish American colonies did not produce as much outstandingly original writing as they did in the previous century. The baroque manner lingered well past the period (roughly the seventeenth century) that is generally regarded as the baroque period. One often hears it said that the baroque permanently marked Spanish American expression. While even casual observers have made observations along these lines, the idea has also been formulated by celebrated intellectual figures. For example, Alejo Carpentier (1904–1980), the celebrated Cuban novelist and essayist, asserts, "Our art was always baroque: from the splendid pre-Colombian sculpture and the codices, up to the best present-day novel-writing in [Latin] America, by way of the cathedrals and colonial monasteries of our continent."[78]

The eighteenth century stands out for a growing spirit of criticism, directed especially against institutions of social control. The principles and general outlook of the Enlightenment were spreading throughout Europe and the Americas. As people gave greater importance to liberty and equality, and less to established authority, royalty, the aristocracy, and ecclesiastical officials all became fair game for criticism and satire. In the Americas, both British- and Spanish-ruled, colonial government was increasingly under attack. For some time, many intellectuals in Spain's American colonies continued to voice the hope that colonial government could be reformed. But even those thinkers who were not yet calling for a break with Spain were increasingly willing to point out the shortcomings of colonial rule.

Representative of these tendencies is the writer known as Concolorcorvo (Alonso Carrió de la Vandera), who was born around 1715 in Gijón, Spain, and died probably in 1773. The real-world Carrió de la Vandera came to the New World colonies as a young man. He first lived as a merchant and then began to seek posts in the Spanish colonial government. He became a figure of controversy after he was appointed to inspect and improve postal service, which had just then come under the control of the crown. As Carrió de la Vandera traveled the route from Buenos Aires and Montevideo to Lima, surveying the chaotic and corrupt running of the postal system, his reformer's zeal came to the fore. Though his charge actually was to reform the postal organization, the unanticipated thoroughness with which he went about his task created friction with his superior, and he came to be regarded as a thorn in the side of the colonial administration. A characteristic gadfly, Carrió until his last days wrote in criticism of the government, the church, and local folkways that he considered disorderly and wasteful.

Concolorcorvo is the name used by this official to publish an underground text, *Lazarillo de ciegos caminantes* (*El Lazarillo: A Guide for Inexperienced Travelers between Buenos Aires and Lima*). The word *lazarillo*, besides denoting "guide," links this book to the picaresque tradition; the best-known picaresque novel in Spanish is the anonymous 1554 *Lazarillo de Tormes*, whose protagonist spends time as a blind man's guide. The Spanish American *Lazarillo*, full of social and moral criticism as well as some rollicking narratives, made its appearance surrounded by secrecy and deliberate misinformation. A good deal of the research on the *Lazarillo* has been devoted to discovering what is behind the false indications provided by the author and publisher. The work was published, most likely without authorization, in Lima in 1775 or 1776. Yet the publication data in the volume indicate that it appeared in Gijón in 1773. The title gives the impression that the work is a travel guide, which it is, but only among many other things. As the book begins, someone who appears to be responsible for the composition of the text presents himself, not as a Spanish colonial official, but as an indigenous Andean man, Calixto Bustamante Carlos Inca, known by the nickname Concolorcorvo (Crow-colored). In an enormously lengthy title, Concolorcorvo credits Alonso Carrió de la Vandera—now known to be the actual author—with coming up with the subject matter for the book as they chatted during their trip from the neighboring cities of Montevideo and Buenos Aires to Lima. Concolorcorvo was a real-life figure and did accompany Carrió de la Vandera on this trip. However, the Spaniard was the one to compose the book. The misattribution of authorship is not just the real author's attempt to avoid reprisals for some inflammatory observations contained in the *Lazarillo*. The work's uninhibited criticism of Spanish colonial society would make sense coming from a disaffected outsider such as an Amerindian. Concolorcorvo displays no interest in defending the government, church, or other authority-wielding institutions; his narration has a cheerful air of "nothing to lose."

While the *Lazarillo* exemplifies the newly critical spirit that would eventually lead to the wars of independence, readers should remember that it is not actually a revolutionary or even anti-colonial text. Indeed, the speaker defends the Spanish campaign of conquest and establishment of colonies in the Americas. Columbus, Cortés, and Pizarro appear favorably portrayed in the *Lazarillo*. However, eighteenth-century Spaniards do not receive the same respectful treatment. As Concolorcorvo none too diplomatically states, with reference to the city of Cuzco: "There is no doubt that it could be better managed in times of peace, and I maintain that the early Spaniards who settled it in tumultuous days were men of sounder judgment than those of today." [79]

Although Concolorcorvo did not recommend replacing colonial government with home rule and espoused reform rather than revolt, he can be considered a precursor of the independence movement. A number of passages in the *Lazarillo*—though not all—manifest an egalitarian outlook. An Enlightenment rationalist, Concolorcorvo takes the position that superstitious, senseless, and harmful practices should be denounced, whether the responsible party is a nomadic herdsman or a highly placed church or state authority. In a few respects, Amerindian society is superior to European. Concolorcovo has a pronounced horror of waste. Many episodes in the *Lazarillo* serve to denounce prodigality, a sin more typical of the Spanish than of the Amerindians, who use resources sparingly. In its judgments, the work distinguishes between the subjects of the great imperial states and native peoples living in less hierarchically organized societies. In Chapter 19 Concolorcovo repeats verbatim a dialogue he had with Carrió de la Vandera. Concolorcovo remarks to the Spaniard, "From all you have said I infer that you consider the Indians civil people." Carrió de la Vandera is then reported as saying, "If you are speaking of those Indians subject to the emperors of Mexico and Peru and their laws, bad or good, I say that they not only have been, and are, civil, but they are more obedient to their superiors than any other nation in the world." [80] Despite this limited appreciation of Amerindian ways, the *Lazarillo* on the whole strongly favors those individuals, whether Spanish or Spanish American, who possess a European-style, rationalistic education.

There is a link, though not a direct one, between the movement for Spanish American independence and the satirical, didactic, and moralistic writing exemplified by Carrió de la Vandera. Certainly this author was not anti-Spanish, and his goal was to reform the colonial system, with no mention ever made of doing away with it. Yet his eagerness to criticize authority and his generally Enlightenment outlook are indications of a lessening acceptance of the existing system of social control. The next chapter will survey the period when Spanish American intellectuals moved toward overt criticism of Spanish rule, the era of the armed struggle for independence (1810–1824), and the period of reorganization following the attainment of political independence for most of Spain's American colonies.

At the same time as the themes of independence, cultural autonomy, and nation-building are coming to the fore in the nineteenth century, significant shifts are occurring in the public's perception of literature. Fictional narrative attains greater respect and more accomplished practitioners among Spanish American writers. The result is a flourishing of the nineteenth-century Spanish American novel and short story.

| 𝒯HE STRUGGLE FOR NATIONHOOD
AND THE RISE OF FICTION

*W*hile the eighteenth century provides relatively few outstanding narrative works, the nineteenth offers an abundance. It was during the first half of this century that the novel and the short story emerged in Spanish America. Fictional narrative was beginning to win a place as a serious form of expression. During most of the colonial period, the reading of novels was linked in many people's minds with idleness, addiction to fantasy, and mental thrill-seeking. There was some reason to associate novel-reading with escapism, since medieval and Renaissance Europe saw the proliferation of lengthy fictional narratives full of such fantastic touches as magic rings, cloaks, and weapons, enchanted castles and mountains, and mirrors that revealed remote or future events. Spain prohibited novels in its New World colonies, apparently on the grounds that they might overexcite the imaginations of the inhabitants and give rise to insubordination. The ban did not prevent the colonists from acquiring and reading works of fiction, some of which arrived in the New World shortly after their original date of publication in Spain.

As the nineteenth century progressed, the novel gained ground as a vehicle for social criticism and as an art form. Although it was still not as prestigious as, for example, heroic poetry, more and more Spanish American authors took up the novel. John S. Brushwood summarizes the situation: "Fiction was not widely cultivated during the colonial period; after independence, novels appeared more frequently, but they were still relatively isolated. As for the number of titles published, it is probably safe to guess that more than 80 percent of nineteenth-century Spanish American novels appeared during the second half of the century." [1]

Of course, for Spanish American countries, the nineteenth century is deeply marked by the effort to win independence from Spain. In the early years of the century, the campaign for political independence is dominant. After the wars of independence conclude in 1824, the focus of attention shifts. Intellectuals encourage the achievement of cultural and intellectual autonomy and map out projects for national growth.

Much of nineteenth-century Spanish American narrative, until the last years of the century, is dominated by nationalistic concerns. In Francine Masiello's words, "Defining the nation, a topic that has once again attracted the attention of scholars, was an obsession with intellectuals of the nineteenth century." [2] Even works that do not overtly treat the theme of nation-building may deal with it in other ways. They may present a figure (usually a woman) who allegorically represents the nation, suggest the direction in which the country should develop, and describe local landscape and customs in an effort to develop a distinctive national literature. Doris Sommer, whose *Foundational Fictions: The National Romances of Latin America* (1991) examines nationalistic elements and founding national myths in nineteenth- and early twentieth-century Latin American novels, states: "Romantic novels go hand in hand with patriotic history in Latin America. The books fueled a desire for domestic happiness that runs over into dreams of national prosperity; and nation-building projects invested private passions with public purpose . . . Romance and republic were often connected . . . through the authors who were preparing national projects through prose fiction and implementing foundational fictions through legislative or military campaigns." [3]

While Sommer here refers specifically to romantic novels, a preoccupation with national questions is even more widespread than the above-cited passage would indicate. Whether written early in the nineteenth century, when neoclassicism was still the prevailing norm, during the mid-century period when romanticism was the dominant mode, or later in the century when realism commingled with romanticism and eventually became the stronger tendency, nineteenth-century Spanish American narrative makes national self-definition and development a major theme. Only at the end of the century, when *modernismo* became the leading tendency, did the topics of nation-building and the creation of national literature move out of the center of attention; yet even at the height of *modernismo* there was still a good deal of nationalistic literature.

The first prominent figure in this process is José Joaquín Fernández de Lizardi (Mexico, 1776–1827), a political journalist who also composed novels, poetry, plays, pamphlets, political broadsides, and annotated calendars (akin to Benjamin Franklin's almanacs). He is known as El Pensador Mexicano (The Mexican Thinker) after the title of his much-noted newspaper of 1812–1814; the term "thinker" is a reminder of Lizardi's Enlightenment-style rationalism. This writer is often singled out as the author of the first novel written and published in Spanish America, the 1816 *El Periquillo Sarniento* (*The Itching Parrot*). Such firsts are always disputable, and it is possible to argue that earlier Spanish American narratives possess some features of the novel. Yet *The Itching Parrot* is unquestionably the first Spanish American novel to win general recognition as such.

Because it is widely hailed as the first Spanish-language novel of the Americas and as, in Nancy Vogeley's phrase, "the innovative book" in Lizardi's oeuvre, *Periquillo* will be singled out for discussion.[4] It should be noted, though, that the same author published other successful novels. The 1818 *La Quijotita y su prima* (Little Miss Quixote and her cousin) is of interest for presenting Lizardi's recommendations concerning the upbringing of young women, while *Vida y hechos del famoso caballero don Catrín de la Fachenda* (Life and deeds of the famous gentleman Don Catrin de la Fachenda), of 1825, stands out for its satirical qualities.

Although Lizardi wrote *The Itching Parrot* before Mexico attained independence, and so technically it could be classified as a colonial text, it is widely regarded as an early work of Mexican national literature. *The Itching Parrot* exemplifies the assertion, made by Jorge Ruedas de la Serna, that throughout the nineteenth century Mexican literary intellectuals were pursuing "the mission of the writer" to build up a body of literature useful to Mexico.[5] Celia Miranda Cárabes summarizes the prevailing judgment on the novel's complicated relation to Mexico's sense of itself as a nation when she calls it a work "in which elements of an incipient nationalism stand out as it portrays life in colonial Mexico shortly before the beginning of independence."[6]

Lizardi had already begun his literary career shortly before the first outbreak of the Mexican independence struggle in 1810. He continued to write and publish throughout the struggle to overthrow Spanish rule, which lasted until 1821, and the early years of Mexico's independence. During this period, Lizardi was a highly visible public figure expressing dissatisfaction with the colonial authorities, but his relation to the anti-Spanish insurgency was tortuous.

Lizardi chastised colonial society harshly. José Luis Martínez sums up Lizardi's activities during the period when freedom of expression was declared in still-colonial Mexico in 1812 and the writer seized the opportunity to publish *The Mexican Thinker:* "In it, he defended freedom of the press, openly censured the colonial government, and even went so far as to publish a cruel satire of Viceroy Venegas, which resulted in freedom of the press being revoked and the brave writer sent back to jail."[7] We would like to think of him as one of those calling for a revolt against Spanish rule, but he long hesitated to do so. Though he was a perennial gadfly, Lizardi's position was that of a reformer rather than an advocate of the overthrow of the colonial regime.

A complicated historical event has confused the issue of Lizardi's position. In 1810 Lizardi, whom the viceroy had appointed acting mayor of the town of Taxco, was arrested for aiding and abetting the insurgents. His apprehension would seem to indicate pro-independence leanings. However, when Jefferson Rea Spell researched this incident, he discovered that Lizardi had authorization from the viceroy to feign submission to the insurgents when they reached Taxco. Since Taxco was poorly defended, "to save the town from pillage and its residents from wholesale slaughter . . . they planned to dissemble."[8] The idea was that later royalist troops would arrive and deal with the independence fighters, as indeed happened. The commanding officer of the pro-Spanish troops was unaware that Lizardi had acted with the viceroy's consent and arrested him, but the viceroy freed him.

Evidently Lizardi was slow to speak out in favor of the movement to overthrow Spanish rule. (It should be recalled that the insurgency began in rural areas; Lizardi was based in the viceregal capital of Mexico City, where the Spanish retained their hold until the latter phases of the lengthy struggle.) Throughout the 1810s, Lizardi was a thorn in the side of the colonial regime. He spent time in jail but hardly emerged chastened. Because of Lizardi's attacks on authorities, the insurgents at times saw him as a de facto ally, even if he would not openly take their side. At other moments, though, Lizardi alienated the insurgents by appearing to curry favor with the colonial government. Spell finds that it was not until March 1821 that "Lizardi, for the first time, voiced the opinion that it would be for the good of both countries if Mexico should be free of Spain."[9] The pamphlet was banned and Lizardi jailed for some days. In May or June of 1821, Lizardi came out in support of the insurgents.[10] Jacobo Chencinski, reviewing Lizardi's initial reluctance to support independence, remarks, "It seems almost absurd,"[11] given that his ideas were so similar to those of the insurgents. Chencinski reminds readers that Lizardi, a great rationalist, was hoping that the Spanish and their colonial subjects could reason together and bring about a "new order" without resorting to violence.[12]

It was during the lengthy struggle for independence that Lizardi published *The Itching Parrot* in installments, two chapters a week. The novel was divided into four books; the fourth did not become available until 1830–1831 owing to censorship. *The Itching Parrot* is not easy to characterize. It has some, but not all, of the features of the picaresque novel. Many critics have debated how close *Parrot* is to the Spanish picaresque novels that were widely read in Lizardi's day. In an especially careful analysis, Sonia Mora seeks to show that Lizardi, by reworking the traditional Spanish model, helps establish a distinctively Spanish American narrative. In Mora's judgment, Lizardi is not dependent upon or imitative of Spanish narrative; rather he is transforming it to create a literature better suited to the Mexican situation.[13] In an important change, Lizardi characterizes his protagonist not as a *pícaro* or rogue as such but rather as a solid, churchgoing citizen recalling episodes from his wild early years. Toward the end of the novel, the protagonist's confessor seeks to ease his shame over his misdeeds by referring to them mildly as "the adventures of a poor boy lacking experience and control."[14] In contrast, the rogue in a standard picaresque novel is an incorrigible sinner who fails to change his character no matter how many disgraceful experiences he suffers.

However ambiguous its relation to the picaresque tradition, *The Itching Parrot* qualifies unequivocally as a didactic novel. Lizardi designed his novel to appeal to as broad a reading public as possible. (Of course, most of the population was illiterate.) The novel is a vehicle for his social criticism, ethical teachings, and beliefs about education. Current-day, educated readers may experience impatience with the narrator's explicit and long-winded moralizing and other signs that Lizardi is reaching out to a relatively unsophisticated audience.

The Itching Parrot takes the form of an old man's account of his life, composed on his deathbed for the benefit of his offspring: "My beloved children, I have wanted to leave you a written account of the not-so-unusual events of my life, so you will retain them and avoid many of the dangers that threaten and indeed injure man in the course of his life."[15] The reader receives moral instruction along with the protagonist's offspring.

The first-person narrator is Pedro Sarmiento, who has been a drifter, a gambler, an assistant to unscrupulous masters, and at times a con artist, as well as a draftee, a castaway, and a kidnapping victim. He reformed in midlife and has since been an upstanding and productive member of society. In the last two segments of the novel, Pedro has already died, and "El Pensador," presumably Lizardi, takes over the narration, recounting the protagonist's end. The Pensador comes into possession of the manuscript that Pedro has left his children. Though it is a private document, the Pensador publishes it in the hope of improving the morals of society.

The work's title, *El Periquillo Sarniento,* refers to a derisive nickname that the narrator acquired as a schoolboy. *Sarniento,* meaning "mangy," is close to the surname *Sarmiento,* and of course *Pedro* and *periquillo* (parrot) are somewhat similar. The nickname fits the protagonist well during his shiftless youth, but once he becomes reintegrated into society, he reclaims the name Pedro.

The novel does not dwell exclusively on the hero's degradation but rather makes a determined effort to show uplifting scenes. While Pedro sees human nature at its worst, at other times he is treated with kindness and loyalty. During his years of drifting, a number of figures try to set him straight and offer him wise advice, which is reproduced at length in the novel. Indeed, he has the opportunity to witness a perfect society when he is shipwrecked on an imaginary Asian island. These chapters allow Lizardi to illustrate his ideas of how society should be regulated.

A well-defined program characterizes Lizardi's outlook and writing. He favors the Enlightenment ideal of independent, critical thought and opposes the old scholastic mode, with its emphasis on trusting the word of authorities. Education is a major concern of Lizardi's. He believes that young people should learn to think clearly, make fair and rational judgments, have good self-discipline and healthy habits, and contribute to society. Boys should be trained to earn an honest living, whether or not the livelihood confers any special prestige. Even if they will not hold paying jobs, girls should also be educated so that they will be judicious, prudent adults; they should learn to occupy their minds with serious matters rather than becoming preoccupied with luxury and diversions. Lizardi includes in *Parrot* a defense of the intellectual equality of men and women and devotes much of his novel *La Quijotita y su prima* to the best method of raising girls. Ornamental education, which enables professionals and aristocrats to spout Latin phrases but provides few skills beneficial to society, is one of Lizardi's targets of derision. Lizardi ridicules the traditional notion, especially strong in Spain and its colonies, that manual labor demeans the honor of high-born individuals. In Lizardi's vision, not only is the concept of hereditary honor preposterous, but the nobility's avoidance of mechanical labor makes this elite a burden upon society. The argument that the practical skills enhance an individual's worth had been gaining currency in progressive circles, propagated by Jean-Jacques Rousseau and others struck with his approach. The narrator of *The Itching Parrot* is set on the wrong course in life when his mother, who views herself and her son as nobility, overrules her husband's plan to have Pedro learn a trade. An exclusively humanistic education leaves Pedro, as he frequently observes, unable to do anything useful with his hands.

To turn over a new leaf, Pedro must exert himself in a hands-on job, managing an inn and store. By this time, he has overcome his aristocratic aversion to practical labor. He realizes that his regeneration can occur only when he begins making a productive contribution to society. The novel chastises idleness of any variety, whether that of the nobleman who cannot bear to soil his hands or that of beggars. In Lizardi's mind, work is redemptive both for the worker and for society as a whole.

Like many satirists, Lizardi targets the professions, with medicine receiving the lengthiest treatment. Pedro has a number of encounters with various types of health-care practitioners. An ignorant midwife brings about his wife's death by intervening too aggressively in a birth. Pedro serves as assistant first to a barber (at that time, barbers performed bloodletting, surgery, and dental extractions) and then to a pharmacist. After being a house servant to a physician, he poses, with some success, as a doctor. These episodes provide the point of departure for the protagonist to give voice to Lizardi's views on medicine. The medical field appears rife with opportunism and fraud. In Lizardi's judgment, physicians are overly aggressive in their treatments. He recommends a more conservative approach, placing greater trust in the healing powers of nature. The novel includes criticism of bloodletting and purges, which of course were mainstays of early nineteenth-century medicine, as harsh remedies that can kill debilitated patients.

Lizardi places some of the blame for poor health on the Mexicans' habits. Pedro believes that he would have been healthier if as a child he had exercised outdoors, eaten more spartanly, bathed in cool water, and kept regular hours. Another problem is in the artificial separation of the physician's and the pharmacist's roles. When Pedro is shipwrecked on the Utopian island, he learns that healers there are required to learn and practice every aspect of medicine, from diagnosis to the prescription and administration of treatments, the making and use of pharmaceutical remedies, and follow-up care. Moreover, they are paid only if the patient's health improves.

Lawyers, and the many scribes and clerks connected with them, come in for briefer but even more condemnatory treatment. In the perfect island society that Pedro visits, there are no professional lawyers. Instead, the entire population is involved in the administration of law. Lay people are taught to cooperate and to understand that they must abide by regulations. The little society's laws, together with the invariable penalties for breaking them, may be read from stone tablets distributed all over the island. Every attempt has been made to eliminate ambiguity from the legal system. The community's ability to solve its own problems also obviates the need for career soldiers and a standing army.

The clerical calling receives more respect than the professions, though the failings of certain priests, friars, and churchgoers are pointed out. The novel shows the attraction that religious institutions exercise on would-be idlers. Pedro becomes a theology student, thinking that it will be easier than military training. He fails to apply himself and makes an inglorious exit from seminary. Later Pedro talks his way into a Franciscan monastery, his real motive being "to avoid the dishonor that would come my way if I were to become an apprentice."[16] The monastic rule is too rigorous for the comfort-seeking Pedro. In the course of his wanderings, Pedro observes some venal and corrupt habits among local priests. These include charging destitute parishioners for their services and entering into collusion with the wealthiest and most powerful men of the community.

On the other hand, the clergy appears as an institution useful in guiding sinners. When the protagonist goes into crisis and decides to reform, he turns to priests for spiritual orientation. To distance himself from his old life, he retreats to a Jesuit monastery.[17] There he comes under the guidance of an old friend who has reformed and is becoming a Franciscan lay brother; Pedro confesses his sins and is reintegrated into the church as well as into respectable society.

Marriage and family life are the subject of some of Pedro's guidelines to his children. Lizardi clearly believes that married men make more solid citizens. However, the novel criticizes the way in which marriage partners are often chosen. There is condemnation of both arranged marriages, whereby prominent families consolidate their financial empires and bloodlines, and impetuously contracted love matches. Lizardi would like for men to marry only after they have matured and for both men and women to use rational criteria in their choice of mates. As an unreflective youth, Pedro rushes into an ill-fated marriage based on superficial attraction. Following his reform, he contracts a second marriage only after seriously discussing all aspects of the situation with his prospective father-in-law.

Lizardi's satire and moralizing target many other practices, including miserly hoarding, the habit of valuing women exclusively for their looks, racism, rudeness to persons of lower social class, and love of ostentatious luxury. The novel comes out repeatedly in favor of moderation: trouble is in store for those who are too rich, too poor, or too good-looking.

Researchers have, as noted above, scrutinized Lizardi's life for clues to his beliefs about Mexican independence. In more recent times, Nancy Vogeley has shifted the basis of the inquiry, instead looking for comments on colonial relations in Lizardi's fiction, especially *The Itching Parrot.* This scholar's thorough analysis shows that Lizardi was still sorting out his own thoughts on colonial rule when he composed *The Itching Parrot.* The novel's message concerning Mexico's colonial status is not uniform throughout, but in certain passages, such as those describing the ideal island society, readers may glimpse a critique of imperialism. For example, Vogeley finds that the discussion of work in the Utopian episode "reproaches . . . colonial economic notions" such as "the concept of colonial territories as part of the *real patronato,* the theory of wealth as bullion from American mines, Spanish monopolistic control of the colonies represented as protection, even the sordid trade based on slavery."[18]

It is fair to see *The Itching Parrot* as an effort to launch a Mexican literature clearly distinct from Spanish writing. In his "Prologue, Dedication, and Advisories to Readers," Lizardi shows his awareness that the situation of "American talents" is unlike that of Spanish authors.[19] New World writers face an uphill struggle to publish and must appeal to a relatively broad reading public to finance their work. Convinced that his work is unlikely to be sold in Spain, Lizardi focuses on Mexican readers.[20] In the same preface Lizardi tells his readers that he realizes that they may represent a broad spectrum: "I know that you may be plebeians, Indians, mulattos, Black people, plagued with vices, stupid, and sly."[21] Though Lizardi's Mexican public is less than elite, he accepts it as the one he needs to reach, and dedicates the book to his readers. This author's literary nationalism is especially evident in his decision to depict characters who were typical of various sectors of the national population and to employ words and phrases that are markedly Mexican. Vogeley asserts that the author's unadorned style distances his work from Spain and its power: "Lizardi's literary language is a model of decolonizing discourse . . . Lizardi's simple style, therefore, although designed to modernize colonial language, must be seen as an effort to repudiate the inherited Peninsular taste for linguistic virtuosity that so often disguised intellectual deficiency and blocked American thinking."[22]

A short way into the nineteenth century, independence movements were operant throughout Spain's American colonies. Around 1810, colonies began declaring their independence, although of course these declarations were usually only the start of a long armed conflict. By the end of 1824, all of Spain's New World colonies except Puerto Rico and Cuba had successfully broken away from the mother country. The wars of independence produced a good deal of writing, though not often in the form of narrative prose. Simón Bolívar (Venezuela, 1783–1830), the celebrated liberator who led the campaign for independence in the northern part of South America, was an intellectual as well as a soldier and politician. His writings consist of letters, speeches, manifestos, position papers, and other historical documents. José Joaquín de Olmedo (Ecuador, 1780–1847) specialized in composing poetry on the theme of the independence wars. Andrés Bello (Venezuela-Chile, 1781–1865), known as "the intellectual father of Spanish America," analyzed the situation that Spanish American countries faced following independence. This interdisciplinary thinker promoted the ideal of cultural autonomy and encouraged the citizens of Spanish American nations to develop their own distinctive intellectual life and artistic forms. His work took the form of essays, treatises, and poetry.

The definitive 1824 victory over the Spanish brought a short-lived euphoria, evident in the enthusiastic nationalistic poetry published in the ensuing months.[23] Soon after, the newly independent countries entered a period of social disruption. Bolívar had envisioned the former Spanish colonies making common cause, and pan-American solidarity was important in the agenda of independence-era intellectuals like Olmedo and Bello. The new nations proved unable to pull together, and internal divisions eroded unity within national borders.

Especially lacking in cohesion were the United Provinces of the Río de la Plata or River Plate, the vast, newly independent area out of which current-day Argentina, Uruguay, Paraguay, and Bolivia emerged. During the colonial period, this expanse of land had been governed from

Buenos Aires, which was finally granted the status of viceregal capital. After independence, the new power holders in this thriving port city still sought to dominate the same territory. Buenos Aires was able to shake off Spanish rule with relative ease, compared with areas in which the battles for independence wrought heavy damage. A tougher challenge was organizing the expanse of recently liberated land into a nation.

By the late 1820s, Buenos Aires had lost hold of the outlying provinces, which became Bolivia, Paraguay, and Uruguay. The remaining territory occupied roughly the same geographical area as present-day Argentina but was still far from constituting one nation. A troublesome point, which would never be fully resolved, was the relation between Buenos Aires and the rest of the country. The provinces were rapidly straying out of the orbit of the dominant city. Local *caudillos* (strongmen) were turning areas of the country into breakaway fiefdoms, and civil war had broken out. At this moment of chaos, Juan Manuel de Rosas (1793–1877) began gaining power. He exercised the type of iron-fisted one-man rule, *caudillismo,* that became common in nineteenth-century Spanish American countries. While establishing his hold, which depended considerably on popular support and the help of the church and cattle-related business, Rosas was also consolidating Argentina, a feat that is considered the principal redeeming feature of his harsh regime.

Rosas ran Argentina from 1835 until his overthrow in 1852. Technically he was governor of the province of Buenos Aires. But, having gained a grip on the provinces as well, he was de facto head of the country, despite constant challenges to his power. Rural *caudillos* were still trying to go their own way in disregard of any national authority. There was also a more organized nationwide resistance, which eventually led to Rosas's military defeat by opposition forces. Rosas was from an elite landowning family, and Buenos Aires was his home base. Despite this advantaged background, his rough appearance and manner made him seem more like the overseer of a ranch, a job to which he liked to compare the running of the nation. His rustic persona was not just a crowd-pleasing affectation. Rosas had interacted closely with gauchos, learned their skills, and gained firsthand knowledge of all aspects of cattle herding and the production of leather and salt beef. His fresh-off-the-ranch style increased his popular appeal and upset Argentines who desired a more urbane, refined, and European country, and particularly wanted the cities to be a refuge from the coarseness of the Argentine cattle business.

Rosas and his tactics continue to be debated to the present day. He is often abominated as a dictator who terrorized the population with his secret police. Yet revisionists cite his outreach to common people, his anti-elitism, and his achievement in bringing some stability and cohesion to a region that had been in chaos. Argentine populist movements, in particular Peronism, typically look to Rosas as a forebear. Though some Argentine intellectuals later came to respect Rosas, for the most part those of his own day hated him. A great many contemporary Argentine writers spent time in exile and often wrote with the undisguised purpose of building up resentment against Rosas's regime. While the overthrow of Rosas was their immediate goal, these displaced intellectuals often had agendas for Argentina's development in the post-Rosas era. At times they expressed their goal as a return to the freedom-loving spirit of the May Revolution (which led to Argentine independence). May of 1810 appeared as the moment when Argentine independence leaders, guided by Enlightenment thought, had held a clear vision of where to take the country. *May,* then, became the watchword for libertarianism, the overthrow of tyranny, and Enlightenment ideals. The intellectuals promoting these goals regarded themselves as the progressives of their era. Yet, in their desire to model Argentina on the most modern aspects of Europe, they were often racist and elitist.

It was one of the Argentine exiles, the romantic poet Esteban Echeverría (1805–1851), who wrote what is generally regarded as the first short story in Spanish America, "El matadero." While the English version is entitled *The Slaughter House,*[24] "The slaughtering ground" might be more accurate, since the story is set in an open-air area on the edges of Buenos Aires where cattle are brought for slaughter. It is a good guess that Echeverría composed this narrative between 1839 and 1840, since it contains references to the nationwide mourning during that period for Rosas's wife.

The author had spent this time in active opposition to the Rosas regime, founding an underground resistance organization in Buenos Aires, participating in a failed revolt, and having to flee to Montevideo. His hatred of Rosas and his supporters is manifest in "The slaughtering grounds." It remained unpublished until 1871, when the influential scholar Juan María Gutiérrez included it in the first volume of his *Revista del Río de la Plata.*[25] Gutiérrez's foreword to the 1871 publication warns readers that they may be shocked by the story's crudity and violence. The editor clearly sees the story as flawed by its harshness and hypothesizes that Echeverría had written it out in draft form and had never had the opportunity to go back and polish it. As Leonor Fleming points out, Gutiérrez's outlook was not unusual; late-nineteenth-century Argentine readers often rejected violent narratives as tasteless and lurid. Fleming wonders whether Echeverría might have refrained from publishing his story because he harbored "reservations or insecurities" over his violations of decorum.[26] Today's readers more often admire the power of the story's roughest scenes, including descriptions of cattle being slaughtered and carved up with abandon. In addition, by breaking with genteel conventions, Echeverría appears ahead of his time. For example, Noé Jitrik believes that the story "has the distinction of anticipating the realism that was starting up in its modern form in Europe just then,"[27] and Fleming speaks of its "precocity."[28]

Echeverría's story allegorizes Argentina under Rosas as one vast slaughterhouse. It makes sense to link Rosas with slaughtering, not just because of the violence of his government, but because he drew support from the cattle-raising and meat-processing industries. The text opens with a statement in which the narrator, with a series of sardonic observations, sets the scene for the narrative to follow. He notes that, while the people of Buenos Aires have gone without meat during the Lenten season in which his story unfolds, the reason is not religious. The Argentine Catholic church, eager to win support, is free with special dispensations to consume meat. This year, however, flooding has impeded operations at the great open-air slaughtering ground that will be the setting of the story. The narrator suggests an unholy alliance between the church, the Rosas regime and its followers, and the enormous Argentine beef industry.

The opening statement provides clues to the narrator's, and Echeverría's, social vision. The speaker in the story is a libertarian who must denounce any threat to freedom. Speaking of authoritarian organizations generally, he says: "The point is to reduce man to a machine who is principally driven, not by his will, but by that of the Church and government."[29]

Following this bitter exposition, the text moves to a series of scenes crammed with frenzied action. Most of it concerns the public slaughter of fifty head of cattle and the free distribution of their meat, a gift from Rosas to his lower-class followers. This event coincides with Good Friday. The giveaway triggers a mass frenzy, with the impoverished people who dwell on the edges of Buenos Aires, together with some roaming dogs, floundering in bloody mud to seize chunks of the freshly slaughtered beasts. The strongest lay claim to the best cuts; the less desirable parts are gathered by women who glean discarded tripe. This section of the text stands out for its crude details, which at times seem realistic and at others nightmarish and grotesque. At one point a rope shaken off by a bull whizzes through the air and into the spectators: "They saw rolling down from a fence post of the corral, as if a hatchet had lopped it off at the root, a child's head, while the torso remained motionless on its wooden horse, shooting a long spout of blood out of every artery."[30]

In conveying the lawlessness and violence of the slaughter, the narrator also expresses a fascinated revulsion toward the participants, uneducated peasants on the doorstep of the urban center. Their coarse ways and support for Rosas infuriate him. Early in the story of the slaughter, he speaks of "that horribly ugly, filthy, and deformed quality of a little proletarian class peculiar to the River Plate."[31] Current-day readers are disturbed to find the narrator referring to African ancestry as a negative feature of the meat-crazed crowd. He describes a contingent of "black and mulatto women who foraged for tripe, whose ugliness went beyond that of the legendary harpies."[32]

Amid this frenzy, the narrator focuses a mesmerized gaze upon the butchers, who embody both savagery and vitality. They stand "knife in hand, arms and chest bare, long, unruly hair, shirt and *chiripá* and face slathered with blood."[33] The *chiripá,* a loose garment covering the lower body, is an item adapted from indigenous tradition. The butchers' attire is a reminder that, even near the cities, Argentine culture is still highly mestizo. The dominant figure among the butchers is the charismatic Matasiete (Kill Seven), who will emerge as one of the two individualized characters in the story. Matasiete stands out when he cuts the throat of a runaway bull and then castrates it, all in front of an admiring crowd.

After the lengthy description of the meat frenzy, the text changes pace again; it presents a fictional tale rather than scenes and reveals the central opposition around which the story turns. The narrative starts up when a well-dressed young man on horseback wanders into the slaughtering ground. Matasiete, the top butcher, first catches sight of the outsider and yells out "Here comes a Unitarian!"—the term used for the anti-Rosas faction. In a show of defiance, the young man has gone out without pro-Rosas insignia and sporting U-shaped facial hair.

The head butcher rushes to confront the new arrival. The narrator then describes the young man. It become it clear that he differs from the denizens of the slaughtering ground not only in politics but in social class and personal style. He wears a tie and uses an English saddle; unlike the butchers, who are unambiguously Argentine, the young man could be mistaken for a European. The arrival of the Unitarian sets off violent mob behavior. First, the young man is taken in front of the slaughterers' "judge," a local figure who settles disputes.

This character's speech reveals him to be present in the text as a spokesperson for the ideals of May. He addresses the local people using a rhetoric that now strikes readers as stagy and stilted. When asked why he fails to wear the pro-Rosas insignia, he says, "Livery is for you slaves, not for free men."[34] Fleming calls him "a cardboard hero,"[35] judging him a failure as a literary creation. She observes that "although the author intended the opposite, the reader of today does not empathize with him, but rather finds his heroism pompous."[36]

After shearing off his defiant sideburns, the people of the slaughtering ground are about to subject the Unitarian to an unspecified act of sexual violence. They tie him down and begin undressing him, perhaps to rape him or to geld him, just as Matasiete castrated the bull. Before they can do either, though, he dies, apparently of a hemorrhage brought on by indignation.

While references to the Lenten season are present from the beginning of the story, the closing episode includes many links to the narrative of the crucifixion. The Unitarian is unmistakably a figure of Christ; for example, he is tied down in the same position in which Christ is conventionally portrayed on the cross.

Jitrik analyzes a paradox that runs through the story and that has no doubt seemed odd to many readers. The narrator's account of the slaughtering ground and its workers and habitués is much more gripping than the passages focused on the Unitarian, where the language is "limp, rhetorical, emphatic, and solemn."[37] The slaughtering scene is horrible, but it is also full of vitality, and the narrator describes it as if he were mesmerized by its liveliness. Jitrik asks, "Where is Echeverría in all this?" The contradictions in the narrative do not lead to the conclusion that "Echeverría loved Rosas and hated himself." Ideologically and intellectually, Echeverría must be on the side of the Unitarian, who after all is a mouthpiece for the ideas of his creator's intellectual group. At the affective level, however, he leans in the other direction. According to Jitrik, "He was fascinated by the violence, he was fascinated by the basic quality, the action, he was fascinated by that American scene that he saw cropping up everywhere and that he longed to understand, though he could only feel it covertly, like a part of oneself that must be repressed and hidden."[38]

In Spanish American literary history, "The slaughtering ground" is a work ahead of its time in overcoming the inhibitions that often muted literary writers. Ideologically, though, it is very much a work of its era. It sums up the strengths of the exile generation, especially the importance that they gave to civil liberties, but also their unmistakable racism. Readers today are particularly fascinated by the contradictions within the text (and, evidently, within the author's mind) that give the story its tense complexity.

The most noted work of nineteenth-century Argentine literature is a product of the movement of exiled intellectuals to topple the Rosas regime. This document is an essay that first appeared in 1845, the work of Domingo Faustino Sarmiento (1811–1888). Over a century after his death, Sarmiento continues to loom as an unavoidable and controversial presence in the history of Argentine thought and culture. Among many other activities, he served as Argentina's president (1868–1874), reorganized its school system, and campaigned for modernization in many areas of national life. Beyond his public service, Sarmiento sought to define, energize, and systematize Argentina. Born around the time of Argentine independence, Sarmiento gives signs of perceiving himself as emblematic of the nation in its struggles to fulfill its potential. Enrique Anderson Imbert observes Sarmiento's identification of himself with the nation: "Sarmiento's originality lies in this: that [his] romantic philosophy of History came to be intimately commingled with his intuitive understanding of his own life as a historical life. He felt that his Self and the Homeland were a single creature, committed to a historical mission within the development of civilization."[39]

The strange-looking original title of Sarmiento's celebrated essay, *Civilización i barbarie: La vida de Juan Facundo Quiroga i aspecto físico, costumbres, i ábitos de la República Argentina*, uses the reformed system of Spanish spelling that was one of the author's projects. In 1868 Mrs. Horace Mann (Mary, the wife of the educator Horace Mann) published an English version entitled *Life in the Argentine Republic in the Days of the Tyrants (Facundo)*. For convenience, the work is often referred to as *Facundo*, the name of the provincial *caudillo* whose rise and fall Sarmiento analyzes in the second part of the work. Facundo, who at one point dominated an expanse of the Argentine interior, epitomizes *caudillismo*. Although the second section of *Facundo* contains a biography, intermingled with many diverse observations on the part of the author, *Facundo* is first and foremost an essay. As such, it falls largely out-side the scope of this survey. Yet some mention must be made of a text whose influence is impossible to avoid.

Facundo first appeared in installments in *El Progreso*, the anti-Rosas exile newspaper that Sarmiento had established in Santiago de Chile. Its most immediate purpose was to help bring down the Rosas regime. But Sarmiento looks beyond the Rosas era, which he optimistically de-scribes as already nearing its end, to set out his vision of Argentina and his theories concerning the progress of history and to expound various other ideas in his agenda. By including in *Facundo* those facts, concepts, and beliefs that he held most vital to the reorganization of Argentina, Sarmiento created a highly diverse work. As Jitrik observes, "In this way, *Facundo* is sociology, history, novel, biography, but no single one of these things."[40]

The first words of the original title of *Facundo*, *Civilización i barbarie* (civilization and barbarism), are Sarmiento's still-controversial attempt to sum up the internal divisions that have marked Argentine national life. Diana Sorensen Goodrich observes that, while subsequent polemical at-tacks on *Facundo* "were launched from a variety of angles . . . one con-sistent target was the civilization-barbarism dichotomy."[41] At the sim-plest level—which turns out to be too simple to account for everything in *Facundo*—civilization is associated with education, liberal ideals, ur-ban, European-style manners and dress, a government with democratic institutions responsive to public opinion, the desire for modernization, and, of course, opposition to Rosas and his regime. Barbarism is linked with such phenomena as illiteracy, *caudillo* rule, reliance on violence to settle differences, failure to exploit and develop natural resources, living in isolated areas, support for Rosas, and gaucho folkways.

Obviously such a portrait of Argentina is too black-and-white to do justice to the currents and countercurrents at work in national society. Sarmiento must introduce many complications into his basic scheme. In addition, the author's strong personality and his individual traits, espe-cially his pronounced romanticism, enter into the picture. Readers of *Fa-cundo* are often surprised to find Sarmiento expressing empathy and even admiration for entities that would seem to fall on the "barbarism" side of the equation. In addition, the system of oppositions that he de-vises to represent Argentina is subject to change as the work goes along. A reader first concludes that Sarmiento is contrasting cities to the coun-try, in favor of the former. But then the author begins to show Argentine cities in opposition to one another. In particular, Buenos Aires does not share a common agenda with the other cities. The international port city is more continental-European; the others are more traditionally Spanish. Even though it would only later be completely established as the national capital, Buenos Aires is already dominant. It promotes measures that will benefit its own economy but drain resources from the other parts of the country.

One could conclude that Sarmiento simply had not organized his ideas into consistent form before setting them down in *Facundo*. Indeed, in real life, the author does appear to have harbored a number of contradictions. But careful readers of *Facundo* have often found it to be not so much a self-contradictory text as one that is very complex, dense, and rich with meanings. Jitrik argues that the real issue is that, in *Facundo*, Sarmiento has produced a literary work, utilizing the irrational rhetoric that is part of literature, rather than a treatise argued along strictly rational lines:

> That is to say, Sarmiento moves simultaneously on different intentional levels; he needs to convey complex notions for which the bare language of facts or interpretation is not enough. And this complex formulation can only be realized if there is a spirit of literature, that is to say, an ambiance that allows the greatest possible number of values to be compressed together in the text, and, moreover, to be presented all at the same time because any imbalance would throw them off. That is what is literary about *Facundo*, and moreover it is its greatest truth. . . .[42]

Moreover, Jitrik identifies the manner of expression used in *Facundo*—though not the majority of the concepts contained in the work—as romantic.[43] With these observations, Jitrik provides useful guidelines for readers struggling to reconcile the seemingly conflicting ideas and sympathies expressed in different passages of this intricate work.

In the first part of *Facundo*, Sarmiento presents his portrait of Argentina, its geography, history, peoples, problems, and needs. It is a frankly opinionated and partial account. Sarmiento favors, for the future of Argentina, a fundamentally European-style type of civilization and highly institutionalized forms of representative government. In his vision, these developments offer a way out of the boss rule and backwardness into which Argentina has been sliding. Sarmiento represents an era in which Argentine intellectuals were unembarrassed about urging the nation to follow the example of foreign countries. Readers of later eras often perceive this thinker as lacking confidence in Argentina's ability to find its own path. Sarmiento would like to see Argentina become modern and efficient in the manner of the United States and those European countries that were the earliest to industrialize. He promotes rapid expansion, material progress, building up the infrastructure, increased foreign trade, and the installation of all types of technical improvements. Ever the educator, Sarmiento assigns great importance to the school system and to any other means of achieving a highly literate nation.

In fact, during the latter part of the nineteenth century many of Sarmiento's urgings were acted upon. Argentina achieved and maintained a high literacy rate. The nation's economy became increasingly linked to those of the long-industrialized countries. The Argentines have been through some bitter experiences as a result of dealings with foreign investors and in international commerce, and here Sarmiento is a convenient target of blame, since he pointed the nation down the road to global involvement. Goodrich sums up the accusatory outlook toward Sarmiento: "During the seventies, when the governments of Cámpora and Perón were giving voice to populism, *Facundo* was indicted as the document of the *vende-patrias* [those who sell out their own country] who had betrayed Argentina and had literally given it away to foreign interests."[44]

Given Sarmiento's pro-growth vision of the nation's future, readers are sometimes surprised at the lyricism with which, in the first part of *Facundo,* he evokes the wild, solitary life of the gauchos. Here Sarmiento, who was to some extent a romantic writer, displays that movement's idealization of nature and of living close to the natural world. Romantics admired rustic ways and oral poetry and narrative; the gauchos exemplified this type of preliterate folk culture with their much-noted singing duels, their elaborate leather crafts, and other highly developed traditional skills. However, in Sarmiento's rationalistic scheme for reorganizing the nation, the gauchos are illiterate nomads whose low-tech way of life has no place in an Argentina ready to take its place among the modern nations.

Facundo Quiroga is the central topic of the second part of the book. Yet Sarmiento is not principally concerned with constructing the narrative of a life and often digresses away from Facundo's story. He focuses on those aspects of Facundo's career that help him argue his own case. In Sarmiento's account, the backlands *caudillo* is manipulated by the Buenos Aires–based dictator. Rosas for a time exploits his ally in the provinces, but has him eliminated as soon as he becomes an obstacle.

Facundo is a very different type of barbarian from Rosas, and it becomes clear that Sarmiento is heavily favoring the provincial *caudillo* over the national dictator. The latter is from a well-off family, enjoys the advantage of being from Buenos Aires, and is a sophisticated calculator. In Sarmiento's analysis, Rosas has turned his back on civilization to become an immensely powerful pseudo-gaucho who oversees Argentina like a ranch. Facundo is an authentic and spontaneous primitive. He eventually makes some ineffectual attempts to govern the provinces in a more systematic manner. Though these initiatives lead nowhere, they demonstrate that the benighted Facundo is trying to grope his way in the direction of civilization. As Facundo's story continues, Sarmiento, who was also from the provinces and had acquired much of his education on his own, exhibits increasingly obvious sympathy toward this figure, even though such an unruly man is of no use in advancing the nation.

In the third part of *Facundo,* which is quite brief, Sarmiento expounds further his vision of Argentina and the need for the nation to advance and progress. The straightforward argumentation in this section points out, by way of contrast, how enriched the earlier parts are by their literary and, in some cases, narrative elements.

Though *Facundo* has been discussed almost continuously since its appearance, it continues to attract literary critics and social scientists eager to unravel its significance. Jitrik's study, *Muerte y resurrección de Facundo* (Death and resurrection of Facundo), appeared in 1983, 138 years after *Facundo*'s initial publication, yet it offers an original interpretation. Jitrik analyses *Facundo* as one would a literary text and concludes that Sarmiento is really coming down on the side of the provinces and against Buenos Aires. This reading at first seems counterintuitive, since one would imagine that Sarmiento would favor the most modern and European of Argentine cities. However, Jitrik's interpretation is consistent with some almost self-evident characteristics of *Facundo.* As noted above, in narrating the relations between Facundo and Rosas, Sarmiento is much more lenient with the provincial *caudillo,* for whom he harbors an obvious sympathy.

To pursue this hypothesis, Jitrik analyses minutely the details of Sarmiento's lexical choices, sentence construction, and other features of the discourse of *Facundo.* According to Jitrik, Sarmiento shows the provinces as backward and miserable, but the reason for their depressed condition is their continual exploitation by Buenos Aires, which feeds its prosperity by draining the rest of the country. In this critic's summary, "Buenos Aires turns out to be, at the heart of [Sarmiento's] expression, the truly guilty party, as 'the shame of America,' in opposition to that other piece of history and life that is the interior, treated with disdain, ruined, made barbaric, enslaved."[45]

Since the late twentieth century, many researchers have examined the way in which much nineteenth-century Spanish American writing seeks to build up nationalistic sentiment and national identity. *Facundo* has been a prime case in point for such scholars.[46] Taking this idea further, Diana Sorensen Goodrich analyzes not *Facundo* itself but the uses to which Argentine intellectuals have put this work over the years. Her *Facundo and the Construction of Argentine Culture* (1996) shows the same basic document being interpreted, reinterpreted, praised, denounced, and otherwise utilized in the effort to shape the nation's culture.

*S*lavery was one of the many issues left unresolved by the attainment of independence. Simón Bolívar had promised the president of Haiti, who supported his campaign, that he would make the abolition of slavery part and parcel of independence from Spain. Though Bolívar did declare against slavery, it was difficult to eradicate the practice in all the newly independent nations. Some countries, such as Mexico and Chile, abolished slavery around the time of independence. Of course, these were nations in which the economy did not depend on slave labor. The dates of abolition of slavery in Latin American countries range from the very early (Chile, 1823, Mexico, 1829) to the very late, with Brazil (1888) the last nation in the Americas to free its slaves. Puerto Rico and Cuba, which had remained Spanish colonies, were slow to emancipate slaves. Puerto Rican slaves were freed in 1873, and Cuba followed in 1880.

Cuba has drawn special attention, both because of the large proportion of the population living in slavery and because the long-running debate over the "peculiar institution" involved many of the nation's intellectuals. Cuban writers produced a number of works that are often grouped together as "the antislavery novels," although the theme of slavery is not equally prominent in all of them. The word *antislavery*, applied to intellectuals who protested the conditions in which slaves lived and worked, is by no means identical with *abolitionist*. Well into the nineteenth century, many Cuban and Brazilian thinkers clung to the hope that the institution of slavery could be reformed. They appealed to slave owners to treat their charges more humanely and proposed legislative half measures that would create various types of partial emancipation, free only certain categories of slaves, or phase out slavery gradually.

The idea that slavery could be improved manifests itself in the fictional figure of the benevolent slave owner. Of course, the literary representation of slavery does not necessarily correspond to clear-cut proposals for dealing with the real-world phenomenon.

At times, the topic of slavery provided an opportunity for writers to express the characteristic romantic longing for freedom. By the 1830s, as opposition to slavery emerged as a literary theme, romanticism was widespread in Spanish America. In Brushwood's judgment, "Almost all the fiction in the years following the achievement of independence is romantic."[47] Many Spanish American antislavery novels demonstrate clearly the links between romanticism and protest against slavery.

An early and well-known antislavery novel is the 1841 *Sab*, the English version of which also bears the name of its title character. This brief, romantic fiction is the work of Gertrudis Gómez de Avellaneda (y Arteaga) (1814–1873), a Cuban-born writer who spent most of her adult life in Spain. Avellaneda eventually became a literary celebrity and a highly successful playwright. At the time she composed *Sab,* though, she was quite young; most likely she began it at about twenty-two and completed it two years later.[48] When she arrived in Madrid in 1841, she was able to publish this novel, with its potentially inflammatory subject matter. The novel was banned in Cuba, where of course slavery was still legal and widespread. After Avellaneda had become a well-established figure, she omitted *Sab* from the 1869 edition of her complete works. This suppression is a topic of debate. In Nara Araujo's summary, "According to some, Gertrudis was frightened by the progressive statements of her youth; according to others, she followed the recommendation of friends and spiritual advisors."[49]

Sab was a daring novel for its time and in 1844 was banned in Cuba. The censor's letter first notes that the novel protests slavery, into which the ill-fated hero Sab has been born. However, the censor secondarily notes, not very specifically, that the novel is "contrary to morality and good custom."[50] Perhaps in this category are the novel's references to the Catholic church's collusion with the sugar-plantation aristocracy. The title character criticizes priests for urging the slave "to obey and be silent, serve his lawful masters with humility and resignation, and never to judge them."[51] In addition, the entire institution of marriage comes in for an unflattering portrayal.

Jerome Branche believes that the disturbing element is "the female writer's freedom of expression regarding sexuality."[52] The amorous plot includes, by the end of the novel, two occurrences of interracial attraction. Sab, a mulatto, harbors an unrequited love for Carlota, the beautiful daughter of his master. The two have been brought up virtually as siblings. In effect, the family recognizes Sab as Carlota's first cousin, the illegitimate son of the heroine's paternal uncle. Because he is the owner's nephew, Sab has been educated and spared rough work. This benevolence has placed him in a painfully dual situation. Sab is a refined young man who can converse with the white members of his family as if in a gathering of equals. There is only the illusion of equality, since the others can give him orders. Sab is said to be like a brother to Carlota, but he has been assigned to her as her personal slave. Carlota, a hyperemotional romantic heroine, is blindly devoted to a handsome but odious blond man and seems oblivious to Sab's devotion. Yet after Carlota grows disenchanted with her marriage and takes a more realistic view of life, her mind returns to Sab.

At the same time, Teresa, also an illegitimate cousin but unambiguously white, who has been secretly pining for Carlota's fiance, becomes drawn to Sab for his nobility of character. The latter development leads to an episode that must have electrified many contemporary readers. Teresa first urges Sab to seek a wife, then, when he replies that no woman could love him, counters: "'I!' she exclaimed, 'I am that woman which entrusts herself to you: we are both orphans and unfortunate souls . . . we two are alone on earth, and each of us needs compassion, love, and happiness. Allow me, then, to follow you to remote climes, to the heart of the wilderness. I will be your friend, your companion, your sister!'" [53]

Sab does not accept Teresa's proposal, but they feel a special empathy. Despite their racial difference, they occupy similar positions in the household; both are illegitimate cousins of the pampered heiress Carlota and form her retinue. Hugh A. Harter's description of Teresa emphasizes her lack of independence: "As she has no money, she has no status in the household, but serves as a sort of companion-servant to Carlota, obviously less than happy with her lot." [54] Teresa's closeness to Sab gives rise to talk in the household. Carlota's by-now husband guesses, through misinterpretation of evidence, that "Teresa loved the mulatto." [55] He finds malicious amusement in what he sees as the discovery of a forbidden passion and ascribes Teresa's behavior to the capricious instability of women.

Carlota also recognizes Teresa's special affinity with Sab, but treats it with respect and sees it as essentially well founded. Voicing the progressive outlook of the novelist, Carlota observes that "she deserves compassion and not censure," since Sab "had a beautiful heart." [56] Carlota is beginning to grasp a commonality between Sab, Teresa, and herself that sets them apart from a society dominated by white males with mercantile values. As Susan Kirkpatrick observes, "By the end of the novel, Sab, Teresa, and Carlota form a new triad unified by . . . shared values and common experiences of powerlessness within the social structure." [57]

The institution of marriage, as it affects women, is denounced along with slavery. Indeed, the two phenomena are paralleled implicitly throughout *Sab*. Finally the comparison surfaces openly. Having been a slave and an empathetic observer of the plight of married women, Sab judges the status of a wife to be worse than slavery, an assessment that has provoked some expressions of incredulity among critics.[58] The dying Sab writes in a letter,

> Oh, women! Poor blind victims! Like slaves, they patiently drag their chains and bow their heads under the yoke of human laws. With no other guide than an untutored and trusting heart, they choose a master for life. The slave can at least change masters, can even hope to buy his freedom some day if he can save enough money, but a woman, when she lifts her careworn hands and mistreated brow to beg for release, hears the monstrous, deathly voice which cries out to her: "In the grave." [59]

The novel often uses Carlota's markedly fair-skinned fiancé as a counter to Sab. The former does not deserve his good fortune and is particularly unworthy of the love of the two heroines, while the latter merits a better lot in life. The third-person narrator, who fills readers in on the characters' less-visible aspects, draws attention to Enrique's weak character. This commentator notes that he is "accustomed always to give in to his father's forceful will," which is driving his courtship of Carlota.[60] When the fiancé and Sab appear in the same scene, the latter's superiority is apparent. Sab is more generous, thoughtful, altruistic, and noble than his rival. For all his refinement, Sab possesses immense physical strength and displays skill at whatever he undertakes, from gardening to cave exploration. The white fiancé appears weak and clumsy in comparison. His most grievous flaw, though, is the poverty of his love for the heroine. For a time, Sab harbors the hope that Carlota will come to see that her intended is unworthy of her. But he resists two opportunities to let his rival die and eventually makes a great personal sacrifice to salvage the engagement. Before the novel ends, Carlota has married a man who makes her unhappy. Her female cousin, who lacks beauty and a fortune, takes refuge in a convent, but paradoxically enjoys greater happiness than her comely, wealthy relative.

Appearing at a time when many people still believed that slavery could be reformed, *Sab* clearly delivers the message that the institution itself is immoral. Unlike many novels written to protest slavery, *Sab* contains no scenes of abuse. The slaves of Carlota's family receive benevolent treatment; Carlota exhibits "enchanting kindness" to them.[61] But even as the slaves are blessing her for her generosity, Carlota points out that the real problem is going unaddressed: "They judge themselves fortunate because they are not receiving blows and abuse, and they calmly eat the bread of slavery." Carlota appears to speak for the author when she states that the only true solution is outright emancipation: "'When I am Enrique's wife,' she added after a moment of silence, 'no unhappy soul around me will breathe the poisonous air of slavery. We will give all our blacks their freedom.'"[62] Sab speaks against slavery, making such assertions as "slaves have no country." Not only do the characters voice the principle that the evil is slavery itself and not its implementation, but the plot makes the same point. Sab, who has received preferential treatment as the owner's nephew, suffers slavery more keenly because his lack of freedom is all the more evident to him.

Sab's thorough intertwining of the issues of race and gender has fascinated current-day critics. Doris Sommer's "Sab C'est Moi," which first appeared in 1987, shows how the novel produces a "productive confusion" of the hard and fast distinctions between black and white and between male and female human beings.[63] The character Sab is the most radical example of a figure who seems to inhabit a space between racial and sexual categories. The novel's opening scene makes the point that a stranger who encounters Sab cannot identify his race by observation. The narrator observes that Sab does not appear white, black, mulatto, or Amerindian, and does not suggest any other category that would correspond to his appearance.

In Sommer's analysis, the features that create Sab's nobility also feminize him. He is worthy insofar as he is sensitive, emotive, and passionate. The traits assigned to Teresa also go against standard notions of gender. Teresa, whose character grows more complex and sympathetic as the plot unfolds, possesses the supposedly masculine power to suppress her emotions and appear impassive. Sommer concludes that, by exposing racial and gender categories as leaky constructions, the novel works to undermine the patriarchal order. *Sab*'s anti-patriarchal slant is furthered by the characterization of the two figures who are male heads of substantial households. Both are too flawed to qualify as patriarchs. Their weakness makes the traditional social order appear to be an arbitrary construction, and, as Sommer puts it, "In this social vacuum, 'author-ity' can pass on to new hands, feminine and/or mulatto hands." [64]

Readers with a feminist perspective often value *Sab* for its focus on the outlook, desires, and feelings of the women characters. Kirkpatrick characterizes the situation, typical of romantic literature, in which a male subject's relations with the world are represented through his desire for, pursuit of, and disillusionment with figures of women. "However," she states, "Avellaneda reverses the gender positions in this paradigm: women become the subjects rather than the objects of desire." [65]

This 1841 novel commingles elements of romanticism and realism. The coexistence of the two tendencies is especially evident in the characterization of Carlota. When she first appears as a betrothed adolescent, Carlota is the quintessential romantic heroine, ruled by passion, blindly devoted to a handsome young man, and oblivious to the petty realities of life. In the sections of the novel that take place after her marriage, this character is portrayed in a more realistic manner. Carlota discovers that her father-in-law has falsified her father's will so as to prevent her sisters from sharing the legacy. Whereas earlier she inhabited an ethereal realm above material concerns, now she becomes involved in a dispute over her inheritance. Having no rights, she loses the struggle and comes to view most of humankind as materialistic. Some characters in the novel, such as the money-grubbing father-in-law, are more typical of realistic than of romantic fiction. The use of both romantic and realistic features typifies many subsequent Spanish American novels.

Sab is the first antislavery narrative to be published in Spanish. Other narratives with similar themes were also being written during the late 1830s, but they would not be published, at least not in Spanish, for many years. Anselmo Suárez y Romero (1818–1878) finished the composition of his novel *Francisco* in 1839; it circulated in manuscript form but did not appear in print until 1880. Another well-known novel, *Cecilia Valdés* by Cirilo Villaverde (1812–1894), has a complicated history. The nucleus of it was published as a short story in 1839, then expanded to novel length, but without bringing the theme of slavery to the fore. In 1882 Villaverde published the definitive version of *Cecilia Valdés*, in which slavery stands out as a major issue. These works that appeared in the 1880s will come in for discussion in Chapter 5.

In recent times, a contemporary nonfiction narrative of slavery has been attracting increasing attention from critics. This is the first-person account of the life of Juan Francisco Manzano (Cuba, 1797–1854). Referred to as *Autobiography of a Slave* or just as *Autobiography,* it is the only known firsthand account of the slave experience in Spanish America. Several contemporary Cuban literary intellectuals were of African ancestry, but the others were apparently free blacks. Manzano, a poet and slave, was uniquely qualified to write an account of slavery that was both firsthand and of literary quality. There is some uncertainty and dispute over the exact dates of composition of the autobiography, but Manzano wrote it over the second half of the 1830s and had completed it by 1839.[66] It appears that Manzano began setting down his experiences while still a slave and was already a free man by the time the completed manuscript began to circulate.

Domingo del Monte, a pro-reform intellectual who headed a gathering or *tertulia* of like-minded friends, was behind both the autobiography and Manzano's manumission. His group's agenda included the promotion of Cuban literature and of social reform, though it stopped short of advocating the immediate abolition of slavery. When del Monte introduced into the *tertulia* a noted poet who was still living in slavery, it aroused concern. Members of the circle took up a collection to purchase Manzano's freedom. It was del Monte's idea for Manzano to write a narrative of his life. This influential figure gave Manzano some indications of what he would like the autobiography to include.

In Cuba the autobiography could only be passed around in handwritten form, but it quickly appeared in English. The Cuban progressives gave this and other texts about slavery to the Irish abolitionist Richard R. Madden. Madden then oversaw the publication of Manzano's autobiography and poetry, under the title *Poems by a Slave in the Island of Cuba, recently liberated* (1840), together with other antislavery writings, many of them by Madden himself. Madden assembled the collection to present at the 1840 General Anti-slavery Convention held in London. For this abolitionist, Manzano's account was documentary material useful to the cause, not a text with literary features. The author was not identified by name, supposedly for his protection, although his initials appear in Madden's foreword and there was only one known poet in Cuba who had recently been a slave. The Spanish-language manuscript was read in progressive circles but not published until 1937.

The text of Manzano's autobiography has a complicated history. The second half has been lost, most likely while the text was being lent to readers in hand-written form. The surviving first half has been through several rewritings. Formally educated editors and translators have felt the need to correct the self-taught author's spelling, punctuation, and syntax, to organize the text into paragraphs, and to make other changes. Madden's English version contains a number of other changes. He needed the autobiography to back his cause and evidently deleted passages deemed unhelpful to the campaign against slavery, such as those in which Manzano reminisces about pleasant times and affectionate feelings that he shared with certain of his masters.[67] The liberties that white editors took with Manzano's text are disturbing to many students of the autobiography. For example, William Luis, after reviewing in detail various versions of Manzano's autobiography, states, "The editors, as surely as slave masters, continue to mold and control Manzano's life."[68]

Of the published versions of the *Autobiography*, scholars prefer José L. Franco's edition of 1937. It is generally considered the one most directly transcribed from the manuscript of the autobiography, believed to be Manzano's own, located in the José Martí National Library in Havana.[69] Yet the fidelity of the 1937 version has also been questioned.[70] One should remember, though, that no transcription is ever identical to the original. Even a facsimile edition requires some editorial decision-making.

The writing of the autobiography was closely linked to Manzano's manumission, and to a certain extent it is a commissioned work documenting the abuses suffered by slaves. Manzano gives a hair-raising account of the cruelties he underwent. In several episodes Manzano undergoes extreme punishments for actions that are either someone else's doing or else beyond his conscious control. In one case, a mix-up results in Manzano's being accused of stealing a chicken. The overseer ties Manzano's hands and makes him run while following on horseback. In Manzano's recollection: "We had gone about a fourth of a league when, tired of running in front of the horse, I tripped and fell. No sooner had I hit the ground than two dogs or two beasts, which were following him, attacked me. One of them, holding my entire left cheek in his mouth, sank his fang all the way through to my molar. The other one perforated my thigh and my left calf, with the utmost voracity and speed. These scars persist in spite of the twenty-four years that have transpired since then."[71]

As well as physical abuse, Manzano is the victim of exploitation: when his mother leaves him money intended to purchase his freedom, his mistress pockets it and retains her slave.

In two passages Manzano points out that he is not narrating every-thing that happened during an episode of abuse, saying that it is best to draw a veil over certain occurrences. These moments of reticence have intrigued critics. They are the point of departure for the article by Robert Richmond Ellis, "Reading through the Veil of Juan Francisco Manzano: From Homoerotic Violence to the Dream of a Homoracial Bond."[72] Ellis surmises that what was left untold was episodes of rape, "in Manzano's case, male-male rape."[73] Ellis suggests that Manzano may have been unable, not just unwilling, to discuss what happened; he "seems to be the victim of childhood sexual trauma that has never been fully registered in language."[74] In this critic's speculative reconstruction, Manzano may have wanted to divulge an experience of rape but may have been unable to overcome the constraints of "the gendered discourse of identity"; sexual violation would go against the author's sense of his own masculinity.[75]

Yet the narrative is not simply a documentary or a text tailor-made to advance the agendas of reformers. A number of elements of Manzano's autobiography have no direct bearing on the issue of slavery and cannot have been added at the urging of del Monte or members of his circle. They are clearly there because Manzano, when he sat down to write, made the decision to include them. The current critical tendency is to see Manzano as not just a bearer of witness but a creative intellectual who has placed his own stamp on his writing project. For example, Sylvia Molloy traces the signs of Manzano's becoming "the author of his text, in control of his material."[76] Molloy perceives Manzano to be "valuing something else in himself besides the story of his misfortunes."[77] She finds particular significance in Manzano's account of his relation to read-ing and writing. These activities are off limits to slaves, but Manzano pursues them with passion and tenacity. After observing his master read and write, Manzano determines to practice these activities:

> That was another problem. I did not know how to start . . . I, never-theless, bought myself a penknife, quills, and very fine paper, which I placed over a discarded sheet written in my master's hand in or-der to accustom myself to the feel of fashioning letters. I worked along tracing the shapes on the paper below. With this method, in less than a month I could already write lines that imitated my master's handwriting . . .
>
> Even during the day, when I had time, I also practiced. I would station myself at the foot of some painting whose title was in capital

letters. With many strokes I was able to imitate the most beautiful letters.[78]

Molloy directs attention to Manzano's writing itself. In her analysis, the "awkward syntax" of a particular passage is what "lends a sense of urgency to his writing, contributing effectively to its compelling quality."[79] Manzano's uncorrected writing, with its peculiarities of style and organization, "is the best self-portrait we have" of a slave who became an author.[80]

Sonia Labrador-Rodríguez accurately summarizes the prevailing view today: "Manzano accepts the proposal that he write a testimonial account of his life as a slave because he sees in it, not only the possibility of obtaining his liberty, but also the opportunity to express what he knows and feels."[81] As Labrador-Rodríguez observes, Manzano does not portray himself as a standard figure of the slave and does not use the word *slave* until late in the narrative. He draws attention to features that make him unique. Manzano points out that, as a child, his protectress "would dress me, comb my hair, and take care that I did not mix with the other black children."[82] These assertions made some readers uncomfortable even at the time; as Luis notes, "Manzano's dissociation from other black slaves has been suppressed in the English edition."[83] Manzano's insistence that he has grown up apart from black people can easily appear a case of identifying with the oppressor. Labrador-Rodríguez, though, suggests that Manzano is instead constructing a particular type of persona for himself: "The narrator replaces the image of the enslaved black man with that of an intelligent, sensitive being who is a victim of arbitrariness and fate . . . he seeks to convince the reader that he or she can identify with the speaker of the narration and moreover he presents a denunciation of the slave-holding regime from another point of view, that of the repressed poet."[84]

From about the 1970s forward, researchers have sought to discover and study more texts by Spanish American writers of African ancestry. Such well-known researchers as Marvin A. Lewis, author of many books and the founding editor of *Afro-Hispanic Review* (1981–), and Richard L. Jackson have centered their careers on this concern. Most of the authors whose work has come in for fresh attention are writers of the twentieth and twenty-first centuries. While nineteenth-century black writers are fewer in number and much more difficult to research, tenacious investigators continue to pursue leads. In Cuba it is known that a number of freemen cultivated intellectual and literary life. The one really celebrated example is "Plácido" (1809–1844; real name, Gabriel de la Concepción Valdés); many others remain to be rediscovered.[85] One easily associates black intellectuals and creative innovators with the Caribbean; yet other regions offer research possibilities. Lewis surprised many readers with the extent of his research into black expression in Argentina, the results of which appear in his 1996 *Afro-Argentine Discourse: Another Dimension of the Black Diaspora*.[86] Since many other Spanish American nations had a significant population of African descent in the nineteenth century, one may expect further information to come to light.

C learly, though the concluding battles of the Wars of Independence took place in 1824, Spanish American nations had scarcely begun the struggle for self-definition. In some cases, it remained unclear for some time what exactly would be included in a particular country. A prime case is Argentina, which well into the nineteenth century had not fully consolidated into its current form. In other instances, national borders were clear enough, but the population was still struggling toward a sense of itself as the collective citizenry of a nation. The newly independent countries lagged in some aspects of their development, owing to centuries of colonial rule. Literary and intellectual life was one area in which the young nations possessed considerable resources at the time they attained political independence. So it made sense to look to literature as a means of strengthening nationalistic sentiment and of airing national concerns. This preoccupation with the nation is evident in many of the works that the next chapter examines.

In addition, the period following the wars of independence saw a great flourishing of romantic expression. Romanticism remained an important force in Spanish American writing until late in the century. However, after mid-century this literary current became increasingly commingled with realism, which eventually emerged as the dominant movement before both tendencies eventually lost ground to *modernismo*. The rise of romanticism and realism in Spanish American narrative will be another major element in the following chapter.

| 𝒯HE MID-NINETEENTH CENTURY

Romanticism, Realism, and Nationalism

*B*y the middle decades of the nineteenth century, the novel was well established as a form of both art and social commentary. Romanticism continued to exercise a powerful hold on writers as well as the reading public, although it was usually a heterogeneous type of romanticism. It is characteristic of Spanish American narrative, and of Spanish American literature generally, to blend movements and tendencies that in Europe might have been considered to be at odds with one another. A particularly common fusion is that of romanticism with realism.

In literary-historical terms, realism is a movement that emerges in the mid-nineteenth century, in some measure as a reaction to romanticism. Realist writers seek to depict reality in all its aspects. Attention is to be focused on the material world as perceived through the evidence of the senses. According to the realist agenda, the writer should avoid using pre-set concepts and tenets in selecting what to show the reader. The realist attempt to be impartial and nondoctrinaire is one feature that distinguishes it from the later movement of naturalism, whose practitioners openly promoted certain beliefs about the human being and society.

The goal of realist writing is to give the effect of describing people, their behavior, and their surroundings exactly as they would ordinarily be found in the real world. In Michael Winkler's summary, realist writing "satisfies normal rather than intensified perceptions of reality [and] provides plausible rather than imaginative explanations."[1]

In line with the ideal of reproducing life as it may be perceived in the course of everyday existence, realist writers tended to concentrate on commonplace people and events. The realists' focus on the ordinary can perhaps be better appreciated when set against romantic writers' fondness for extremes, stark contrasts, and occurrences that would be rare in real life. In romantic narratives characters may be aristocrats or undergo abysmal deprivation in the wilderness. The same figure may live in penury and wealth, since drastic changes in fortune are a staple of romantic plots. Romantic characters may occupy such unusual roles in society as those of pirate, poet, visionary, hermit, penitent, castaway, revenge-seeker, or disillusioned wanderer. In addition to these exceptional human characters, phantoms and other supernatural entities function in the story lines of some romantic narratives.

The characters in realist narratives are likely to be bourgeois, middle class, or lower class and to hold the occupations that are most common among the real-world population. Many merchants, clerks, landlords, low or middle-level authorities, small-time criminals, and servants figure in realist narratives. Perhaps needless to say, among realists it was taboo to predicate a plot on supernatural phenomena. Realism often upset contemporary readers by referring openly to the less agreeable aspects of human beings, such as petty greed and poor hygiene. For advocates of realism, it was not so important that writers display a powerful imagination as that they demonstrate accuracy in observing life and imitating it in literature.

One strong motive behind the development and acceptance of realism was the ascendancy of the social sciences in the nineteenth century. Many contemporary intellectuals were struggling to attain a more objective outlook on human behavior, whether as social scientists or as writers. From today's perspective, the struggle to attain an impartial vision of society appears doomed to fail. We now tend to stress that every observer and commentator is viewing and speaking from a particular position. The triumph of realism depended on widespread confidence that human beings could shed their theoretical and personal biases and look directly at reality. The erosion of this confidence makes the concept of realism, at times, alien to readers of the present era. We tend to perceive the campaign for impartiality as itself motivated by an ideology of knowledge and the fact worshipper's desire for infallible information.

Complicating the issue, the term *realism* is not applied exclusively to literature produced under the impetus of the realist movement. Sometimes "realism" is employed in a more general way to refer to any writing, from any era, that uses little evident stylization and gives the effect of direct observation. In these cases, there is no programmed effort to study society impartially. Rather, writers are simply turning attention to everyday matters and to what is regarded, by consensus, as being real. These two meanings of realism are particularly likely to cause confusion in the case of Spanish-language literature. Writing influenced by the realist trend is difficult to distinguish from the unadorned, matter-of-fact accounts of social phenomena that writers had already been producing in

Spanish. Well before realism was labeled, a number of Spanish-language writers had been frank in portraying the less exalted parts of human existence. In its lack of idealization and focus on concrete, material phenomena, much literature written in Spanish resembles the writing that would subsequently come out of the realist movement. Shortly before realism appeared as a trend, some of this naturally occurring realism was already present in Spanish American romantic narratives. As John S. Brushwood observes, "The natural realism of the Hispanic tradition obscured further the line of demarcation between Romanticism and scientific Realism, which was none too clear at best."[2] The mixture of romanticism and realism, already evident in *Sab,* is one that will grow more marked as the century progresses.

Despite the frequent occurrence of spontaneous realism in Spanish-language writing, realism as a movement was not as strong in Spain as it was in such countries as France, England, and the United States. It is a reasonable conjecture that the limited extent of the realist movement in Spain can be correlated to less of a drive in that country to establish a scientific approach to studying society. In some Spanish American countries realism as a movement was more pronounced than in others. Following the same pattern, those countries with a strong realist movement, such as Chile, also experienced a vigorous effort to promote social-scientific thought.

Spanish American writers of the post-Independence period place romanticism, realism, and various combinations of the two at the service of literary nationalism. Virtually all Spanish American intellectuals of the mid-nineteenth century take up, in some way, the issue of how their nations should best evolve, whether politically, socially, or culturally. Novelists often reveal a keen awareness that they are contributing to the making of a national literature.

The previous chapter pointed out the disruption in Argentine intellectual life brought about by the regime, lasting from 1835 until 1852, of Juan Manuel de Rosas.

Many, perhaps nearly all, important Argentine intellectuals were forced into exile. At the same time, the Rosas regime stimulated literary production by providing abundant thematic material to writers who passionately denounced its repression. After Rosas's downfall in 1852, writers continued to revisit the years of his government, during which Argentina's internal divisions stood out even more vividly than usual.

Esteban Echeverría's anti-Rosas short story "The slaughtering grounds" (1838–1840) was discussed in the previous chapter. Two other Argentine writers reached a wide audience with their fictional, and highly romantic, narratives of the Rosas era. José Mármol (1817–1871; full name, José Pedro Crisólogo Mármol), otherwise known as a romantic poet, composed the lengthy novel *Amalia*. Very popular in its time, this work was first published as an incomplete serial in 1851–1852 and in definitive book form in 1855. As the setting for several of her best-known narratives of love, conflict, and betrayal, Juana Manuela Gorriti (1818–1892) chose the Rosas years, when the divisions in Argentine society grew extreme. Gorriti has been rediscovered in recent years, in part for the daring independence with which she led her life and her campaign for women's participation in national society and cultural life. In her narratives women protagonists often struggle to heal the wounds inflicted by factional violence.

Mármol's *Amalia* is indisputably a romantic work; this novel and the 1867 *María* by Jorge Isaacs of Colombia, to be discussed later in this chapter, are the most widely read narratives to emerge from Spanish American romanticism. Like many narratives of its time, *Amalia* sustains reader interest by repeatedly placing the characters in situations of hair-raising danger or painful dilemmas. It exemplifies the plot conventions of the serial novel, some of which Brushwood summarizes in his analysis of Mármol's novel: "overstatement of emotion, violence, mystery, and rare coincidence, in various combinations. Protagonists or other important characters tend to fit into clear categories of good or bad ... A frequently used technique is the withholding of information in order to create suspense."[3] Jorge Ruedas de la Serna observes another feature common to novels published in installments, at least to those that won favor with readers: "The most noteworthy formal characteristic of these works was their length or bulk. When a work turned out to be a success, the goal was to keep it running as long as possible."[4]

Amalia and a member of the resistance live out one of the ill-fated love affairs that are a staple of romantic narrative. Melancholy signs augur the tragic end to which the characters are predestined. Just as the couple declares mutual love, a white rose falls from Amalia's hands to the floor, filling her with dread. As she is dressing for her wedding, a second white rose sends the same signal, and one of Amalia's songbirds emits a single note "with a strange accent, more like a moan than the natural modulations of those members of Nature's choir."[5] The heroine's foreboding proves prescient, since the characters are submerged in a final bloodbath.

Romantic as it may be, *Amalia* is primarily a work of social activism that encourages resistance to Rosas and makes a number of statements about the direction that Argentine society should take after the leader is overthrown. It should be remembered that while Rosas and his followers dominated Buenos Aires and nearby areas, not all of the country was under Rosista control. The *unitarios* were still waging battles and, as the end of the regime neared, were holding more and more ground. Mármol loaded the novel with information about the military resistance to Rosas and with essaylike passages setting forth his vision of Argentina's problems and future promise.

The novel was first published in a supplement to *La Semana* (The week), a newspaper that Mármol had founded in Montevideo, at that time the center of anti-Rosas activity among Argentine exiles. It came out at a moment when the exiles' hopes were soaring. Opposition to Rosas was finally gaining sufficient military strength and foreign support to defeat the strongman. The publication of *Amalia* was interrupted by the battle of Caseros (February 1852), which brought about the fall of the Rosas regime. *La Semana* announced the victory and ceased publication; as Juan Carlos Ghiano notes, Mármol was in a hurry to reestablish himself in Buenos Aires.[6] Mármol published a farewell, "To the Subscribers of *La Semana*." In it he announces that the installments of the novel "are suspended for fifteen or twenty days" and reassures readers that in Buenos Aires he will research and polish the ending.[7] However, as Beatriz Curia observes, "The readership that had followed, week after week, the twists and turns of the novel had to wait three years to learn how it all came out."[8] Curia, who has carried out a comparison of the serial *Amalia* and the 1855 book version, concludes that the complete edition "is a different novel." Mármol had toned down many potentially inflammatory aspects of the novel "to avoid conflicts between the factions locked in struggle."[9] Though *Amalia* appeared during an era of renewed hope, its action is set in 1840, known as "the year of terror" for the intense activity of Rosas's secret agents.

For today's readers, a major obstacle to appreciation of *Amalia* is the novel's method of characterization. In his portrayal of characters Mármol does not seek to imitate the contradictory and ambiguous nature of real-world personalities. The title character is a beautiful, selfless young widow who throws herself into succoring a fugitive dissident from the Rosas regime. Rosas maintained an extensive and much-feared secret police force, so the novel stresses Amalia's self-abnegating heroism in harboring a known enemy of the nation's strongman. The narrator's descriptions of Amalia point out that readers should not expect the realistic representation of a woman. In the midst of a highly idealized portrait of the heroine, he comments, "At that moment, Amalia was not a woman; she was one of those goddesses that the mythological poetry of the Greeks conceived." [10] The narrator often alludes to Amalia as an angel or goddess, calls her "divine," likens her to a marble statue, or otherwise sets the heroine in a category apart from human women. In the logic of the novel she serves as an embodiment of the best of the Argentine nation. The two male heroes, members of the anti-Rosas resistance, are both of high moral character and, as is conventional for romantic heroes, strikingly handsome. One of the two men, who is sheltered by Amalia, falls in love with her and eventually dies beside her after Rosas's secret police raid their home. He is a pure idealist whose portrayal seems especially two-dimensional. The other principal male character, Bello, has a pragmatic streak and a chameleonlike adaptability that make him the novel's most complex figure. As both the son of a Rosas supporter and a member of the dissident underground, he moves between the two worlds. Able to fit into any environment, Bello roams all over Buenos Aires; his far-flung adventures allow a wide variety of characters to enter into the narrative.

Those who side with Rosas come in for a schematic portrayal. In the majority of cases, they are associated with blood, gore, the color red, cruelty, and coarseness. Many of the supporters of Rosas are physically grotesque. Nonetheless, a few innocent or potentially redeemable souls are found within the Rosas camp. The most prominent of these exceptions is Rosas's daughter Manuela. Mármol took a special interest in this young woman and composed her biography (1849) as well as portraying her in his celebrated novel. She appears as a victim who is forced by her birth to live inside the sinister apparatus of her father's regime. The novel is also benign in its treatment of Rosas's two sisters. Perhaps more surprisingly, the chief of the Buenos Aires police is represented as a basically decent individual who, enmeshed in the dictator's web, has no opportunity to work for the good. But Mármol surrounds these few sympathetic characters with an unruly mass of gauchos, street brawlers, stereotypically mysterious and sinister Amerindians, hangers-on, spies, hit men, and schemers.

Readers today are often distressed by the novel's persistent association between African or Amerindian ancestry and such traits as treachery, poor hygiene, disorderliness, and love of violence. For example, when the narrator takes the reader inside the home of Rosas's sister-in-law, which is also a nerve center for the repressive secret police, the first person described is "an old mulatto woman, whose cleanliness could be vouched for about as well as that of her mistress."[11] The narrator and the characters are uninhibited in attributing characteristics to entire racial groups. Perhaps the strangest of these race-based characterizations comes from Bello. When he shelters the wounded resistance fighter in Amalia's house, he tells her to dismiss two sets of servants, "the white people because they're white, and the black people because they're black"; only biracial household help are allowed to remain. Bello explains the rationale behind these orders. In his vision of Argentina, a large proportion of the lower class has been turned into spies and traitors for the regime. He goes on: "There is only one exception in the lower class, and that's the mulattos; the black people have grown conceited, the whites are prostituted, but the mulattos, because of that propensity that there is in every mixed race to raise oneself and to gain dignity, are almost all enemies of Rosas, because they know that the *unitarios* [members of the faction opposed to Rosas's *federales*] are the enlightened and well-educated people, whom they always take for a model."[12]

Elitist beliefs about social class and cultural tastes are aired as freely as racial prejudices. As noted in the previous chapter's discussion of "The slaughtering grounds," Rosas cultivated the support of every aspect of the cattle industry, from ranching to meat packing, and enjoyed popularity among the lower classes generally. Argentine writers who portray the regime in fiction reveal an acute awareness that *federales,* the followers of Rosas, are for the most part of a lower social class than themselves. Even those Rosas supporters who are white and wealthy, such as the owners of vast haciendas, have not mastered the style that the nation's intellectuals tended to prize most highly: European, urban, and upper class.

This consciousness, and with it an elitist disdain for the *federales,* is evident throughout *Amalia.* The novel includes a highly detailed account of the interior of Amalia's house, decorated in the most refined style that the author can evoke. As is often noted in the novel, Amalia seldom enters into contact with the general run of humankind, associating only with a few select friends and relatives. Her house is on the outskirts of Buenos Aires, and the characters hope that it will escape the reach of Rosas and his spies, who dominate the city. The descriptions of the heroine's home, a refuge of wealth and aristocratic European taste, are in contrast with the novel's accounts of the backward conditions of the streets of Buenos Aires, where dirt and chaos predominate and little attempt has been made to install modern urban amenities.

Rosas and his guards do not lack for money, but live as if on the ranch, even while in the city. The narrator expresses an almost obsessive disdain for these country bumpkins. He ridicules their rustic furniture, inadequate interior lighting, uncouth joshing, and inability to make civilized dinner-table conversation. As noted in the previous chapter, Rosas had strengthened his populist appeal by cultivating a style that was markedly rural and Argentine and surrounding himself with gauchos. The narrator expresses revulsion at the incursion of this ranch culture into the city.

Mármol's belief in the essential superiority of European urbanity is most evident when Amalia, Bello, and another anti-Rosas woman infiltrate a ball thrown by the Rosas faction. The three dissidents are an island of aristocratic European manners in a sea of down-home crudity. The narrator comments, "Daniel, we were saying, was the purest man at that gathering, and the most European man who was there." [13] Rosas's sister Agustina is the belle of the ball until Amalia makes her entrance. The latter, who wears nothing that is not imported from France, immediately outshines the homespun beauty of Agustina. Among other disadvantages, Agustina has not learned to compose her features into the artfully "tender and spiritual" expression favored in the romantic era. Her face ingenuously betrays "an animation that only the *unitarias* [anti-Rosas women] would find shocking." [14] Trinidad Pérez expresses the queasiness that current-day readers feel over the way the novel ridicules characters for their low social class and down-home tastes: "The author's deeply class-biased vision turns this novel into one of the most reactionary and discriminatory in all of Latin American literature. Its intention is to point out the class difference among the human groups and sectors that it presents." [15]

The well-known Argentine critic David Viñas is particularly outraged by Mármol's practice of dividing the nation into two groups: noble souls, distinguished by their urbane European culture, and coarse thugs whose culture is unmistakably Argentine. In Viñas's analysis, Mármol is distorting the program of his generation of liberal intellectuals. The original agenda of these intellectuals, who struggled to maintain a democratic vision, included a "synthesis between the American and the European." In *Amalia*, though, "the parallelism becomes polarized in its content and meaning until it goes out of balance." [16] Throughout *Amalia*, Mármol creates extreme contrasts of refinement and crudity, which come to "underlie and shape the architecture of the book." [17] When the two cultural styles are perceived and portrayed as incompatible, the project of the mid-century liberals, theoretically intended to promote unity, is thrown off track.

At the time of its appearance, *Amalia* attracted readers with its plot full of perils and heroic deeds, anti-Rosas sentiment, and romantically ringing assertions in support of freedom. Over the years, though, it has lost much of its appeal. Sommer, who is relatively kind to *Amalia,* observes that the novel once offered guidance to the direction in which the nation should evolve, "a design for the new Argentine citizen . . . Yet today it is read more as a period piece than as a founding text."[18]

The career of Juana Manuela Gorriti is not as closely linked with opposition to Rosas as is that of Mármol, yet she was preoccupied with the Rosas era and its violence. Criticism on Gorriti often mentions her life, which was, for a woman, far ahead of the times. She was born on a ranch in the province of Salta, in the north of Argentina at the edge of the Andes. Gorriti, who spent many years in Peru and Bolivia, is an Andean as well as an Argentine writer. She took an interest in the cultures native to the region, promoting indigenous folk music and featuring Andean lore in her novels and stories. As Hebe Beatriz Molina observes, after Gorriti's death, her works underwent a period of neglect; few new editions appeared, so this author's books became difficult to locate.[19] Since the late twentieth century new editions and many critical studies have appeared.

As Gorriti reminds readers of her biographies of national heroes, her family played an important part in the independence campaign and continued to be prominent in politics and military affairs. Her father was General José Ignacio Gorriti, who fought with the *unitarios* during the civil wars preceding Rosas's consolidation of power. General Gorriti and his family fled to Bolivia.[20] At fourteen, Juana Manuela Gorriti married Manuel Isidoro Belzú, an officer in the Bolivian army, and followed her husband into exile to Lima. He returned to Bolivia, where he was president at the time of his assassination. Meanwhile, Gorriti was attracting readers. In Molina's summary, "Juana Manuela Gorriti published her stories bit by bit in newspapers and magazines in Bolivia, Peru, Argentina, and, at times, Chile and Venezuela."[21]

Gorriti left her husband and in 1848 set up residence in Lima on her own. She was a charismatic presence in this literary capital, which would be her primary base for years. Between her moves and her travels, Gorriti did not reside again in Argentina until the 1870s, long after Rosas's fall in 1852. Francine Masiello sums up the significance of Gorriti's career: "Traveling through countries dominated by eminently masculine struggles for power in the aftermath of independence, Gorriti chose to address questions of feminine rights and to initiate a dialogue—among men and women—of international scope."[22]

Though Gorriti had little direct contact with the Rosas regime, she was intensely aware of it and of its polarizing effects on Argentina. Many of her action-filled, often melodramatic novels and short stories portray the dissolution of Argentina into violent factions. Gorriti often brings *unitarios* and *federales* together in her narratives. Her short stories and novels set in the Rosas era resemble *Amalia,* but with significant differences. As noted, the main complaint against Mármol is that his narratives exacerbate the split between Rosas's supporters and opponents. He idealizes the former, ridicules the latter, and leaves little hope for reconciliation. In her writing Gorriti favors the *unitarios* but expresses horror at a society that has broken down into two hostile camps. Critics have been fascinated by Gorriti's willingness to probe Argentina's conflict using characters from both sides of the national divide. Cristina Iglesias argues that Gorriti's writing takes a much more sympathetic look at *federales* than can be found in such male-authored texts as Mármol's *Amalia* or the essays of the celebrated statesman Domingo Faustino Sarmiento, discussed in the previous chapter. Iglesias makes the bold assertion that this unusually flexible writer empathizes with her beleaguered *federal* characters until, at moments, "Gorriti is writing literature that goes against her own political convictions."[23]

Iglesias here raises a complicated issue. Gorriti does at times project in her texts a longing for national unity. Yet her hatred of the Rosas cause interferes with any effort to view the division from both sides. In reviewing the evidence for and against Gorriti as a writer who promotes reconciliation, it is worth remembering a sagacious observation of Masiello's: "The work of Juana Manuela Gorriti is highly contradictory."[24]

Gorriti's heroines often maintain ties to characters from both factions, venturing out of their homes to meet with members of the opposition. In some cases they are seeking a way to heal and to mother Argentine society. Their actions are an attempt to ameliorate the damage that the conflict wreaks. Mary G. Berg accurately summarizes the efforts of these women: "Women are often portrayed as the mediators between the political divisions that have locked their men into bloodthirsty frenzy."[25] The male characters are more unbending and partisan. They remain first and foremost opposing warriors, whether *federales* or *unitarios.*

The first volume of Gorriti's *Sueños y realidades* (Dreams and realities), published in 1865, collects her earliest short stories and novels. (In the nineteenth century it was common to refer to short fictional works as novels, and Gorriti follows this practice.) Several of these narratives refer to some aspect of the Rosas regime. Berg notes that the volume contains work written as early as the mid-1830s as well as more recent stories.[26] The stories of national conflict feature resolute women who defy their families to reach out to members of the opposition. Among these is the often-reprinted *La hija del mashorquero*, a very short novel. The title identifies the heroine as the daughter of a member of Rosas's secret police, the Mazorca, feared for its summary executions of suspected dissidents. Clemencia, whose name is the Spanish word for clemency, is conscience-stricken after she discovers the nature of her father's work, which essentially consists of commanding an assassination force. She seeks to make amends by clandestinely assisting the widows and children of her father's victims. The plot leads to a melodramatic climax in which she is killed by her own father while taking the place of the wife of an *unitario*. A similar concept is at work in *La novia del muerto* (The dead man's bride). Again the heroine is the daughter of a *federal* and attracted to the other side. She falls in love with an *unitario*. The doomed couple is seen literally seeking common ground on which to meet.

Iglesias argues that "The dead man's bride" to some extent "inverts the story of *Amalia*." Both Gorriti's heroine and Amalia are from Tucumán. Iglesias points out that the dead man's bride lives on the outskirts of Tucumán because the city is under the control of the *unitarios*, while Amalia lives on the outskirts of Buenos Aires because the city is dominated by *federales*. In her analysis, "The dead man's bride" to some extent replicates the plot of *Amalia* but moves away from its sectarianism. For example, both narratives feature a secret wedding, but Mármol's story features the union of like-minded *unitarios*, while in Gorriti's novel it is a risky mixed marriage.[27]

Despite these signs of a desire for reconciliation, with women as the most empathetic of mediators, Gorriti does not abandon the fundamental principle that the *unitarios* are in the right. In her fiction the *federal* women who become involved with *unitarios* are not themselves enthusiasts of Rosas. Rather, they are from pro-Rosas families, but have come to harbor a forbidden sympathy for the *unitarios*. The violence in the stories is nearly always exercised by *federales*. Amelia Royo represents the critical view that Gorriti never wavers in her opposition to Rosas and his followers. She observes of Gorriti's narratives of *federales* and *unitarios* that "curiously . . . there is a repetition of the Manichean formula of the most unalloyed anti-Rosas sentiment of the times."[28] For Royo,

Gorriti's characters continue to be "stereotypes of good and evil who represent the conflict" between the nation's factions.[29] After examining the various oppositions that come into play in Gorriti's stories of the Rosas regime, Royo concludes that behind them all is one schematic division: "It is a pure and simple matter of placing *unitarios* at the positive pole and *federales* at the negative pole."[30]

Gorriti's tendency to link Rosas and his supporters with almost satanic malignancy is painfully evident in *El lucero del manantial* (The morning star of the spring). A lurid short novel from the same volume as the above-discussed narratives, *Morning star* makes Argentina under Rosas seem like a delirious fantasy. As a young woman, the heroine surrenders to a mysterious lover who at first seems to be part of a dream. He appears amid a vision of gruesome phantasmagoria, and the narrator characterizes him as a "vision":

> One night a vision came to trouble the placid sleep of the virgin.
>
> She saw a vast field covered with half-open graves and sown with beheaded cadavers. From all those split necks there flowed rivulets of blood that, joining in a deep riverbed, formed a river whose red waves murmured mournful moans and grew wide and tall as a tidal wave.
>
> In the noxious fumes along its banks, sure-footedly treading on the bloody faces of the dead men, there walked a man whose naked arm brandished a dagger.
>
> That man was beautiful; but with a somber beauty like that of the accursed archangel; and in his eyes, blue as the sky, shone sinister flashes of lightning that made one freeze with fear.[31]

Though the episode seems like an erotic dream, the heroine bears a child. She becomes the wife of a legislator who opposes Rosas and is assassinated by the latter's agents. During this crisis, the heroine recognizes the nation's much-feared leader as the transient lover of her youth. Her son is about to be executed as well, and the heroine rushes to plead with Rosas to spare the young man's life. Exhibiting the intransigence typical of Gorriti's male characters, the condemned youth would rather die than have his mother approach Rosas: "Do not ask your husband's killer for mercy, or your son will curse you from eternity."[32] The mother's effort to appeal is unsuccessful, and Rosas has his son put to death.

Although the heroine enters into contact with both factions, bearing the child of a *federal* and marrying an *unitario*, this blood-soaked narrative could hardly be considered conciliatory. The narrator uninhibitedly describes Rosas as a demonic being, and the plot makes him responsible for the death of his son.

While Gorriti failed to rise above the rift that split Argentina, it would be difficult to name any of the nation's intellectuals who did not display a factional outlook during and long after the Rosas years. Whatever Gorriti's vision of the Rosas phenomenon may have been, she is unambiguously pro-woman. Her stories of the Rosas regime portray women as more altruistic and less absolutist than men. Gorriti's heroines are typically pure-hearted, angelic creatures intent on protecting and succoring others. Like Mármol's *Amalia,* they resemble familiar images of the Virgin Mary and also serve as figures of Argentina, or at least of the nation's noblest aspects. The male characters are more likely to view political violence as normal and inevitable, while the sensitive, motherly heroines regard it with horror and look for some way to ameliorate the situation. An exception is the Gorriti heroine who, in *El guante negro* (The black glove), kills her husband. But she is defending her son, whom the pro-Rosas father was planning to kill to prevent his defection to the *unitarios.* Though Gorriti's female protagonists have little success in their attempts to protect others from violence, they succeed in establishing the author's view of women as the great reservoir of kindness and understanding in society.

Native Andean themes appear occasionally in Gorriti's work. As did many writers and readers during the romantic era, she found more grandeur in the past than the present, and this nostalgic vision is evident in her treatment of indigenous themes. Gorriti was enthralled by vanished civilizations and ancient legends. She particularly relished narratives involving centuries-old lore, tribal secrets of the royal Incas, electrifying disclosures, prophecies, curses, omens, and, a particular favorite of hers, a secret, underground Inca city constructed of gold. Like many nineteenth-century Spanish American writers, Gorriti dwells upon two great themes: the splendor of the great Native American empires and the cruel injustice of the conquest. Typical of this past-minded outlook is the reaction of a Gorriti heroine upon learning that her beloved had an indigenous mother. She exclaims, "The one my heart has chosen is a child of the Incas!"[33] By "Incas" she refers to the imperial aristocracy; she then invokes the names of the first and last Inca emperors. The heroine exults at the thrilling link to the fabled nobility, "vanished beings," rather than connecting her beloved with everyday native peoples of the here and now in which they are both living.[34]

With the romantic fondness for weaving secrets and revelations into narratives, Gorriti creates stories around characters whose Inca ancestry remains a secret, to others and at times to themselves, until it is divulged during a crisis. The idea that the native peoples of the Americas harbor privileged tribal knowledge, not to be disclosed to outsiders, exercises a perennial appeal upon the popular imagination. Gorriti provides her indigenous and *mestizo* characters with many secrets that they share with one another while the reader is allowed to listen in.

Elena Altuna has examined and evaluated the representation of indigenous culture in Gorriti's narratives and, by way of comparison, among the participants in her above-noted salon, the *veladas literarias*.[35] Altuna finds that Gorriti and her colleagues, all of whom belonged to the dominant white culture, viewed the Andean peoples as worthy of greater recognition, courageous, and noble. Amerindians were also emblematic of the new Spanish American nations' drive to become independent from Spain, not just politically but in outlook and culture. Through her presentations at sessions of the salon, Gorriti encouraged her associates, who had been brought up with European music, to appreciate the *yaraví*, a folk-music form based in large part on native tradition.[36]

On the other hand, Gorriti and her fellow intellectuals tended to see Amerindian peoples as exotic and picturesque others. Altuna asserts that Gorriti's fiction reveals a deep-seated belief that the native Andean peoples were not part of the same social world or nation in which she and her colleagues dwelt. In her narratives on indigenous themes, Gorriti tended to repeat the same plot line, featuring a doomed love between representatives of white and native Andean cultures. In Altuna's analysis, the impossibility of these inter-ethnic loves "reveals the inability to imagine a nation that could integrate its majority sector, the indigenous population."[37] At the same time, Altuna recognizes that this writer's outlook on and portrayal of Andean culture was typical of the progressive intellectual circles of her day.

Like many readers of Gorriti's stories, Altuna notices that this writer is inconsistent. At moments, Gorriti seems ahead of her time in her portrayal of native Andean characters. Altuna is impressed that in one story, "Si haces mal no esperes bien" (If you do evil, don't expect good), Gorriti creates for a wronged indigenous woman a fiery speech denouncing her exploitation and that of the native peoples of the Andes. Since writers on indigenous themes were slow to create articulate native characters, Gorriti appears advanced in her decision to have the woman set forth her own case.[38]

Gorriti's stories on Inca themes were popular in their time, but today they seem to lack relevance to the pressing real-world problems of the indigenous population of nineteenth-century Peru. The poverty and exploitation of the native Andean population did not lend itself to Gorriti's highly romantic mode of storytelling, but these social problems would be taken up as subject matter by later writers with a more realistic approach.

It was the resurgence of feminism that led to the rediscovery of Gorriti, not just as Argentina's first female novelist but also for her unconventional life, progressive views, and support of women's participation in intellectual life. In 1980 widespread interest in Gorriti was ignited with the popular success of a novel based on her life. *Juanamanuela, mucha mujer* (Juanamanuela, a lot of woman) by the Argentine novelist Martha Mercader, portrayed Gorriti as a determined woman who lived in defiance of social norms.[39] Gorriti's life, whose basic facts were noted above, raises a number of gender-related issues. From its early years, her marriage gave rise to much gossip about both partners. It was a bold step for Gorriti to create an independent household in Lima after her husband, Manuel Isidoro Belzú, had returned to Bolivia to pursue his political ambitions. In mid-nineteenth-century Lima, while widows could respectably head their own households and manage various types of enterprises, for a woman from a prominent family to leave her marriage was not yet accepted. Moreover, Gorriti made no effort to downplay her status as a separated wife. According to María Laura de Arriba, "She abandoned the last name Belzú and took back the one designating the name of her father."[40] Gorriti was even more marked as a sexual nonconformist when she bore two children while living independently in Lima.

While Gorriti's freedom in personal matters fascinates her admirers, perhaps more significant are her efforts to make room for women in intellectual life. Gorriti was renowned as an organizer of *veladas literarias*. These were cultural and literary salons, evening sessions that lasted several hours and featured writers reading from their own and others' texts along with performances of music, parlor entertainments, occasionally exhibitions of visual artworks, and lectures and discussion of topics of the issues of the day among progressive thinkers. Gorriti supervised these salons in the various cities where she resided, though the most celebrated were her *veladas* in the two major cultural capitals of South America, Lima and Buenos Aires.[41] She welcomed women, and many attended and participated.[42]

The subject matter of the lectures often had to do particularly with women and the desirability of strengthening their education. Obviously, women's schooling had improved greatly since colonial times, when, as Sor Juana noted with horror, even wealthy men might leave their daughters illiterate. Even so, in Gorriti's day, the education of girls was incomplete compared with that of boys. Pupils of both sexes learned to read and write. In fact, throughout the nineteenth century, it was generally assumed that women were fonder of reading than were men. The reading of novels, a genre that was slow to gain prestige, was sometimes denigrated as a typically feminine form of escapism. There is some factual basis to the association of very popular fiction with women readers. Jorge Ruedas de la Serna asserts that "the serialized novel drew a largely female readership. The husband would buy the newspaper or magazine, not so much for its party affiliation or political outlook as for the latest installment of the novel, which would be clamored for by the wife, who saw this reading as perhaps the only chance to escape from an oppressive existence."[43]

Boys were much more likely to study subjects that required the exercise of reason, such as sciences, philosophy, and statesmanship. Girls spent more school time on nonacademic subjects, such as etiquette, needlework and other domestic arts, and religious devotions. The goal of girls' education was to produce faithful wives, devoted mothers, and competent household managers. In the upper classes there was an effort to produce cultivated women whose refinement would bring prestige to their future husbands. Perhaps needless to say, boys spent more years in school than did girls. Nineteenth-century progressives often stressed the benefits that Spanish American societies would reap if the mothers of its future (male) leaders were better educated.

Gorriti, who was clearly the best-known woman novelist living in mid-nineteenth-century Spanish America (Gertrudis Gómez de Avellaneda being in Spain), was eager to see other women writers exercise their talents. In Lima she encouraged a number of younger female authors. Though the numbers of women writers had risen greatly since Sor Juana's time, women whose work appeared in print were often subject to harsh criticism and ridiculed in an openly sexist way. Gorriti extended her support to many of these writers who were just then struggling to establish themselves. The most celebrated of these are Matto de Turner, who called herself Gorriti's "daughter" (and will be discussed in Chapter 5), and Matto's friend and colleague Mercedes Cabello de Carbonera (Peru, 1845–1909).

While it is clear that Gorriti was an early feminist who promoted improvements in women's status, a more complicated proposition is the identification of a distinctively woman's outlook in her writing. The noted feminist critic Lucía Guerra Cunningham has sought to demonstrate that Gorriti's writing manifests "a feminine perspective belonging to that time period."[44] In the opinion of Guerra Cunningham, women's vision was necessarily different from that of men; nineteenth-century Spanish American women had less training in logic, spent more time reading romantic fiction and adventure tales, were more pious, and, of course, were excluded from direct participation in affairs of state.[45] Guerra Cunningham, comparing Gorriti's narratives of the Rosas regime with Mármol's *Amalia,* observes that the woman writer offers less rational analysis of the political situation and accords greater prominence to elements of the supernatural and the power of intuition, among other differences.[46]

It is an exceedingly difficult critical task to identify a vision or manner of writing distinctive to women. However, nearly any reader of Gorriti's work would recognize that women characters dominate her narratives. Both Masiello and Guerra Cunningham point out that Gorriti spotlights characters from groups excluded from power.[47] This category includes not only women but also Amerindians, the demented, and all types of, in Masiello's words, "peripheral beings, abandoned by society."[48]

An important point to remember about Gorriti is that, while she wrote in the nineteenth century, the critical study of her work only began in the late twentieth century. Her rediscovery is still under way, and research into her career and writings still offers many opportunities to future critics. Though Gorriti is the only nineteenth-century Argentine woman writer discussed in this study, readers should be aware that there were many others whose work is not as well known but who are coming in for rediscovery. The 1992 publication of Masiello's *Between Civilization and Barbarism: Women, Nation, and Literary Culture in Modern Argentina* greatly stimulated research in this area. This study, which covers the nineteenth century and the early decades of the twentieth, examines both female- and male-authored texts that either state or imply the part that women are to play in defining, humanizing, educating, and morally strengthening the nation. Masiello examines "the kinds of interventions provided by women: their meditations on the public sphere, their participation in literary traditions, and their struggle for access to the symbolic realm that determines the cultural imagination of a nation."[49] To do so, this researcher draws upon an amazing archive of Argentine women's texts that she has gathered. Extending beyond literature to essays and journalism, the body of female-authored writing to which Masiello alludes demonstrates that pre-twentieth-century women wrote much more than has commonly been assumed.[50]

T he 1862 *Martín Rivas* continues to be one of the most widely read of nineteenth-century Spanish American novels, especially in the author's native Chile, where it is regarded as a landmark in the development of the Chilean novel. The work of Alberto Blest Gana (1830–1920), *Martín Rivas* first appeared, as did many nineteenth-century novels, as a serial. Published in installments in the Santiago newspaper *La Voz de Chile* (The voice of Chile), *Martín Rivas* gripped its readership with a complex plot full of secrets, revelations, and sudden changes in the characters' fortunes.

While *Martín Rivas* has many subplots, its central thread is a narrative of hard-won success in both love and economic well-being. Martín Rivas is a young man from the northern mining regions of Chile. As the novel begins, he has just arrived in the capital, Santiago. His goal is to become a lawyer and so support his family, whose finances have suffered a disaster. Martín must overcome, through his tenacity and quick thinking, numerous obstacles. He at first endures snobbish rejection for his provincial roughness and lack of means; his classmates and associates perceive him as a country bumpkin or a member of a lower social class. For most of the novel, Martín is tormented by an excruciatingly unrequited passion for Leonor, the beautiful, outwardly cold and aloof daughter of the rich man who is providing him lodging in Santiago. Though the family members are hardly welcoming, Martín makes himself indispensable to them, helping the father with his business and quick-wittedly extricating the son from an embarrassing entrapment.

Various misadventures befall Martín, but he always emerges with his fortunes improved. He is an assiduous positive thinker who, when he experiences a moment of insecurity, forces himself to be resolute: "The voice of reason persuaded him to abandon his childish discouragement before it dampened his spirits."[51] At one point, he must leave the family's elegant house in disgrace, suffering the scorn of the young woman he loves, because a good deed on his part has been misinterpreted as a sexual escapade. As he confidently predicts, he is soon redeemed in the family's eyes. His brief absence makes them realize how beneficial he has been to them, and he is warmly welcomed back. Shortly afterward, Martín is condemned to death for his participation in a revolt against the government. Even this adversity proves opportune. Leonor, who has been keeping her love for Martín secret, is so disturbed by the death sentence that she states, in front of her astonished family, "I love him."[52] Her campaign to rescue Martín not only saves his life but solidifies their relationship.

While his struggle is an uphill one, Martín eventually wins over all the wealthier and more urbane characters, including the initially haughty Leonor. The final chapter begins with the transcription of a letter from Martín to his sister: "The proud girl, who disdainfully greeted a poor provincial who sought her family's patronage, now bestows upon your brother a treasure of love that brings him to his knees in adoration."[53] Leonor's father is to blame for the financial ruin of Martín's family. So justice is served when the marriage to the man's daughter establishes the young man securely for life. Wrapping up the plot at the novel's end, the narrator informs readers that "Don Dámaso Encina turned all of his business affairs over to Martín Rivas in order to devote himself more freely to the political fluctuations which he hoped would one day land him in the House of Senate."[54] Indeed, Martín, who initially struck the family as a rustic, has emerged as the household member best qualified to manage a fortune.

Interpretations of the novel vary widely. As Jorge Román-Lagunas puts it: "According to most critics, we are looking at a novel that makes a statement. There is no agreement, however, on the nature of this statement."[55] Clearly the hero rises above adversity to achieve a well-merited success, but over what does he triumph? Is *Martín Rivas* the story of an individual who makes good, summoning such personal talents as superior intelligence and organizational skills? Or does the protagonist stand for a sector of society, such as a social class or regional population? Most critics see Martín as the idealized representation of a group, but they disagree on which one. The influential critic Alone (real name, Hernán Díaz Arrieta), who for many years wielded great influence in Chile, makes the case that Martín overcomes a class barrier. In his reading, Martín represents "the triumph of the poor, yet intelligent and hardworking middle class."[56] This class is shown occupying, and deservedly so, places in society that have previously been reserved for the bourgeoisie.

Jaime Concha, though, objects to this interpretation, calling it a "common misreading of Blest Gana's *Martín Rivas*."[57] In his outlook, the novel gives readers the impression that Martín is from a lower social class than Leonor. Yet, in Concha's reading, Martín is already upper middle class when the novel begins. His disadvantage is that he is from the newly emerged mine-owning bourgeoisie of the northern provinces. He stands out in contrast to the established Santiago families whose wealth derives from land holdings and financial dealings. Martín is temporarily poor as a result of his father's financial ruin, but displays the outlook of the upper middle class; he has an elite bearing and fully expects to become a successful lawyer. Concha argues that Blest Gana's political position, a tepid liberalism, explains the lack of clarity surrounding the hero's class standing. Blest Gana was eager to see a limited degree of social mobility so that the newer branches of the upper middle class could take their place in Chilean society. While the offspring of mining entrepreneurs might initially seem rough-hewn to the stylish financiers of Santiago, the new arrivals possessed expertise needed to make Chile part of the world economy of modern capitalism. The novel gives the impression of endorsing an open, democratic society; according to Concha, though, Blest Gana seeks to preserve class stratification with only minor modifications.[58] Juan Durán-Luzio also sees in Martín's success the union of old money and rising new capitalists, but does not fault Blest Gana for half-hearted liberalism.[59] For Durán-Luzio, *Martín Rivas* makes a worthy contribution to the progressive thought of the 1860s.[60]

Martín Rivas is another case of the commingling of romantic and realistic elements. In this case, the author was a student of the French realist movement, but often reproduced elements of the romantic narrative with which his generation had grown up. The novel offers a cross section of Santiago society at mid-century. Its multiple plot lines permit the inclusion of many characters, ranging from the wealthy bourgeois family to lower-middle-class characters and a few poor people. Yet, as Hernán Poblete Varas puts it, "The characters are surrounded by a romantic nimbus."[61] This critic also cites as a romantic trait the sudden revelations, reversals of fortune, and seemingly desperate crises that advance the plot.[62]

Characterization in *Martín Rivas* is not entirely along romantic lines. Poblete Varas observes that the descriptions of both Martín and his best friend conform to "romantic images"; both have pale, intense, brooding faces.[63] The idealized portrait of the title character and his devotion to what he believes to be a hopeless love make him resemble the hero of a romantic work. Yet he can also be efficient, practical, and cool-headed, qualities far removed from the romantic ideal. His wealthy mentor takes him on as a clerk but comes to depend on his talents for business and crisis management, unromantic traits.

During most of the novel, Leonor does not exhibit the gentle sweetness that readers have come to associate with romantic heroines. Instead, she has a dominant personality and delights in tormenting her suitors. While romantic writers often idealized fragile women, Blest Gana characterizes Leonor as an indefatigable horsewoman. In an emergency, she exhibits unusual strength and dexterity to save Martín: "Leonor turned the key in the lock, pulled back the unwieldy crossbar as if it were weightless, and opened the door within seconds." [64] It must be admitted, though, that once Leonor falls in love, she bears a greater resemblance to other heroines of romantic novels than she has to that point.

Youthful love is a major component of the novel's subject matter, but it does not always come in for an earnest romantic treatment. The narrator points out, at times clearly relishing the irony, that considerations of finance and status enter into the most passionate courtship. The novel's plot involves two amorous triangles. In both, love at times is portrayed as a lofty, ennobling passion. At other moments, courtship and marriage appear to be handy footholds for characters seeking to climb the social ladder or improve their economic status. Martín's sponsor was a clerk with a loan firm before his marriage. The narrator, in revealing this fact, makes a sly comment on the link between love and money: "Back then, Doña Engracia's want of beauty was compensated by an inheritance of 30,000 pesos, which so incited the passions of the young Encina that he asked for her hand in marriage." [65] Blest Gana finds it humorous to introduce a note of cold commerce into an amorous scene. For example, Leonor's cousin and Martín's best friend are in love, but their union depends upon the successful outcome of negotiations, in which both lovers' families are involved, over the renewal of the lease on an hacienda. When the two are alone together, the young man bursts into avowals of his devotion. "But," as the narrator wryly puts it, "he momentarily abandoned the topic of eternal love to discuss some obstacles in the real world" [66]—the lovers must keep one another up to date on negotiations over the lease.

Leonor prefers Martín over other suitors in great part because he does not appear to be attracted by her fortune. Nonetheless, their marriage benefits both parties. Martín has outstanding business skills but lacks capital, while Leonor's family needs a new head to manage its fortune. The father is losing interest, and the oldest son has repeatedly demonstrated a lack of common sense. It may well have occurred to later readers that Leonor's determined and resourceful personality would qualify her to head the family businesses. Yet plainly her father never thinks of turning the helm of his enterprises over to a female successor.

Readers who approach *Martín Rivas* expecting a purely realistic narrative may find it oddly lighthearted and sweet. Though Blest Gana started out as a romantic writer, by the time he composed *Martín Rivas* he had become a student of literary realism and especially the work of its most visible representative, the French novelist Honoré de Balzac. Yet he does not follow these models all the way. As George D. Schade puts it, "Blest Glana wanted to be the Chilean Balzac . . . though he never really fulfilled this aim." [67]

The ending of *Martín Rivas,* in which the protagonist wins the hand of the rich and beautiful heroine and the respect of everyone else, scarcely qualifies as a realistic statement about current social conditions. In another departure from realism, Blest Gana avoids the scenes of unpleasantness and squalor that are a hallmark of realistic narrative. When realist novelists portrayed lower-class characters, they sought to give a straightforward, socially conscious account of life in poverty. *Martín Rivas* is fundamentally about the upper and lower strata of the middle class, but it depicts some lower-class figures, such as servants, street merchants, and a ribald carriage driver. Their portrayal is in the time-honored literary and theatrical tradition of using members of the lower class to provide comic relief rather than to expose their problems. Román-Lagunas concludes that Blest Gana's work "cannot even be classified as realist in the strict sense . . . realism meant the right to state everything without hiding anything and it is evident that Blest Gana's work comes into being more or less restrained, prudent, hinting not stating; it does not wish to wound; it seeks to portray without showing the sore and shameful aspects." [68]

Whatever its exact relation to literary movements and tendencies, *Martín Rivas* was indisputably a major step toward establishing the Chilean novel. It also affected Spanish American narrative as a whole. Blest Gana, a dignified-looking gentleman who had a successful career in diplomacy as well as literature, helped make the composition and consumption of novels appear as worthwhile activities. The public was letting go of the idea that novel reading was an indulgence in fantasy, leading to an overheated imagination, and especially dangerous for impressionable young women. Though novelists now could be viewed as serious writers, readers still expected them to provide entertainment in the form of gripping plots and memorably dramatic scenes.

The year 1867 marked the appearance of a novel that would gain a firm hold on readers' imaginations, eventually becoming the single most often read work of Spanish American narrative. This text is *María* by Jorge Isaacs (Colombia, 1837–

1895). *María* is known first and foremost as a tale of adolescent love frustrated by the heroine's early death. The story has been told, years later, by Efraín, who had hoped to marry the beautiful and sweet-natured María. A brief note at the beginning of the novel indicates that Efraín has since died, leaving an account of his great loss to his brothers and sisters.

As is the case in a number of nineteenth-century novels, passionate love develops between characters so closely linked—genetically, by background, or both—as to be virtual siblings. María is Efraín's cousin but seems almost like his sister. The orphaned María was taken in and raised by Efraín's parents, whom she calls "Mama" and "Papa." This background creates some unusual situations; when Efraín talks to his father about a possible marriage with María, the patriarch must speak as both the young man's father and a man whose foster daughter's hand is being sought.

Efraín recalls coming home to the family ranch after boarding school and renewing his love with the now fifteen-year-old María, although the two have been fond of each other since infancy. Hardly have the two young people begun their courtship than María is diagnosed with an aggressive form of epilepsy that is at one point said to be fatal, although the novel leaves open the possibility that she could have lived with the disorder. The knowledge that María may die young fills the couple with melancholy and foreboding; deepening the gloom, the older Efraín who is telling the story in retrospect reveals from the outset that it will have an unhappy ending. Many tragic portents, especially lowering storm clouds and ominous black birds, serve as reminders of the impending death. The above description makes *María* sound similar to many other contemporary novels, both European and Latin American, featuring star-crossed lovers in exotic (that is, South American) settings. A vogue for this type of narrative had arisen following the international success of the 1801 novel *Atala* by the then widely read French writer (François Auguste) René de Chateaubriand (1768–1848). It is plain that Isaacs was among the many Spanish American writers who were influenced by Chateaubriand, since Efraín reads the French author's work aloud to María and his sister. Even so, the Colombian novel goes well beyond the romantic-exotic formula established by Chateaubriand.

While the ill-fated romance provides the main plot thread, the novel contains many elements of social commentary. Racial, ethnic, and class issues are among Isaacs's preoccupations. Although all the principal characters belong to the same family of white landowners, the numerous secondary figures are more diverse. They include white peasants, some of whom live together with their animals in backwoods rusticity, and slaves of African descent. *María* includes a lengthy section, almost a short novel embedded within the main one, dedicated to the denunciation of slavery. The antislavery narrative is somewhat surprising in that this practice had already been abolished in Colombia in 1852. The section concerned specifically with slavery portrays it in a negative light, but the novel as a whole sends a less clear message. Efraín's family, which is nostalgically idealized, owns slaves. The family treats them with the utmost benevolence and, whenever Efraín and his father encounter slaves on their lands, the latter appear delighted to see their masters. Here the antislavery theme appears to have been overridden by a concept that the novel promotes insistently: Efraín, in his youth, enjoyed universal love and respect.

A second, more shadowy ethnic theme appears occasionally in the novel. Efraín's father was born in Jamaica to a Sephardic family (as was that of the real-life author), while his mother is a Catholic Colombian. María's father was the brother of Efraín's father, and her mother was a beautiful Jewish Jamaican woman. Yet, owing to very thorough conversions to Catholicism, the two young people apparently have no acquaintance with Jewish observances, folkways, history, or intellectual tradition. María, born Ester and baptized in early childhood, is a particularly fervent Catholic, devoted to the Virgin Mary. Early in the novel, allusions to the family's unusual origin pique curiosity by leaving this ethnicity unspecified. In Chapter 3 Efraín says that he could see in María's eyes, downcast in modest shyness, "the brilliance and beauty of those of the women of her race." [69] In Chapter 4 he divulges that he, too, bears the exotic, unnamed trait. Efraín recalls gazing at María's feet and noticing that "her light and dignified step revealed all the unvanquished pride of our race, and the seductive modesty of the Christian virgin." Only in Chapter 7 is the Jewish community of Jamaica revealed as the original home of Efraín's father, María, and her parents.

Isaacs uninhibitedly evokes the mystique surrounding Sephardim, reputed to possess exceptional charm and good looks, and the stock romantic figure of the beautiful, exotic Jewess. Jewishness is associated with mysterious forces, as when Efraín states that it is the Jewish background of his now-Christian father that leads the latter to read the future in portents and omens. (However, belief in augury is not limited to the novel's Jewish characters; omens appear frequently in *María* and accurately reveal faraway or future events.)

Critics who have examined the topic of Jewishness in *María* have had to work with scant material. For some time after its publication, critics seemed determined to find evidence of some type of Jewish outlook in it. Since the author had grown up in a Christian home and his writing reveals no acquaintance with the history of Jewish thought, this line of inquiry proved fruitless.

More recent critics have sought to see how ideas about being Jewish function within the novel. For example, Sylvia Molloy notes that the father's Jewish ancestry and foreign birth correspond well to the novel's theme of painful separation from one's home base. Molloy admits, though, that the novel only vaguely suggests the father as a figure of Jewish exile.[70] This critic's comments contain worthwhile reminders that allusions to Jewishness remain shadowy and undeveloped throughout *María*.[71]

Doris Sommer takes a more unusual approach in her 1991 essay "María's Disease: A National Romance (Con)Founded."[72] Sommer argues that "the Jewish race bears a stain in this novel"[73] and that María's Jewishness is the reason why, in the logic of the novel, she cannot live to have a family with Efraín. This highly provocative analysis has won attention but has not established itself as a standard or widely accepted reading of *María*.

The main plot progression, involving María's decline and death, is linked to another tale of deterioration and loss. During Efraín's childhood and adolescence, the family is one of the most established and respected in the region. As well as owning a large ranch house, family members enjoy roaming over a scenic stretch of land in the Cauca Valley and receiving deferential and affectionate treatment from a large community of workers.

The ranch, named El Paraíso, is for Efraín an earthly paradise, but one that he can never inhabit for long. His great desire is never to be separated from the family home. His father's insistence that he be sent away to study heightens Efraín's fond idealization of El Paraíso. According to Molloy's analysis, when Efraín imagines what it is like to be back on the ranch, he is envisioning "a life suspended outside of time," a bucolic rural world where little changes except the seasons. In his nostalgic mind, going home and staying home would be "the reintegration of the son into the family community," "getting back to the origin."[74]

Almost as soon as the novel opens, this paradise is imperiled. During the time that Efraín is courting María, the father discovers that his partner has lost a good portion of his capital, and the family's fortunes also head downhill. By the time he is writing his reminiscences, Efraín has lost not only María but also the idyllic family ranch and the pleasant land-scape with which she is closely identified. He expresses regret over the loss of this beloved and prestigious home in much the same lamenting mode that he assumes to speak of María. In Chapter 33 he broods nos-talgically: "Nevermore will I admire those songs, breathe those aromas, contemplate those landscapes filled with light, as I did in the happy days of my childhood and the beautiful ones of my adolescence: Strangers now live in my parents' home!"

John S. Brushwood condenses into a single sentence the relation be-tween María's death and the old estate passing out of the hands of Efraín's family: "*Efraín suffers the loss of María and the region to which he be-longs* [italics in original]. The expansion of this statement repeatedly associates María with the region as the protagonist's sense of separation develops."[75]

The definition of gender roles is an overt issue in *María*. The heroine is not just the particular young woman that Efraín loves. Rather the novel idealizes her as the perfect female. She represents a very traditional ideal of womanhood. María has extremely little education, devotes herself to caring for the children in the household, and appears docile and sub-missive. Throughout the novel, characters make a number of remarks about relations between men and women, some of which have proved disturbing to later readers. Perhaps most strikingly, in Chapter 20 María appears to imply a belief that men are more intellectually advanced than women. She tells Efraín that, if she should ever do or say anything dis-pleasing to him, he need only tell her and she will discontinue that be-havior. He asks, "And should I not expect you to do the same for me?" Her answer is "No, because I cannot give you advice, nor know whether what I think is the best thing; besides, you know what I am going to say to you before I say it."

While Efraín's reminiscences draw attention to the chastity of his relations with María, they also show that the young woman is accom-plished in traditional female wiles to win male attention. For instance, she will hastily cover up an exposed foot or shoulder just as Efraín looks at her. Donald McGrady, in examining early commentary on *María*, dis-covered that some critics have always expressed shock that the novel's feminine ideal is a sophisticated flirt.[76]

For all her coquettish playfulness, María is a self-sacrificing creature eager to keep Efraín happy. When she discovers that he is dissatisfied with the way the servants press his shirts, she surreptitiously masters ironing to suit his needs. Since one of the family's preoccupations is preserving the women from work that might roughen their aristocratic hands, María's ironing strikes Efraín as risk taking on his behalf. While María never reaches adulthood, she gives every sign of heading toward a life dedicated to husband, children, and religious devotions. The adult equivalent of María is Efraín's selfless mother, who automatically submits to her husband. Rodolfo A. Borello summarizes the mother's involvement in the plot: "She incarnates—always—the will of her husband; she functions in the work by softening or attenuating the harshness of the orders and opinions of the head of the family, but she seconds him like a double who incarnates the same ideas and feelings as he does."[77] The novel's linkage of María with Efraín's mother is one of the elements that leads Raymond Leslie Williams to identify an "Oedipal structure" in the novel.[78] Williams, analyzing *María* in his 1991 *The Colombian Novel, 1844–1987*, finds in its plot an intricate and uneasy set of relations between the characters, with incestuous attraction a major source of tension.[79]

María illustrates well the earlier-noted co-occurrence of romanticism and realism in Spanish American narrative. The romantic elements are the most salient. Of course, the tale of doomed love is quintessentially romantic. The characterization of María is also typical of the romantic tendency. Like many other heroines created under the impetus of this movement, she is ethereally beautiful, young and inexperienced, and touchingly vulnerable (in her case, she is an orphan with a fatal disorder). Also romantic are the harbingers of doom, especially black birds, whose appearance fills the characters with foreboding. Romantics cultivated melancholy, and Efraín, lamenting the loss of his beloved, the family's ranchlands, and the privileged situation that he enjoyed in his youth, incarnates sadness. The novel's idealized descriptions of the Cauca Valley are in the romantic tradition of worshipping nature.

On the other hand, many passages in the novel exhibit the realist drive to represent reality in all its aspects. The peasants and slaves who work the ranchlands are realistically portrayed. While Efraín's family assiduously cultivates refinement, the peasants share living space with their animals and exchange bumptious jokes.

While the minor characters of lower social class provide the main source of material for realistic writing, at times males of the landowning class come in for warts-and-all portraiture. Efraín's father is a patriarch whose pronouncements must be obeyed; Williams characterizes him as "overwhelmingly dominant."[80] He exhibits unsteady judgment, brings misfortune upon the family, and can be coarse, especially compared with his sensitive, idealistic son. His habit of trusting others too much in financial matters leads to the downturn in the family's fortunes. The father inadvertently causes María's death by sending Efraín to Europe to study medicine. His rationale is that strong emotions provoked by Efraín's presence will damage María's health. Instead, the anguish of separation from her beloved kills her.

The father also represents a bourgeois, mercantile, bargain-striking approach to life. In sending Efraín to Europe, his concern is less for María's well-being than for his son's career, threatened by devotion to a sickly girl. The father is frank in stating that he is funding his son's medical studies because the family needs a well-paid professional to strengthen its financial situation. Borello notes that the father's method of dealing with the cousins' inconvenient love is the negotiation of terms and conditions, "the typical bourgeois contract." [81] Molloy observes that the father, in forcing Efraín to get down to business, is driving him out of the timeless idyll that the young man desires. The father seeks "the son's entry into an adult bourgeoisie, profitable and conscious." [82] Even pettier is the behavior of Efraín's schoolmate Carlos. While Efraín sees María as the one woman in the world for him, Carlos asks for her hand because she seems an advantageous match.

Nationalistic issues do not surface openly as themes in the novel. The concern with building up regional pride and identity manifests itself in other ways, particularly the protagonist's adoration of a South American landscape, that of the Cauca Valley. María is at times almost coterminous with this gorgeous American scenery, and Efraín desires never to be parted from either. The family patriarch, epitomizing a Eurocentric bias, is determined to separate his son from his rustic home. He sends him, against his will, first to Bogotá, with its relatively European urban society, and then to Europe itself. His rationale is that only in these settings can Efraín gain the knowledge needed to launch him on a brilliant and lucrative career.

In recent decades critics have been drawn to *María* for the more covert messages that it may send about such issues as gender, sexuality, patriarchy, and race. At times, there is a perception of *María* as a novel that is not always aboveboard in the way it communicates. An example of this suspicion is the work of Margo Glantz. While most readers have probably noticed that *María* is a story of sexual attraction as well as spiritual love, and many have found in it a hint of incest, Glantz goes beyond these observations to discover a highly erotic, and even kinky, narrative underneath the novel's chaste surface. She notes that every family member who crosses the path of Efraín and María becomes involved in transmitting encrypted sexual messages between the lovers. The youngest sibling, who as a child may be caressed by anyone, serves as a useful proxy when the two inflamed young people must keep their hands off one another. In addition, the patriarch of this oddly intimate household at several points appears to be competing with his son over María and flirts with the girl, who is his niece and foster daughter. In Glantz's judgment, "Incest is global, that is to say, it includes the whole family, the living and the dead."[83] She also finds an element of fetishism in the description of María, who is almost covered with elaborate nineteenth-century finery and set against a tropical background.

In addition, *María* has attracted new attention for a pervasive instability concerning who exactly is in control of the story. Williams points out that, although the text of *María* presents itself as Efraín's reminiscences, inconsistencies complicate the picture, and Efraín appears as a fragmented entity. For Williams, these oddities create sufficient ambiguity to call into question "the assumption of an Efraín who is a clearly defined self."[84] Rather than fault the novel for its fluctuations, Williams appreciates the innovative complexity of creating "a protagonist who is far from the unified personality which the traditional unified text would require."[85]

*T*hough realism gradually displaced romanticism during the last third of the century, decidedly romantic fiction, and especially texts that employed romantic conventions in the service of nation-building, continued to appear late in the century. An example is the 1879 *Cumandá o un drama entre salvajes* (Cumandá or a drama among savages) by the Ecuadorean Juan León Mera (1832–1894). *Cumandá* is often referred to as the first Ecuadorean novel, and it is undeniably the first well-known one. Such claims as "first national novel" can never be established with certainty, since many nineteenth-century novels appeared in serialized form, were never published as books, and subsequently fell into oblivion. The narrative, whose third-person narrator often interrupts his story to expound his views on social issues, is set in the eastern part of Ecuador. Its characters are either white missionaries or members of various Native American tribes. The most prominent of these are the relatively hospitable and law-abiding Zaparos and the Jibaros, characterized as fiercely aggressive. Missionary activity in the region has exposed its native dwellers to Christianity. A few communities practice this religion, while the rest have an inactive knowledge of the rudiments of Christianity that, in the novel's view, needs only encouragement to be transformed into living faith.

Cumandá, named for its heroine, as are many nineteenth-century novels, is organized around a tale of impossible love, though the amorous theme is not predominant in the novel. The reasons for the impossibility are so convoluted that they take the entire novel to untangle. From the point of view of Cumandá's Amerindian family, the problem is straightforward. She is a maiden of Zaparo descent, one of the virgins participating in ancestral religious rites, and should not have fallen in love with Carlos, the son of a widower who has become a Dominican missionary priest. However, from very early in the novel, the reader receives broad hints that Cumandá is of European ancestry. As a child, she survived an Amerindian raid, provoked by the whites' harsh treatment of native peoples, which killed her mother and all but one brother. Apparently, she was taken in by an indigenous family and raised as their own. Not only is Cumandá white, but she is, by her own declaration, a Christian.

If Cumandá is a Christian white woman, then she would seem to be a socially acceptable match for Carlos, but there are further complications. Following the clues that the narrator divulges, one quickly concludes that Carlos must be the brother who survived the massacre. This circumstance would make their love incestuous, were it not for the fact that Carlos has always treated Cumandá more like a sibling than an object of desire. Both Carlos and the narrator assert that no worldly passion enters into his bond with Cumandá. The narrator explains insistently that "both of their loves were chaste." [86] While willing to marry Cumandá if she so wishes, "Carlos was content for his love to be on a fraternal basis." [87] In Chapter 15 Carlos takes exception to his father's statement, intended as an expression of support: "You will marry the beautiful Cumandá, you will make her yours, you will be happy." [88] Although Carlos is engaged to be married to Cumandá, he tells his father, "When you say 'you will marry her, you will make her yours,' I see that you do not grasp the nature of my passion, that you are confusing me with common lovers, that you are lowering my thought from the region of the angels to the mire of the material world." [89] When Carlos and his father discover Cumandá's identity, the young missionary is elated rather than dismayed that the woman he loves is his sister. He rejoices, "How right I was to feel for her that pure and generous love that only an angel could inspire!" [90]

Clearly the story of the couple is designed to draw readers' minds toward something other than passionate love. The novel places more stress on the conflict and disunity in the society of Ecuador, where the white population exploits the native Andean one and is distrusted and hated in return. *Cumandá* advocates an effort to achieve inter-ethnic reconciliation and harmony, turning the divided nation into a close-knit family. In particular, the novel identifies Christianity as the force that can both civilize Amerindians and heal the wounds left by the whites' conquest and subsequent mistreatment of the indigenous population. The many misfortunes that befall the characters in *Cumandá* all have their origins either in the cruelty with which white conquistadors and landowners have treated the indigenous people, or else in what the narrator uninhibitedly refers to as the barbarism of Amerindians unconverted to Christianity.

During the later chapters of the novel, Carlos's father becomes more prominent, representing the struggle for Christian reconciliation between whites and native peoples of the Andean region. He sets out to save Cumandá from ritual sacrifice, but his attention turns to saving the soul of Tubón, the indigenous man who has haunted him for years. Back when Carlos's father was an abusive landowner, Tubón was one of his mistreated workers and the leader of the raid that killed most of the family. At the end of the novel, Carlos's father and the dying Tubón forgive one another. The priest appeals to Tubón's latent knowledge of the Christian faith, whose seeds were planted by earlier missionaries, to convert him to Christianity moments before death. Though the effort to save Cumandá fails, her death appears providential in averting incest and promoting conversion. The novel ends by offering hope for nationwide amity based on the Christian ideal of fraternity between human beings. As Doris Sommer explains, "The sacrifice was Cumandá, the woman over whose dead body Spanish and Indian fathers can love each other."[91]

Beyond urging the spread of Christianity generally, the narrator of *Cumandá* advocates a Jesuit presence in Ecuador. He often laments the 1767 expulsion of this order from Spain's American colonies. According to the version of history that *Cumandá* presents, the Jesuits, by establishing settlements (*reducciones*) for native Ecuadorean converts, had begun a labor of civilization that lost ground after their expulsion. Mera, in his career as a member of Congress, was an advocate of reestablishing the Jesuits in Ecuador.[92]

Critical opinion is divided as to whether *Cumandá* is a backward-looking work that promotes an authoritarian ideal of social governance or whether it should be seen as overall a progressive work, though reflecting the author's pro-clerical beliefs and the ethnocentrism of his times. Antonio Benítez Rojo takes the former view, emphasizing Mera's connections to the Ecuadorean dictator Gabriel García Moreno (1821–1875; president, 1861–1865, 1869–1875). In this critic's view, the novel's "project wants the Ecuadorian nation of the 1870s to 'evolve' toward the past, or to be exact, to seek modernity in the first half of the eighteenth century, the period of the Jesuit missions . . . This peculiarity can be better understood if one takes into account that Mera was an extreme defender of García Moreno's regime, whose ideological foundation recalls somewhat the eighteenth-century Spanish Bourbon model (enlightened despotism) as it combines religious fanaticism and political absolutism with commercial capitalism and the scientific thought of the Enlightenment."[93]

Readers of the twenty-first century may be shocked by Mera's assumption that, without Christianity, indigenous peoples would live a less than human existence and their communities would not qualify as societies. In the second chapter the narrator of *Cumandá* tells readers: "More than a century ago, the indefatigable dedication of missionaries had begun to breathe the first glimmerings of civilization into this barbarous people; it had humanized them in great part at the cost of heroic sacrifices. [These sacrifices] bore fruit by winning thousands of souls for heaven and bringing numerous peoples into social life."[94] Francisco E. Aguirre V. notes "a marked ethnocentrism that is apparent in the definitive importance that Mera gives to the missionary efforts of Catholic priests, who with every cross they planted worked a mysterious power and prevented the indigenous tribes from living divorced from the human species."[95]

When evaluating such observations by the narrator, one should take into account that when *Cumandá* appeared in 1879, few non-Amerindian readers considered indigenous societies to be on a par with their own. Manuel Corrales Pascual, surveying late-nineteenth-century criticism of the novel, observes that "although the author cannot avoid a strong ethnocentrism in his judgments, from the very first he drew criticism from his contemporaries for the way he idealized the Indian."[96] The examples that Corrales Pascual cites show critics of the time unable to accept that a woman raised in an Amerindian society could be beautiful or sensitive. While both Aguirre and Corrales Pascual cite evidence of Mera's ethnocentrism, both argue that this author was more respectful of indigenous communities and more aware of their rights than were most intellectuals of his time.

There is no doubt that Mera supported the dictator García Moreno and believed that humankind must become Christian to achieve civilization. It is not so certain that his overall social vision is retrograde. To give a picture of Mera's politics, Aguirre identifies the legislative proposals that the author supported as a member of the 1861 National Constitutional Assembly. These items include such advanced measures as the granting of citizenship to illiterate inhabitants of the country, the abolition of the death penalty, freedom of the press, and strengthening congressional activities as a means of limiting the power of the executive.[97] Aguirre goes on to find the same democratic principles illustrated by the plot of *Cumandá* and expounded in the narrator's often lengthy summaries and editorializing.[98]

Corrales Pascual also supports the idea that the social outlook inherent in Mera's novel is unusually progressive for 1879. This critic proposes that *Cumandá* be regarded as the first Ecuadorean example of the *indigenista* novel, that is, the novel used to draw public attention to the problems afflicting native peoples and the need to remedy them.[99] While generally literary *indigenismo* in Ecuador is seen as beginning in the 1920s, Corrales Pascual identifies in *Cumandá* the chief distinguishing features of this tendency.[100] These include reminders that European conquerors seized land belonging to Native Americans and subjected these dispossessed people to inhumane treatment. The narrator's habit of breaking away from the story to denounce the ill treatment of Amerindians also typifies the later *indigenista* novel. Corrales Pascual observes that while *Cumandá* contains the basic elements of an *indigenista* novel, these features may go unrecognized because Mera softens his social criticism. For example, he portrays white characters as good at heart but liable to succumb to the temptation to exploit Amerindians.[101]

While *Cumandá* still has its defenders, in recent decades it has received relatively little attention outside Ecuador. It has scarcely benefited from the revival of interest in nineteenth-century narrative that has drawn new readers to such works as Gómez de Avellaneda's 1841 *Sab*. Perhaps potential readers are discouraged by the prospect of making their way through the narrator's obtrusive editorial comments. In addition, *Cumandá* seems outmoded because, while Mera clearly means his novel to benefit Amerindians, he exhibits no concern for what today is called "cultural survival"; he does not consider it important for traditional indigenous folkways to continue. As for one significant component of indigenous cultures, native religions, Mera plainly states that they should all be eradicated, along with their associated rituals, and replaced with Christianity. This outlook seems alien to current-day readers, who by and large consider Amerindian cultural traditions worthy of preservation. Antiquated, as well, is the idea that universal Christianity will bring about the solution to the nation's social inequalities and its split along ethnic lines.

The desire to create a myth of national origin is vividly present in another late romantic novel, *Enriquillo* (1882). The work of the Dominican Manuel de Jesús Galván (1834–1910), this novel was successfully translated into English by the distinguished poet Robert Graves. His 1954 English version bears the title *The Cross and the Sword*.

Enriquillo is the novel-length elaboration of an episode that appears in the sixteenth-century *Historia de las Indias* (History of the Indies) by Bartolomé de las Casas (1474–1566), discussed in Chapter 1. Enriquillo is an indigenous nobleman who has converted to Christianity and serves as the overseer on a Spanish-owned estate. Though Enriquillo is peace-loving and law-abiding by character, the abusive treatment that he and his wife suffer from the Spanish landowner drives him to escape. Enriquillo becomes the leader of a band of indigenous workers who have run away from the virtual slavery in which they are kept. Las Casas emphasizes that Enriquillo seeks to avoid bloodshed and is eager to negotiate an end to his rebellion and rejoin Spanish-dominated society.

Subsequent generations of readers have pointed to distortions of historical fact in *Enriquillo*. One of the principal complaints is that, while Las Casas shows the cruelty of the conquerors, Galván portrays the Spanish as, with exceptions, humane rulers. Another objection is that Galván creates a national myth in which Dominicans arise from the indigenous legacy, ignoring the African component of the nation. Benítez Rojo summarizes the latter problem: "Although a great part of the [Dominican] population was black and mulatto . . . nationalistic practices sought the explanation for the more or less dark color of the people in a fictional indigenous ancestry, an approach which *Enriquillo* strengthened."[102]

Sommer, though recognizing that *Enriquillo* is faulty if read and judged as a historical novel, nonetheless asserts its validity as a national romance. This critic admits that Galván's vision of the Dominican Republic exhibits, upon close inspection, some major omissions and that his work is designed "simply to exclude blacks from the national epic."[103] Yet she argues that *Enriquillo* functions best for readers who grasp that it is "closer to what Galván himself called it, a 'leyenda histórica' (historical legend)."[104] In Sommer's view, while one may point out *Enriquillo's* distortion of historical fact, "it would be better to recognize the work as a romance and thus identify it by the very qualities of verbal sumptuousness and sublime conceptual simplicity that distinguish it from novels." [105]

The 1879 *Cumandá* and 1882 *Enriquillo* may seem to be unusually late examples of the use of romantic narrative to promote the formation of a unifying national identity. They are by no means the last. Although its verse form places it outside the scope of this survey, the narrative poem *Tabaré* by the Uruguayan Juan Zorrilla de San Martín (1855–1931) deserves brief mention because of its 1888 date. *Tabaré* is yet another work that reflects both the exotic romanticism of Chateaubriand and Spanish American intellectuals' desire to encourage national pride, identity, and solidarity.

As difficult as it is to establish a starting date for Spanish American romanticism, it would be even less feasible to say when this movement ended. In subsequent chapters romanticism will be seen yielding more ground to realism, with which it continues to coexist for many years. Toward the end of the nineteenth century, romanticism's hold on the reading public is further weakened when this long-running movement begins to be upstaged by *modernismo*. Romanticism continues to be one element in Spanish American narrative throughout the nineteenth century, but it never recaptures the dominant place that it held at mid-century.

Chapter Five

'L̲ATE-NINETEENTH-CENTURY
NARRATIVES OF SOCIAL COMMENTARY
AND NATIONAL SELF-REFLECTION

A s the nineteenth century moved into its latter decades, literary life continued to grow more organized in Spanish American capitals. Increasingly, the writers of a given nation established journals, salons, and literary circles, to learn from one another and to promote the idea that they were carrying out serious work. Writers of fiction were eager to win greater respect for the novel and short story, which had often been regarded as lightweight genres. By the late decades of the century, the novel was flourishing. While there are relatively few Spanish American novels from the early decades of the nineteenth century, by the 1860s examples of the genre are far too numerous for anything more than a sampling to be discussed here.

Writers of fiction continue their involvement with the great issues troubling the still fairly new nations. Topics include slavery, Amerindian peoples, curbing ecclesiastical power, and national unity. Until the late nineteenth century, Spanish American writers still promote the development of national literature. Only in the next chapter, in the section on *modernismo,* will I be discussing literature that is no longer so preoccupied with national questions.

T he previous chapter mentioned the interest in late-1830s Cuba in producing narrative works that would stir the conscience of the nation concerning slavery. Some of the most important antislavery narratives from this period were not published until Cuba abolished slavery in 1880. Two of the most significant are *Cecilia Valdés, o La Loma del Angel* (Cecilia Valdés, or Angel's Hill) by Cirilo Villaverde (1812–1894), of which the definitive version appeared in 1882, and *Francisco: El ingenio o las delicias del campo* (Francisco: the sugar mill or the delights of the country) by Anselmo Suárez y Romero (1818–1878), published in 1880 after circulating in manuscript form for years. While the expanded *Cecilia Valdés* appeared two years after the publication of *Francisco,* the two works are virtually contemporaneous. I discuss *Cecilia Valdés* first because of its importance and complexity. Critics often examine *Cecilia Valdés* in search of evidence of contemporary racial and gender concepts. This tendency is especially pronounced in the current era, marked by a preoccupation with the social and cultural messages encoded in literary texts. Still, *Cecilia Valdés* is also an artistically elaborate text, as witness the detailed analysis by Raimundo Lazo.[1]

Chapter 3 mentioned the brief versions of *Cecilia Valdés* that Villaverde published in the 1830s. The author then set the project aside. In 1879 he completed the definitive version in U.S. exile. It was published in New York in 1882.[2] This version became one of the major Spanish American novels, and its title character has, in Reynaldo González's words, "become a myth unto herself."[3]

Although *Cecilia Valdés* is commonly classified among antislavery novels, it is not always focused on slaves and masters. Quite a few characters, including the protagonist, are free mulattos and blacks. *Cecilia Valdés* makes the point that Cuba is not a nation with one white population and a different black one. The novel shows Cuba as composed of people of widely varying shades and degrees of freedom.

While presenting a statement about Cuba's racial situation and national identity, *Cecilia Valdés* is also a page-turner, full of secrets, revelations, unexpected reversals, a beautiful, ill-fated heroine, and allusions to taboo phenomena, especially incest. Though Spanish American narrative was becoming more realistic, a trend evident in *Cecilia Valdés,* it still supplied the melodrama that readers savored in romantic novels. For example, Cecilia's grandmother starts to make a deathbed revelation but dies with the key word unuttered.

The narrator of *Cecilia Valdés* is preoccupied with racial categories and their often arbitrary character. He emphasizes that the physiognomy of the title character, the illegitimate daughter of a white man and a mulatto woman, does not reveal her African ancestry. The novel presents contradictory information on this point. The narrator refers to her "lightly bronzed color," and her admirers call her "the little bronze Virgin."[4] But many characters state that Cecilia looks European. Her wet nurse calls her "white as coconut," her grandmother refers to her "mother of pearl complexion," and her father says that "she will pass for white anywhere that people don't know what her background is."[5] She cannot be distinguished from one of the novel's white characters.

Perhaps the explanation for the conflicting descriptions of Cecilia is the influence that beliefs have on perception. When the narrator evokes the myth of the overpowering sensuality of biracial women, Cecilia seems darker. As Cecilia arrives at a dance, the narrator confirms: "There was none more beautiful nor more able to make a man in love lose his senses . . . she could well pass for the Venus of the hybrid Ethiopian-Caucasian race."[6] She produces "the effect of an electrical charge . . . magic influence."[7] Her lover calls her "all passion and fire; she is my temptress, a devil in the form of a woman, the Venus of mulatto women."[8]

Cecilia's near-whiteness and beauty drive the plot. Her grandmother has urged her to avoid identification as black and marry a well-established white man. This outlook leads her to favor Leonardo, a spoiled young white man, over a mulatto musician who loves her and tries to protect her. Leonardo is following the same pattern as his father and other men of their class: they turn to women of color for passion. Their brides are white women who need not inspire love or desire but bring status or wealth or both. In fact, a white bride is already being lined up for Leonardo. Although readers quickly grasp these conventions, Cecilia does not.

Cecilia Valdés adds embellishments to the central conflict. All of the central characters, and some of the secondary ones, have unrevealed aspects: shameful secrets, painful memories, or links to other characters. The narrator possesses complete information about the characters. By referring cryptically to what he knows, he teases the curiosity of readers. In Lazo's analysis, "It is, beyond doubt, a calculated plan to increase the reader's interest by revealing little by little to him or her the origin, the physical appearance, the moral and intellectual makeup, and the ends being pursued by the characters, as well as the plot that deliberately connects them all."[9]

From the first chapter, the reader encounters evidence that Leonardo and Cecilia have the same father. A friend tells Leonardo that many consider Cecilia his half sister, which would explain her perfect likeness to Leonardo's legitimate sister Adela. Leonardo dismisses the notion as "nothing but talk."[10] The novel's many scenes of characters denying the obvious suggest that slavery and the racial hierarchy are tolerated because their disturbing aspects are suppressed from awareness.

Many nineteenth-century novels bring their characters to the brink of incest. In *Cecilia Valdés* the half siblings actually consummate their affair and produce an illegitimate child. Furthermore, Leonardo is having sexual relations with a woman identical to his full sister. The narrator says of Leonardo and Adela: "If they had not been brother and sister, they would have loved each other, the way the most celebrated lovers the world has known loved each other."[11]

Another incestuous figure is Leonardo's mother. The twelfth chapter of Book One details her fixation on him, ending with her gazing rapturously at her son as he lies naked from the waist up. Lazo refers to "the excesses of her disturbed love for her favorite son" and calls this character "sort of, unconsciously, a passionate Jocasta."[12]

The incest pervading Leonardo's family signals the decadence that Villaverde sees throughout Cuban society. Antonio Benítez Rojo observes:

> . . . the problem is much more serious and cannot be reduced to the "Black / White" opposition alone. Leonardo desires Cecilia because of her physical resemblance to his white sister, Adela Gamboa. The incest, however, cannot be avoided, since Leonardo and Cecilia have sexual relations without knowing that both are children of the same father. In this way, the incestuous desire is presented to the reader as a generalized and fatal defect which runs through the Cuban nation, reducing its effectiveness to the extent that it is a slave-owning and patriarchal project.[13]

Leonardo's family exemplifies various features of this malaise. His father is a Spanish merchant grown rich through imports, including slave running, and marriage to a sugar-mill heiress. Leonardo's father strives be a country squire and craves a title of nobility. His wife was born into the Cuban upper class and often reminds her family that she is the source of its wealth. The family's flaws include indolence, snobbery, apathy, frivolity, and selfishness, but the worst is cruelty to slaves.

While the early chapters of the novel proceed at a leisurely pace, describing various scenes and providing clues to the plot's mysteries, the last chapters are hectic. Leonardo's parents decide that it is time he marry. Cecilia sends her suitor, the mulatto musician, to stop the wedding. He stabs Leonardo, who, in one of the novel's many melodramatic flourishes, dies soaking the wedding gown with blood.

There is some suspicion that *Cecilia Valdés* not only treats the theme of racism but also is to some degree a racist text.[14] As Matías Montes Huidobro observes, "If Cecilia Valdés had not been almost white, she would have been almost black, and the fate of the novel would have been different."[15] Cecilia's family is growing whiter with every successive generation, and this move toward whiteness "constitutes an 'evolutionary guarantee' for Cuban society in general."[16]

These misgivings about the novel are supported by María Teresa Aedo's analysis. Aedo concedes that *Cecilia Valdés* is "an attempt" to resolve Cuba's racial conflicts. "However," she goes on to say, "at this level we discover a fundamental contradiction in the narrator between postulating the principles of fraternity and equality as the basis of new social relations and, at the same time, the exaltation of the white race and culture as the bearers of the rationality that must lead the march of this social 'body' made up in its majority of mulattos and black people."[17] People of color are associated with such qualities as fiery spontaneity, while the ability to offer sensible guidance is found in certain white characters.

As an example, Aedo points to the trio composed of the biracial Cecilia, Leonardo's sister Adela, and Adela's black slave. The three women, who represent the island's major racial categories, are, in some senses, sisters. Two have the same father, and all three had the same wet nurse. "Nonetheless," Aedo observes, "in this triangular relation between the sisters, Adela must fulfill the role of 'godmother' and intercessor, that is to say, the white race must guide, shelter, and make possible this union of sisterhood in liberty."[18]

Cecilia Valdés indeed often associates people of color with heat and sensuality and whiteness with a cool temperament. This practice becomes particularly evident when one compares the description of Cecilia with that of Leonardo's fiancée, Isabel. Isabel is not just white, but pale with light eyes. The narrator asserts that she is attractive, although "there was nothing beautiful about her. Her charm was in the way she spoke and moved."[19] Cecilia can instantly captivate a throng of men. In contrast, the narrator says of the "discreet and mannerly" Isabel that "needless to say, she drew the notice of refined people."[20] She has no sensual appeal: "There was no feminine roundness, and of course, nothing voluptuous, as we have noted, in Isabel's shape."[21] The narrator finds Isabel "manly."[22] Her father, boasting about Isabel's success managing his coffee plantation, says that "She does everything like a man."[23]

Isabel stands out for her coolly rational behavior, which further sets her apart from the spitfire Cecilia. Leonardo respects her, but she does not kindle passion. Asked whether he would marry Isabel, since he admits that she leaves him cold, Leonardo replies, "That's exactly how one should pick a wife."[24]

Slavery is indirectly present in all of *Cecilia Valdés,* since the novel makes the point that the slave system is toxic for Cuban society. The narrator several times observes the deleterious effects of slavery on the owners, reflecting, for instance: "That slavery has the power to distort the notion of the just and the unjust in the spirit of the master; that it blunts human sensibility; that it loosens the closest social ties; that it weakens the sense of one's own dignity and even obscures the ideas of honor, one can understand."[25] Sugar-mill owners are singled out: "Could there be happiness, peace of mind for those who knowingly crystallized the juice of sugar cane with the blood of thousands of slaves?"[26]

Leonardo's father owns a slave ship that continues to make runs to Africa, although, under British pressure, Spain has outlawed the slave trade in its colonies. In one scene he complains to his wife about what he views as British interference in his line of work. He tells a story in which his ship is pursued by a British patrol vessel. To lighten the load, the captain throws overboard various items, including "the bundles that were on deck."[27] His wife is horrified to realize that the "bundles" were human slaves. Leonardo's father brushes off his wife's reaction and goes on to describe the tactic of cramming slaves into the hold and nailing the hatches shut. In his outlook, it is good business; even if half the slaves die, the voyage still turns a profit. The father's speech stands out for his enthusiastic approval of inhuman measures and his allusions to African captives as objects such as "coal sacks."[28] His wife, born into a slave-owning family and married to a slave trader for twenty-five years, has managed not to know how slaves are transported.

Two portions of the novel show rural slave labor; the first is set on a coffee plantation and the second in a sugar-producing operation. The coffee plantation is idealized as a gardenlike stretch of Cuban landscape. It is a well-regulated operation; the manager is the just, businesslike Isabel. She protects the slaves from whipping, and they adore her. The passages set on the coffee plantation weaken the novel's statement that slavery itself is damaging to the nation's character. Isabel owns and orders about slaves, yet she stands out for her high moral principles.

Isabel's coffee plantation is contrasted with the infernal sugar mill owned and operated by Leonardo's family. The family's policy is to work their slaves mercilessly and subject them to cruel and arbitrary punishment, yet at the same time to maintain their own peace of mind. Direct control of the slaves is left to a sadistic overseer, who enjoys a free hand with the whip so long as he does not disturb the white owners. This portion of the novel contains detailed scenes of brutal whippings. Two different characters tell the story of an escaped and captured slave who committed suicide by forcing his tongue down his throat. As in the section concerned with the pursuit of the slave ship, the narrator focuses attention on the reactions of the slave owners. Leonardo's mother is upset to awaken one morning to the sound of flogging. She complains to her husband that the overseer "doesn't have the least bit of consideration for us."[29] The novel again suggests that a suppression of awareness is required to tolerate slavery.

Certainly, *Cecilia Valdés* is not written to twenty-first-century criteria of political correctness. Even judged by its own standards, it exhibits some inconsistent ideas about race. In a way, these contradictions make the novel more valuable to critics, since they provide glimpses into the way that progressive white Cuban intellectuals struggled to move away from a background of racism.

Also significant in the history of antislavery narrative, although brief and relatively simple, is *Francisco* by Anselmo Suárez y Romero. The text's second title, *El ingenio o las delicias del campo* (The sugar mill or the delights of the countryside), is ironic; sugar mills are shown as hellish. *Francisco,* originally composed between 1838 and 1839, was slow to make its way into print. Domingo del Monte commissioned the work from Suárez y Romero to give it to the Irish abolitionist Richard Madden. However, Madden did not publish it in the volume he was compiling, which centered on the work of the former slave Juan Francisco Manzano. In Cuba, because of its antislavery message, *Francisco* could circulate only in hand-copied form. In 1880, after the author's death, *Francisco* was published in New York.[30]

Francisco differs significantly from the antislavery novels discussed above. While *Sab* and *Cecilia Valdés* feature multiple themes and elaborate plots, *Francisco* is focused on exposing the evil inherent in slavery. In Doris Sommer's words, "*Francisco* is an open denunciation of slavery. The fatal love triangle that frames the narrative, involving a noble black slave, the mulatta slave who reciprocates his love, and the lascivious white master who stops at nothing to possess her, seems almost a pretext for the novel's relentless and detailed review of slavery's institutional horrors."[31]

The title characters of *Sab* and *Cecilia Valdés* intrigue readers with their conflicted identities, ambiguously poised on the racial borderline. These characters identify with white society and seek entry into it, a desire that often makes readers today squirm. Francisco, though, is plainly a black man. While Sab and Cecilia harbor hopeless attachments to white people, Francisco loves another slave, Dorotea. The lady's maid and seamstress to the mistress of the house, Dorotea is a young mulatto woman who clearly views herself as part of Cuba's black population. William Luis characterizes *Francisco* as an example of "black slaves attracted not to whites but to their own blackness." [32]

Moreover, the love between Francisco and Dorotea is mutual. The plots of *Sab* and *Cecilia Valdés* show only sad loves. In these novels the same stratified Cuban society that supports slavery also poisons personal relations, producing marriages of convenience, unrequited love across racial barriers, and exploitative affairs like that of Leonardo with Cecilia Valdés. Francisco and Dorotea would be happy if not for two slave owners, a mother and son. The mother is not evil, but self-centered and capricious. Her chief flaw is to treat Dorotea as her personal possession, which in fact a slave is, and to resent her maid having wishes and desires of her own. The son is the villain of the story, an exploiter who torments Francisco to force Dorotea to accept his sexual advances. His cruelty drives both lovers to early deaths, Francisco by suicide and Dorotea consumed with grief. The novel left many contemporary readers moved over both the unhappy fate of the fictional lovers and the plight of real-world slaves in sugar mills. [33]

Francisco is considered a step forward in placing front and center characters who are unambiguously black people and who form part of African-Cuban culture and society. Though a number of Cuban writers were concerned with the island's racial problems, they had been slow to give black characters significant roles in their novels. However, there is some controversy over Suárez y Romero's decision to make both Francisco and Dorotea behave submissively toward their mistress and master. Of course, real-world slaves, like any other oppressed people, at times made a display of bending to their masters' will. But might such a portrayal risk suggesting that slaves accept their lot? Critical analysis has brought out a good reason for the submissive behavior that the novel attributes to Francisco and Dorotea. Eduardo Castañeda observes that, while there is a strong element of realism in the novel, the characterization of the protagonist is clearly not designed to be true to life. In Castañeda's summary, "Suárez y Romero idealizes Francisco; he takes him out of his social context and tries to convert him to a Christian stoicism." [34] Francisco models the Christian virtues of mildness, patience, and forbearance. This analysis is consistent with the many Christian allusions in the short novel. Luis makes a very similar analysis, explaining the meekness of both Francisco and Dorotea as part of their characteri-

zation as Christian and even Christlike figures: "Within a religious context, the slaves' passivity suggests the sacrifice of Christ and thus harks
back to the Bible. There is an intertextual link between *Francisco* and the
Bible."[35]

In addition to making an emotional plea on behalf of slaves, based on
their right to liberty and happiness, the novel *Francisco* contains a considerable supply of detailed information about nineteenth-century
Cuban sugar mills and the existence of those who worked there. Suárez
y Romero had spent some months on a sugar-producing estate during
the time he was writing *Francisco,* and he seized the opportunity to make
an accurate observation of the details. The noted Cuban anthropologist
Fernando Ortiz (1881–1969) quotes liberally from *Francisco* in one of his
earliest studies, the 1916 *Los negros esclavos* (Black slaves). (Ortiz turns
to literary narratives, including *Cecilia Valdés,* in search of descriptive
accounts, since contemporary essays on slavery focused more on legal
and moral aspects of this intensely debated institution.) Del Monte appears to have seen the principal value of the short novel as offering an ex-
posé of slave labor conditions in sugar mills. While the author called the
novel after its ill-fated hero, del Monte suggested instead the title, today
generally used as a subtitle, that draws attention to the account of the
horrors of sugar production.[36] Del Monte was perhaps the first of many
readers who have turned to this novel not so much for its literary qualities as for the information it contains about real-world sugar mills and the
experience of the slaves on whom sugar-making depended.

*L*iterary nationalism did not always manifest itself
in allegorical narratives of a particular nation or in
literary contributions to great national debates, such as the discussion of
slavery. In many cases, literature is nationalistic in the sense that it relies
on themes, settings, and language that are highly particular to a given nation or a region within a nation. Jorge Ruedas de la Serna summarizes
the way in which Mexican intellectuals approached literature: "Mexican
literary activity of the past century [i.e., the nineteenth century] was accompanied by a widespread reflection, or we might say 'self-reflection,'
on the part of those who served as writers and contributed to giving the
role of writer a special place among human activities, mainly by emphasizing its usefulness and its importance in improving society, ridding it
of poor habits, strengthening public morality, recognizing more fully the
value of our geographical and cultural identity, affirming our identity,
and, along with all this, strengthening national consciousness."[37] In

Ruedas de la Serna's judgment, Mexican writers of the early to mid nineteenth century were aware that they would not be the ones to produce the most accomplished works of Mexican literature, which appeared later in the century; nonetheless, "They knew that they were toiling at a great collective task and with a mission to accomplish."[38]

Here literary nationalism becomes commingled with *costumbrismo*, the description of the customs typical of a particular region or country. *Costumbrismo* may be used to satirize inane and outdated traditions or to provide a detailed ethnographic account of the everyday life of a given community. In the latter part of the nineteenth century, Mexican writers of prose fiction portrayed life in various parts of the nation as part of the campaign to increase Mexican readers' sense of belonging to the nation and to promote improvements in Mexican life. The characters that are most visibly typical of the nation, and especially of its distinctive virtues, are likely to come in for the most favorable portrayal. Some of the clearest examples of this approach to creating a national literature are the narrative and the organizational activities of Ignacio Manuel Altamirano (Mexico, 1834–1893).

Altamirano is a figure charged with significance in Mexican cultural history. As is often noted, he was of entirely indigenous ancestry. He received a Spanish-language education with assistance from programs designed to bring Mexico's native peoples into the dominant society. Beyond his work in literature, Altamirano was a participant in political life and military actions. He held significant public positions, including seats in Congress and on the Supreme Court. For many years his career was closely linked to that of President Benito Juárez. Juárez figures briefly in Altamirano's novel *El Zarco;* the narrator makes a point of the Mexican president's Amerindian origin. Altamirano is generally regarded as one of the great defenders of liberalism in nineteenth-century Mexico. Despite his active participation in public affairs, Altamirano was first and foremost a writer. He published texts in many genres but is best known as a novelist.

Perhaps even more significant than any one text in Altamirano's oeuvre is his campaign to organize literary life in Mexico and to promote a specifically Mexican literature. Since the Mexican independence movement began, there had been successive efforts to found a forum for the nation's writers. Formal literary groups, known by such terms as *academy* or *lyceum,* had brought together like-minded authors, especially poets. Altamirano sought to move beyond these limited circles to organize all Mexican writers, whatever their age, outlook, or the styles and genres in which they wrote, in the campaign to construct a national literature. Many celebrated figures in Spanish American cultural history have special appellations that summarize the accomplishments for which they are remembered. The one most often applied to Altamirano is "the father of Mexican literature." While this epithet originally honored its bearer, it has taken on a less favorable resonance as critics have denounced a paternalistic current in the author's work.[39]

Altamirano advocated a program for developing Mexican letters. An important tenet was that the nation's literature should be liberated from the need to promote political goals. In Altamirano's view, appreciation for the esthetic aspects of literature had waned in the highly politicized environment of the period immediately following independence. The value of literature needed to be restored in the minds of the Mexican public. Mexican intellectuals had become divided into factions by their varying political loyalties. Altamirano's ideal was that the mission of building a national literature should override such differences, and politically diverse writers should cooperate in activities, such as salons, magazines, and literary societies, that supported this goal. The founding in 1869 of the influential literary journal *El Renacimiento* (The renaissance) was one of Altamirano's projects. In his vision, while writers would promote national pride and sound morals through literature, they would not sacrifice the esthetic quality of their work to deliver social, ethical, and nationalistic messages. Belief in literature as an art that was not be tied to particular political agendas would grow increasingly important. In the late years of the century this principle would be a tenet of the movement known as *modernismo*.

In addition, Altamirano urged writers to cultivate a distinctly Mexican writing in their themes, settings, characters, language, and outlook. One might observe, though, that the nation's writers had already been generating a Mexican literature for some time. Indeed, in some cases they were highly conscious of doing so. A perhaps obvious early example is the above-discussed case of José Joaquín Fernández de Lizardi.

Altamirano follows his own program in his best-known works, the relatively brief novels *Clemencia* (1869), *El Zarco* (The Blue-Eyed Man), which was completed in 1888 but only published posthumously in 1901, and *La Navidad en las montañas* (Christmas in the mountains), a long short story of 1870. *Clemencia* was first serialized in *El Renacimiento* and illustrates the ideals that Altamirano promoted through his journal, especially the precept that Mexican literature should satisfy esthetic criteria. It is admired as one of the first Mexican novels to feature a pared-down, well-integrated narrative structure, unencumbered by essaylike digressions or gratuitous subplots. (Another early Mexican novel singled out for its unusually artful execution, despite its proliferating plot lines, is *Astucia, el jefe de los hermanos de la hoja o los charros contrabandistas de La Rama* [Shrewdness: the chief of the brothers of the blade or the cowboy smugglers of La Rama]. Its author was Luis G. Inclán [1816–1875], a printshop owner who typeset and illustrated his own work; José Luis Martínez suggests that he might have started doing so because there was little outside business coming into his establishment.[40] Although *Astucia,* whose two volumes were published in 1865 and 1866, exhibits some of the literary quality that Altamirano cultivated, Inclán is by no means as sophisticated a novelist as Altamirano.) Manuel Sol summarizes the critical consensus concerning the breakthrough that Altamirano made with his 1869 novel: "*Clemencia* marks the beginning, according to historians of literature, of the artistic novel in Mexico."[41] Stephen M. Bell says that "in form *Clemencia* is a much more sophisticated novelistic construction than any of its predecessors in Mexico."[42] The same judgment is evident in Antonio Castro Leal's statement that the publication of *Clemencia* opened "a new phase in Mexican literary narrative. The new works are better constructed; their style is more polished and efficacious."[43]

As part of his effort to modernize and streamline Mexican narrative, Altamirano sought to avoid what he regarded as an inartistic reliance on narrators, often quite garrulous ones, who could serve as mouthpieces for the author's opinions. In his best-known works the narrators are artful constructions, in line with the author's goal of keeping literature distinct from editorializing and pamphleteering. *Clemencia,* for example, begins with a framing story that introduces the principal narrator, who is himself a fictional creation. The main plot of *Clemencia* is related by a physician and an excellent host, who entertains his guests by retelling a series of episodes that he witnessed in his youth, when he was involved in fighting the French. Present at the physician's party is a writer who later composes a recreation of his host's oral account. This transcript appears to make up the text of *Clemencia,* with the exception of the first chapter, set at the party. In an appended note, Altamirano cheerfully admits that, by nonliterary standards, it is improbable that the physician could tell his entire tale in one evening. He urges readers to grant him artistic license: "It is a literary artifice, like any other."[44] Here Altamirano is promoting one of the key ideas in his program: that imaginative literature should be neither written nor read in a way more suitable for essays or treatises. While the story the physician tells has a moral point, as a charming host and raconteur this fictional narrator is obliged to please and fascinate his guests and not bore them with homilies.

Altamirano likes to set his plots against the dramatic background of turbulent periods in Mexican history. *Clemencia* takes place in late 1863, during the French invasion of Mexico. The novel sets four principal characters, two men and two women of marriageable age, in contrast to one another. Both the heroines are young, beautiful, essentially good-hearted, and clever. But one is dark-eyed and alluring, while the other is a fragile, ethereal, pale creature. One of the male protagonists is a handsome, blond charmer who captures both women's hearts with his looks and flattery. In the course of a narrative full of surprises, twists, and sudden reversals of fortune, this gallant is discovered to be a heel and a traitor. He attempts to seduce both the heroines and tries to involve one in his disloyal dealings with the French. The other principal male character has neither good looks nor social skills, and seems cold and aloof, but possesses a sterling character and high morals. The raconteur-narrator initially says of this man, "He seemed repugnant and, indeed, everyone found him *antipático* [not likable]."[45] At the same time, the physician attributes to him some features, such as thrift, industry, and sobriety, which in Altamirano's fiction are invariably signs of a worthy person.

As the plot unfolds, the narrator reveals more evidence that the unimposing, unsociable young man is the soul of altruism and makes the greatest sacrifices for the good of others. The physician-narrator is the privileged confidant to whom the reserved hero pours out his story before dying a martyr's death. The seemingly alienated young man reveals that he has suffered rejection for his devotion to liberal ideals. The physician, who initially described the hero as having an unappealing appearance, states that just before his execution "The young man was beautiful, heroically beautiful."[46]

As one may surmise from this quick summary, *Clemencia* is designed to dissuade readers from judging their fellow human beings by superficial criteria such as good looks and social charm. In the words of Carlos Monsiváis: "The message is unequivocal: Altamirano is waging a hopeless battle against the belief in 'presentation' (faith in outward appearances)."[47]

La Navidad en las montañas is a perennial Christmas favorite. The story is presented as the reminiscences of a man's transforming experience. As in *Clemencia,* there is the pretense that the principal narrator related the story to a very sharp listener, who then reconstructed the account in written form. Back when the reminiscing narrator was a fighter for the liberal cause and had become "a banished man, a victim of political passions," he spent the holiday in a mountain village.[48] In his account, shortly before he encountered the village, "a feeling of sadness took hold of me."[49] Caught in Mexico's internal strife, he has a less than sanguine outlook on the nation. He also shares with many liberals a distrust of the church and a horror of the clergy. He discovers that the isolated village maintains a communal and egalitarian form of Christianity, similar to that of the earliest Christians with their emphasis on sharing and humility. While the little town does have a priest, he displays none of the ecclesiastical authoritarianism of which reformers complained, and is referred to as a brother of the villagers.

The experience of this pure Christianity and of the good hearts of the Mexican townsfolk has a reinvigorating effect on the main narrator, who is healed of his world weariness. An appended note from the author who transcribed the account reveals that he is "today very well known in Mexico," presumably for his service in the building of the nation.[50] Monsiváis observes that Altamirano has designed this long story so that he can praise the original essence of Christianity without abandoning the liberal campaign to lessen the Catholic clergy's control over life in Mexico.[51]

El Zarco, like *Clemencia,* has four protagonists, two men and two women. Again the women and men are potential mates for one another and again the personal drama takes place in a moment of social upheaval. In this case, rural areas are being terrorized and ransacked by bandits who stand out not only for their lawlessness but also for their love of ostentation, display, and externals. They sport elaborate *charro* garb, which they adorn with a profusion of silver ornaments. The virtuous townspeople express their disgust with the gaudy outlaws by dressing as plainly as possible. However, one of the bandits, a handsome man named El Zarco for his blue eyes, is able to beguile one of the heroines into running away and becoming his mistress. Despite a proper upbringing in a well-established family, the young woman is morally weak and succumbs to the lure of the bandit's physical charm, his sparkling outfit, and the jewels that he brings her. Altamirano, through the events of his celebrated novel, punishes this woman harshly for her love of glitter, even though she comes to recognize her error.

This character makes a second mistake, beyond allowing herself to be beguiled by a dazzling exterior. Her own physical appearance betrays no trace of indigenous ancestry; not coincidentally, she is regarded as the town beauty. In turn, she disparages the physiognomic traits associated with Amerindians. This outlook is especially sinful in the world of Altamirano's narrative; besides its obvious racism, it is an obstacle to the development of national pride. The unusually white heroine disdains a hard-working, agreeable, and morally sound suitor in part because he is a blacksmith, "a poor artisan."[52] But she is even more vehement in rejecting him as "a horrible Indian I can't stand."[53] The other principal female character, who is neither as white nor as haughty, benefits from her friend's escape with the bandit to win a husband who is brave, loyal, and, as is observed on various occasions, likely to provide a steady income.

Though it treats the perennially popular topic of banditry, *El Zarco* has none of the rollicking, anarchical quality one typically expects from outlaw tales, which often bound from one action-packed episode to the next. The robbers are by no means the "merry men" of the legends of Robin Hood, nor is *El Zarco* organized around their forays and exploits. Rather, the novel condemns the bandits as violent deviants who live in squalor. *El Zarco* does not dignify their activities with a central organizing function in the narrative and often does not show them. While she is still living in her sheltered home, the young woman who later runs away with the flashy bandit harbors a romantic notion of life among bandits, no doubt gleaned from fiction that is less edifying than *El Zarco*. However, as soon as El Zarco takes her to the bandits' encampment, she realizes that the outlaws are dirty, coarse, and out of control, and she regrets her involvement with them. Clearly, Altamirano was promoting an ideal of order and careful regulation, whether in everyday Mexican life or in the composition of literature.

A more lenient view of bandits has long been widespread in popular song and tales and in literature. It certainly figured in a number of nineteenth-century Spanish American narratives. In some cases, tales of bandits' exploits appeared only in serial installments, whether in newspapers or as pamphlets, and were quickly forgotten. In others, the narratives of banditry became novels. One of the most celebrated of the outlaw serials to be published in book form was *Los bandidos de Río Frío* (The bandits of Cold River), first published in serial form in 1889–1891, by the highly popular Mexican writer Manuel Payno (1810–1894).

Payno was one of the already-established Mexican writers whom Altamirano invited to his activities, seeking to include a wide variety of authors in a literary life of national scope. In 1867 and 1868 Payno, who was a generation older than Altamirano, participated in the latter's literary salon.[54] While he carries out Altamirano's injunction to write as a Mexican, Payno can hardly be said to have striven for the pared-down, well-integrated narrative construction promoted by the father of Mexican literature.

Earlier in the century, Payno had scored a popular success with his lengthy, loosely knit episodic narrative *El fistol del diablo* (The devil's stickpin), serialized in a Mexico City magazine during 1845 and 1846. Between 1888 and 1891 Payno revised his earlier best-seller and composed *Bandidos*. This sprawling novel was also first published in installments, this time in Barcelona. *Bandidos,* like its predecessor, roams from episode to episode without adhering to an overall plan of organization. Antonio Castro Leal reconstructs, with some conjecture, the history of its composition: "It is certain that Payno, as soon as he wrote each chapter, sent it off to the editor in Barcelona. So when he set to work . . . the author must not have had more than a general idea of the subject matter and a very vague conception of its plan and development."[55] (One should keep in mind, though, that serial publication was a widespread practice in the nineteenth century, and a number of highly regarded novels first appeared in installments. The fact that a novel was published in this manner should not be assumed to indicate that its composition is slipshod.)

While *Bandidos* is a fictional narrative, it takes as its point of departure the real-world career and downfall of Colonel Juan Yáñez. Yáñez was no simple highwayman, although he had many rough thugs in his wide-flung network. While he was the kingpin of Mexican crime, he held a military rank and government posts. This scoundrel dressed with ostentatious splendor and was invited into the drawing rooms of the most respectable families. The press made much of the 1839 trial and execution of this criminal mastermind. Payno transforms Yáñez into the character Relumbrón, an adaptable individual whose reach extends nationwide. This choice of central figure allows Payno to include scenes and characters from many regions of Mexico and to represent all the nation's social classes.

The mixed and divided opinion over *Bandidos* reflects the different and sometimes conflicting expectations with which readers approach literary narrative. There is general agreement that *Bandidos* is successful in entertaining its audience with its colorful portraits, wide variety of settings, cliff-hanging chapter endings, miraculous escapes, and abundant action. Also beyond doubt is the novel's extraordinary range, which allows it to represent Mexico. Roaming around the nation, *Bandidos* covers urban, village, and rural life as well as the rich and the poor. It brings in not only human characters of indigenous, *mestizo,* and Spanish ances-try but also other species, as when a motherly dog serves a key function in the plot. Payno was an informal ethnologist as well as a writer of fic-tion, so *Bandidos* contains detailed descriptions of such phenomena as folk practices combining native religions and Catholicism. Opinion is more divided over the value that *Bandidos* possesses as a work of litera-ture. Readers generally find the narrative rambling, especially in com-parison with the tightly structured, artistic novel and short story exem-plified by Altamirano's fiction.

Margo Glantz, a critic known for her populist views on culture, comes to the defense of *Bandidos.* She notes how often readers have faulted *Bandidos* by attributing to it the typical flaws of a serialized novel, such as disregard for the characters' inner selves and lack of cohesion.[56] In this critic's outlook, such a line of criticism amounts to judging a novel of bold actions by standards better suited to a subtle, concentrated psy-chological novel.[57] To demonstrate her point that *Bandidos* is substan-tial enough to sustain critical analysis, Glantz presents a new reading of the first twenty chapters of the novel. These early sections relate the event-filled childhood and adolescence of a foundling who will resurface later in the novel as part of vast network of bandits. In her analysis, the young man, abandoned by Amerindian witches as an attenuated form of human sacrifice, is a "ritual figure . . . the protagonist of a myth of origin, that of the new Mexican national consciousness, brought to life starting with the independence."[58] For Glantz, the character of this foundling allows Payno to "organize the world of his novel like a na-tional epic."[59]

While Glantz's analysis is original and ingenious, the consensus con-tinues to be the one represented by Carlos Monsiváis, who discusses *Los bandidos de Río Frío* as the quintessential serial adventure novel.[60] In Monsiváis's judgment, readers may admire *Bandidos* for its range and its liveliness; in addition, it is a valuable source of information about daily life in Mexico of the early to mid nineteenth century. Yet it does little to advance the evolution of the novel as an art form in Mexico. Monsiváis summarizes: "The novel does not offer any shrewd literary moves, or the creation of characters who go beyond archetypes, or dazzling prose. But it does have an effective narrative, sociological richness, and an abun-dance of characters."[61] This same critic adds that the outstanding fea-ture of Relumbrón's career—the country's greatest outlaw being a highly visible government figure—is one with which corruption-weary Mexi-can readers can identify.[62]

As the novel continues to shed its image as an escapist pastime and gain respectability, one sees an increase in the number of Mexican intellectuals and public figures willing to devote time to the composition of works in this genre. Public service and literature have many links between them. Many novelists of the late nineteenth century are politicians and public administrators. An example of this career pattern is Vicente Riva Palacio (y Guerrero) (1832–1896, grandson of Vicente Guerrero, the Mexican independence hero). From the late 1860s until his death, Riva Palacio won over and commanded a faithful readership, although his novels are too melodramatic for most readers today. Riva Palacio placed his novels and short stories at various turning points in Mexican history, from the flourishing of the Aztec empire to the recent French invasion, which the author had combated. He is best known, though, for fiction set in the colonial period, crammed with action, intrigue, and many subplots involving love, treachery, and heroism. Riva Palacio was one of the youthful authors whom Altamirano, who was also young but already influential, helped to launch, praising his focus on Mexican history and the encouragement that his work gave to nationalistic pride.

Of the same Mexican generation is José Tomás de Cuéllar (1830–1894), who used both his own name and the pseudonym Facundo. Cuéllar was a moralist whose short *costumbrista* novels satirized the foibles and vices of Mexico City society, with the middle class being his favored target. This prolific author is best known for a series of short novels collectively known as *La linterna mágica* (*The Magic Lantern*), published between 1869 and 1892. *Costumbrismo* is the category most frequently used to classify his fiction, whose main point is to show characteristic human types and customs in a given society. Cuéllar's novels had an enthusiastic contemporary readership; following serialization, they were repeatedly issued in book form. In recent times there has been some critical rediscovery of this author. English-language versions of two of Cuéllar's novels, *Having a Ball* (original, *Baile y cochino*) and *Christmas Eve* (*La Noche Buena*) appeared in 2000 in the Library of Latin America series of Oxford University Press.

To this day, readers are still sometimes taken aback by the relentlessness of Cuéllar's ridicule. In his enthusiasm for satire, he apparently cannot resist making sport even of those characters who represent the virtues, such as a dignified sobriety of manner and dress, that he is encouraging. When portraying characters with moral defects, especially foppish young men, scheming coquettes, and husband-hunters showcasing their physical charms, Cuéllar can be caustic in the extreme.

Largely for this reason, Martínez observes that, while in some ways Cuéllar's writing falls within the tradition of Mexican *costumbrismo,* in other ways he is a singular writer. In this critic's analysis, Cuéllar stands out not only for his special focus on Mexico's middle class, but also for the extreme tartness with which he portrays and then comments upon his characters' flaws. In Martínez's words, "Incapable of bringing empathy in together with his critical spirit, he gave his series of novels the sour tone of caricature."[63]

Cuéllar's fiction expresses his distaste for modernization and its manifestations; he also has a horror of vanity and devotes pages to descriptions of preening and primping. Modern urban women especially disturb him with their cosmetics and other means of altering their appearance, their bold ways, and their newfound ability to move about and mingle with people outside their family and family-approved friends. Glantz realizes that, in ridiculing the mobility and intermingling of contemporary society, Cuéllar is nostalgically lamenting "the disintegration of the nuclear family, which was Christian and often rural."[64] During the late twentieth and early twenty-first centuries, there has been a revival of interest in Cuéllar as an acute observer of a society in transition.[65]

Photography was one of Cuéllar's activities, and it is easy to identify aspects of his fiction that resemble photographic portraiture or other static images. The author himself makes the parallelism evident, especially when he gives his short novel *Christmas Eve* the subtitle *Negatives Exposed from December 24 to December 25, 1882.*[66] The overall series title refers, of course, to an early form of slide projector. While the novels in the series have plots, many passages are devoted to recording the details of a scene rather than to showing actions. The author's preoccupation with representing tableaux, together with his detached outlook toward his characters, link him in readers' minds to photography.

A respected novelist with an unusual literary career is Emilio Rabasa (1856–1930). Considerably younger than Altamirano and his contemporaries, and primarily dedicated to legal and political work, Rabasa had a brief spurt of literary production that coincided with the activity of the established authors. Under the pseudonym Sancho Polo, Rabasa published four novels during 1887 and 1888. These novels are linked by, among other shared features, the characters of an unscrupulous politician and a journalist. The politician is plainly corrupt; the journalist at first appears to be a youthful idealist, but his basic venality becomes increasingly evident. The setting shifts from a small town to Mexico City. Whether in town or city, one finds various forms of bribery and a lack of regard for democratic rule; the novel shows this panorama of laxity, but, compared with many of the novels just surveyed, it contains very little moralizing. After publishing a shorter work of fiction in 1891, Rabasa abandoned creative writing. He published under his own name in such fields as constitutional law and political science. It appears that Rabasa regarded the writing of fiction as a diversion from his serious work.

Of the novels that Rabasa produced during his few years of creativity, the first, the 1887 *La bola* (The melee), is the most highly regarded. The title refers to the violent, messy revolt that the politician sets off to impose himself as boss of a little town. This novel, with its well-paced, unified plot, is more predominantly and distinctly a work of realism than the Mexican novels discussed above. Many earlier works offered passages of realistic description and narration, if one defines realism as an effort to portray reality in all its aspects without embellishment. Yet, in the Mexican novel, elements of realism commingled with melodramatic romanticism, open moralizing, picturesque local scenes in the manner of *costumbrismo,* and the swashbuckling scenes of pursuit, escape, and fighting that were staples of popular serials. Rabasa's *La bola* adheres to its central goal of presenting a fictional exploration of the least attractive workings of power.

Also important figures in Mexican realism are two writers, still read today, whose careers span the late nineteenth and early twentieth centuries. These are José López Portillo y Rojas (1850–1923) and Federico Gamboa (1864–1939).

López Portillo, as well as being a writer of realist fiction, was an important public figure. From the 1880s to 1910 he occupied a number of important government posts. During the first decade of the twentieth century, he served as governor of Jalisco and in cabinet-level national posts, among other roles. After the Mexican Revolution and the fall of President Porfirio Díaz, with whom he was linked, López Portillo was still a visible figure and administrator in institutions concerned with the arts and sciences. He became president of the Mexican Academy, among other posts, and generally wielded substantial influence. This author possessed an exceptional range of expertise. He taught law and political economics and published works in such diverse areas as philosophy, history, biography, literary criticism, and anthropology; he was also a translator from French to Spanish. While he wrote literary works in several genres, it is his fiction that has continued to attract readers.

As a writer of fiction, López Portillo favors rural settings and characters who exemplify aspects of Mexican country people, both the strengths to be found in farming communities and the aspects that need improvement. The most widely read of his narratives is his first full-length novel, the 1898 *La parcela* (The plot of land). It has been through many editions and has often been required reading for courses. The plot of *La parcela* has provided the basis for film adaptations. The 1938 version, entitled *Nobleza ranchera* (dir. Alfredo del Diestro) was distributed in the United States as *Rural Chivalry*. The 1950 adaptation, *La posesión* (dir. Julio Bracho) featured the popular performer Jorge Negrete as the noble-hearted son of an hacienda owner; the story was reworked to provide him opportunities to sing.

The conflict in the novel arises over a plot of land that is claimed by the owners of two adjoining haciendas. Before the dispute over the border property, there is already tension between the two *hacendados*. One has been industriously modernizing agricultural methods to increase productivity, while the other remains a traditional member of the landed gentry. When the more conservative landowner presses his claims on the lot, a feud erupts, involving not only the two *hacendados* but also their loyal farmhands and various advantage-seeking meddlers. While a number of characters have a part in fanning the flames, reconciliation begins with the love between the son of one landowner and the daughter of the other, and the novel ends on a note of forgiveness and neighborly friendship.

La parcela met a favorable reception, owing in part to the widespread desire to see many diverse aspects of Mexican life reflected in literature. Joaquina Navarro summarizes contemporary reactions to the novel: "The entirely rural subject matter of *La parcela* aroused great interest; the work was considered the Mexican novel par excellence, the first novel of the Mexican countryside. Literary intellectuals of López-Portillo's time received it with rejoicing."[67]

While López Portillo continues to figure as an important writer, later critics have not always been so admiring of the way in which he creates rural Mexican characters. Navarro observes that, while the more caricatured characters in *La parcela* stand out, the noble-spirited country people lack complexity and "their personality does not go beyond presenting them as paragons of pure moral qualities."[68] Mario Martín-Flores also complains about a lack of nuance in the novel's characterization. In his analysis, the portrayal of good rural characters as simple and guileless serves to oppose "a childlike America" to "European decadence."[69] This latter comment, in particular, touches upon a problem that will continue to bedevil Spanish American writers: how a worldly writer can present the actions and speech of characters with less formal education.

Though Gamboa is an important figure to be aware of, he will not be discussed here because he made his greatest impact only after the nineteenth century closed. This author began publishing in the late 1880s. His novel of 1896, *Suprema ley* (Supreme law), could be seen either as realistic or naturalistic, depending on which portions are stressed; in addition, some passages are dominated by romanticism and a pro-family ideology. Still, Gamboa owes his renown to his novel of 1903, the equally difficult-to-classify *Santa.* Named after its prostitute-heroine, *Santa* attained great popularity and continues to be reissued. Gamboa's twentieth-century writing is the significant part of his oeuvre. John S. Brushwood observes, "His later work gives a much more complete view of the author's reality."[70]

Since independence, the Andean region had suffered political conflicts and wars between neighboring countries, some of them the cause of considerable devastation. While these events came and went, the entire area faced a perennial problem. The population of the Andean countries was as high as 80 percent indigenous, but the Amerindians of the Andes had little way of participating in national life and were for the most part living in poverty and exploited by landholders and authorities. Progressive intellectuals realized that some action was necessary to make native peoples fully part of the young Andean republics and to provide relief from the miserable conditions in which they lived. However, there was little agreement about what measures were called for. Some reform-minded liberals stressed the need for education, others sought curbs on the power of church and government authorities, and others focused on issues of land holding and use. This debate surfaced in literature as well as the essay.

The single most important literary figure to emerge from the Andean countries in all of the nineteenth century was Ricardo Palma (1833–1919). Palma, whose stories remain entertaining, is the founding figure of Peruvian literary life. He restored the National Library in Lima and developed its collections. As well as being a writer, historian, librarian, and arbiter of tastes, he held political posts.

Palma is best known for developing a form known as the *tradición.* The *Tradiciones peruanas,* the title applied to all of Palma's writings in this vein, appeared between 1872 and 1910, with the exception of the ribald *Tradiciones en salsa verde* (Traditions in hot sauce), withheld from publication until 1972.

The *tradición* is, for the most part, a subtype of the short story. However, it contains elements that are neither fictitious nor narrative. The point of departure is, in most cases, some nugget of information that the narrator has gleaned. The source may be gossip or an archival document. Many of Palma's *tradiciones* feature a framing device in which someone who appears to be the author tells how he came across the subject matter. Often he has discovered a tale while researching some folk saying, striking turn of phrase, or allusion to past events. After coming to the end of the preamble, Palma starts the narrative part of the *tradición*.

Whether or not a given *tradición* begins with opening remarks of this type, once the story is underway it is generally interrupted by segments of nonnarrative material in which history and gossip are freely commingled. The narrator may break off his story to detail the life and times of some respected authority or renowned scoundrel, or offer information about the construction of Lima's historical downtown, before returning to the half-finished tale. The frequency with which these asides occur leads Enrique Pupo-Walker to characterize the *tradición* as "a brief tale that thrives on rambling commentary and that is prone to ironic digressions."[71]

González suggests that it may not be desirable to seek a definition for the *tradición*. This critic observes that Palma's definitions of the subgenre were "always unsatisfactory." Other critics' efforts to pin down the characteristics of the *tradición* "are attempts to impose coherence upon a 'genre' (so to speak) that tends to question such attempts at synthesis." González prefers an open characterization that respects "the diverse and contradictory impulses that converge in Palma's work."[72]

Palma took great pains to make the language of his *tradiciones* striking and noteworthy. He was a collector of archaic words and phrases, popular proverbs and puns, and all manner of unusual and memorable linguistic constructions. These included not only witty and ingenious flourishes but also taunts, insults, and verbal mudslinging; Palma took a special interest in the expression of aggression through language. He was also a collector of ribald narratives and sexually suggestive turns of phrase. The *tradiciones* that Palma published contain only mildly spicy allusions to such phenomena as clandestine affairs and sumptuously maintained mistresses, usually treated with a worldly jocularity. His racy tales composed for private circulation display his connoisseur's knowledge of coarse popular expressions.

Palma's favored setting is Lima, although some of the *tradiciones* take place in the Incan empire or during the conquest. In particular, he is drawn to portray Lima at the height of its magnificence as a viceregal capital, when it was the "City of Kings," a showpiece of urban opulence. Successive viceroys had embellished the city with palatial government buildings and public works projects, while the city's upper crust constructed residences with wrought-iron balconies, arcades, ornamental tiles, and sculpted and carved masonry. The mannered customs of the aristocrats who frequented the viceroy's court also figure prominently in Palma's *tradiciones*.

Detractors and enthusiasts of the *tradiciones* have debated the significance of Palma's preoccupation with the colonial past. The negative view is that Palma is a traditionalist who idealizes the past, specifically colonial Peru with its stratified society and lack of democratic institutions. During Palma's lifetime, he faced derision from Manuel González Prada, who associated the author of the *tradiciones* with nostalgia and himself with forward-looking critical thought. One should take into account, though, that these two prominent figures in Peruvian intellectual life harbored a long-running mutual enmity. Peruvian social critic José Carlos Mariátegui (1894–1930) recognized Palma's mockery of the aristocracy. In his *Siete ensayos de interpretación de la realidad peruana* (*Seven Interpretive Essays on Peruvian Reality*), his highly influential collection of 1928, Mariátegui recognizes "the irreverent and unorthodox spirit of Palma." [73]

The best-known recent polemic against Palma's *tradiciones* appears in *Lima la horrible* (Lima the horrible), the 1964 book of essays by Sebastián Salazar Bondy (Peru, 1924–1965). Salazar Bondy identifies a syndrome whereby residents of Lima delude themselves that they are still living in the City of Kings. Via this fantasy, they avoid the pressing issues of the overcrowded modern city. In this critic's view, despite Palma's liberal political affiliation, in his *tradiciones* he was "the most gifted manufacturer of that literary drug" (i.e., nostalgia for the colonial era). [74] Salazar Bondy maintains that, in populating his imaginary Lima with a wide variety of characters, Palma failed to include "anyone who, being malcontent and free, would want to shake up conformity and change the attitude of deference toward institutions." [75]

Defenders of Palma maintain that his portrait of colonial society is a satirical one. According to this latter reading, Palma finds absurdity in the sumptuous pomp with which the colonial elite surrounded itself and injustice in its wielding of power. Critical discussion of the *tradiciones* often includes arguments intended to demonstrate either that Palma glamorized colonial society or that he satirized it.

There is no doubt that Palma expresses a sense of enchantment with certain aspects of colonial Lima, particularly in its lavish eighteenth-century heyday. His enthusiasm can seem odd for a writer who in real life consistently expressed a progressive social outlook. For instance, the *tradiciones* include admiring portraits of legendary mistresses who plied their wiles on powerful men, as well as of selfless, devout virgins and mothers. One might assume that the author could only envision women as sensuous, scheming vixens or as earth angels. In real life, though, Palma supported women's involvement in intellectual life and encouraged his daughter to pursue a literary career.

Raúl Porras Barrenechea, who argues that Palma was sincerely democratic, at the same time recognizes that the author of the *tradiciones* displayed unmistakable nostalgia for certain aspects of pre-Independence society. Porras Barrenechea points out that Palma was born less than a decade after the wars of Independence, and Peru was especially slow to shed the habits of the colonial era; in some cases, Palma is describing traditions that he had observed in his youth.[76] In this critic's analysis, the affection that Palma shows for certain old-fashioned folkways is a harmless sentiment that does not interfere with his desire to liberalize and democratize Peruvian society.

As an example, Porras discusses Palma's enthusiasm for the *tapadas* (covered-up women) of Lima, who, pulling ample scarves across their faces, tantalized male admirers with fleeting glimpses of their features. Palma's literary work evokes the mysterious allure of these half-hidden women. Porras points out that the writer also favored the continuation of this custom in real life.[77] According to this researcher, the traditional female garb was still in use in Lima during Palma's youth. At mid-century (1853–1854), the enveloping attire fell from favor. The women of Lima adopted so-called French dress, in which the neck and face remained visible while the extravagantly adorned millinery of the era perched atop the head. The abandonment of the old style caused some consternation. According to Porras Barrenechea, Palma "waged a campaign in verse in defense of the *saya y manto* (the traditional concealing garments) and against French-style dress."[78] Palma's advocacy of the time-honored apparel was a comical one, framed as a debate between the old and new articles of clothing. He was not seeking to halt the modernization of women's wear or to require women to cover up. He simply was expressing nostalgia for the intriguingly swathed women who had long been pointed out as one of the distinctive local sights of Lima. As Porras Barrenechea understands the situation, Palma was attracted to bygone or vanishing folkways in a way typical of romanticism, a movement to which this writer had strong links.

Juan Durán Luzio has laid out the evidence that Palma was a satirist critical of the authoritarian character of colonial society. This critic finds no basis for the widespread perception of Palma "as one who idealized the past, as the creator of a colonial Arcadia." [79] To bring the discussion onto more rational ground, Durán Luzio identifies the most frequent targets of Palma's wrath, which expresses itself both in satire and in direct, sometimes harshly accusatory statements. He then examines the reasons for which these entities appear in a negative light in the *tradiciones*. Palma often took aim at the Jesuits, both through satirical portraits of Jesuit priests and through assertions critical of the entire order. Durán Luzio pinpoints the motive for Palma's anti-Jesuit writing: "It's a denunciation made against the religious order that had stood out, more than any other, for controlling liberating and progressive thought and action." [80]

Along with authoritarian clerics, officials of the colonial government come under attack in the *tradiciones*. Durán Luzio cites the case of "Pues bonita soy yo, la Castellanos" (I, Castellanos, am the pretty one), a *tradición* concerning the rivalry between two kept women. While describing the lengths of ostentatious display to which the two women go, the narrator points out that one of them, the famous royal favorite La Pericholi, is maintained at public expense by the Viceroy Amat. This highest of colonial administrators is abusing government funds and his official influence to indulge his lover's whims. Durán Luzio revisits the critical problem of Palma's fixation on the city of Lima, which is often viewed as the sentimental attachment of an antiquarian. This scholar observes that the wealthy administrative center was full of the corruption and abuses of power and finances that Palma sought to denounce. [81]

González believes that the long-running debate over Palma's outlook on aristocratic tradition may be missing an even more significant question. While González clearly states that Palma's *tradiciones* "ridicule the Peruvian elite's aspirations of nobility," [82] this critic is more concerned with Palma's suspicion of the entire concept of genealogy, widely relied upon as a systematizing force. In González's view, Palma had an anarchistic outlook on all systems, and especially hierarchies constructed to benefit one sector of society. Palma's distrust of these ordering and classificatory devices extends beyond family trees to include the way that conventional histories were written and the typical pattern of the nineteenth-century novel.[83]

Much as Palma enjoyed utilizing old-fashioned ways as thematic material, he was innovative in his painstaking effort to produce a carefully worked, highly polished prose. The appreciation for more deliberate, even overtly artificial writing would become one hallmark of *modernismo,* to be discussed in the following chapter.

*P*eruvian intellectuals, during this same period, were growing more concerned over the plight of the native Andeans. At the time, the indigenous population was heavily concentrated in the mountainous sierra; massive migration to Lima came later. Nineteenth-century Peruvians of European descent, if they lived on the coast, had long found it easy to give little thought to the Native American population. The poet, essayist, and speaker Manuel González Prada (1848–1918) exercised a charismatic influence in drawing attention to this aspect of the nation's reality. González Prada's views were highly progressive for the time in which he lived, though in retrospect some of his essays might seem idealistic. He expounded the need to curb the power of landowners, Catholic clergy, and government officials, especially in rural areas where authorities could most easily abuse the indigenous population. Nationalistic concerns were also part of his program, and he encouraged the development of a Peruvian spirit in literature and the other arts.

Women intellectuals were included in González Prada's circle. One of these, Clorinda Matto de Turner (1852–1909), illustrated this reformer's ideas in her fiction. Her 1889 novel *Aves sin nido* (English, *Birds without a Nest* and *Torn from the Nest*) is dedicated to González Prada and exemplifies his concepts. Matto published two other novels, the 1891 *Indole* (Basic nature) and *Herencia* (Inheritance), an 1895 sequel to *Aves sin nido,* but the first remains the most significant.

Aves sin nido has always been controversial. As Ana Peluffo notes: "Even though *Aves sin nido* (1889) today has a canonical status as the first work of *indigenismo* and had a massive circulation in the nineteenth century, as demonstrated by the three simultaneous editions that sold out and its almost immediate translation into English, the publication of this novel generated an acute controversy in the literary world."[84] *Aves sin nido* is the first widely read (not the first) example of literary *indigenismo*, literature about Amerindians, and provides a valuable sample of 1880s progressive thought.[85] In addition, readers are drawn to Matto's difficulties as a reform-minded woman intellectual. In Mary G. Berg's summary, "Burned in effigy, excommunicated, the presses of her feminist print shop smashed and her manuscripts burned by mobs just before her hasty flight from Lima in 1895, Clorinda Matto de Turner may have been the most controversial woman writer of nineteenth-century Latin America."[86]

Matto began by publishing in newspapers her poetry and essays on women, Amerindians, and other topics. She was also influenced by the *tradiciones*. While Palma set many *tradiciones* in Lima, Matto adapted the *tradición* to Cuzco. One of her assets was a knowledge of the Quechua language and Andean culture.

In 1883 Matto assumed the editorship of *La Bolsa* (Market news) in Arequipa. Berg points out that she "became the first woman in the Americas to head an important daily paper."[87] In 1886 she moved to Lima, where González Prada mentored her. In 1889 Matto became editor of *El Perú Ilustrado* (Illustrated Peru) and published *Aves sin nido,* igniting conflict. President Andrés Avelino Cáceres led support for the novel and the Catholic church rallied opposition. In 1890 Matto drew further fire when *El Perú Ilustrado* printed a story by Henrique Coelho Neto (Brazil, 1864–1934) in which Christ responds to the sexuality of Mary Magdalene. The publication was the pretext for Matto's excommunication and the prohibition of *Aves sin nido.*

Aves sin nido opens with a description of an Andean town whose bucolic appearance hides corruption. The plot begins when an Amerindian woman seeks help from the protagonist, Lucía. She tells a story of exploitation by the figures that wield power over the native Andeans. They include the trinity that González Prada, in his celebrated 1888 speech in the Teatro Politeama, had blamed for the native Andeans' oppression: town governor, priest, and judge.[88] In her preface Matto echoes González Prada's words, deploring "the abjection into which this race [Andean Amerindians] is plunged by small-town despots who, while their names may change, never fail to live up to the epithet of tyrants. They are no other than, in general, the priests, governors, caciques, and mayors."[89]

As well as protesting the exploitation of Amerindians, *Aves sin nido* is concerned with women. Its pro-woman position is evident in the characterization of males and females. Male characters may be either corrupt or altruistic; the latter men are either Lima-educated liberals or Amerindians. But whether urban or rural, white or native, women are good. Lucía's husband remarks that in villages "Everyone is out for personal gain and no one corrects that bad or stimulates the good; but it is surprising that women and men are nothing alike in their behaviour." She replies "If the women were bad, too, this would be a hell!"[90]

Sexual exploitation of women is a concern in *Aves sin nido*. Priests prey upon the women parishioners. Native women are forced to become domestic and sexual servants to priests. The novel features revelations of sexual abuse of both native and white women by clerical and civil authorities. Egalitarian marriage is another theme. The main characters are Lucía and Fernando Martín, an ideal couple from Lima who are united by a shared ethical outlook.

Lucía is the one who first seeks to reform the corrupt town. She summons to her house the priest and governor, urging them to right the situation of the Amerindian family whose mother has appealed to her. The officials respond by organizing an attack on the progressive couple's home, during which the parents of the indigenous family are killed.

Eager to incorporate Amerindians into the nation, Lucía and Fernando adopt the orphans. Both are female, providing the occasion for statements about girls' schooling. Fernando tells Lucía: "They are our adopted daughters; they will go with us to Lima and there, as we have already planned, we will place them in the college best adapted to form wives and mothers, without wasting their time in exaggerated repetition of words called prayers without idea or sentiment."[91]

Fernando's desire that the girls' education "form wives and mothers" might seem retrograde. But nineteenth-century feminists typically argued that educated women improve families. Post-Independence Spanish American thinkers often looked to women as mothers of future leaders. Peluffo recalls that the leading figure of nineteenth-century Argentina, Domingo Faustino Sarmiento, recommended women's education for this reason.[92] In Peluffo's analysis, "In Matto de Turner this ideology is utilized to widen the domestic sphere assigned [to women], to acquire economic independence and to advance in an intellectual profession, undertaken with a sense of religious mission."[93]

Readers of *Aves sin nido* may be shocked by the novel's one allusion to feminism. Lucía recalls the anti-feminist *El ángel del hogar; estudios morales acerca de la mujer* (The angel of the home; moral studies of woman) by María del Pilar Sinués de Marco (1835–1893). One passage lingers in Lucía's mind: "Forget, poor women, your dreams of emancipation and liberty. Those are theories of sickly minds which can never be practised, because woman was born to grace the home."[94] Antonio Cornejo Polar points out that women characters in *Aves sin nido* flout this guidance.[95]

Aves sin nido has always been faulted for lack of artistry. To appreciate it, a reader must accept that it is designed to deliver a social critique. As Peluffo accurately observes, "*Aves sin nido* sets itself up, from the first pages of the preface, as a text more concerned with ethical than esthetic issues."[96]

Other critics express concern over the solutions that *Aves sin nido* proposes to the exploitation of Amerindians. Help comes from well-placed reformers of European extraction. Brushwood characterizes the novel's implicit statement: "So far as the redemption of the Indian is concerned, obviously it depends on a more honorable authority, and that condition may be brought about by education. An active role for the Indian is not a point of emphasis, although presumably he might participate in a better educational process."[97] In addition, the novel lacks the concept of broad-based alliances. In Cornejo Polar's words, "In both *Aves sin nido* and its pallid sequel, the 1893 *Herencia* (Inheritance), the inability of Clorinda Matto to imagine collective solutions stands out."[98] This critic also discovers a contradiction in Matto's view of Amerindian culture. In the preface to *Aves sin nido,* she states: "I love the native race with a tender love, and so I have observed its customs closely, enchanted by their simplicity."[99] Yet, in some passages, Matto does not seem to want indigenous culture to survive. In Cornejo Polar's judgment: "Isolated [indigenous] characters are the ones who are able to escape their miserable fate and if they manage to do so, it is to the extent that—in more than one sense—they cease to be Indians."[100] It is easy to find examples that support Cornejo Polar's assertions. When Lucía first undertakes to help the exploited indigenous family, she becomes the foster mother of one of their daughters, giving her the upbringing of a Peruvian lady of European background. After the girls are orphaned, they are both brought up in this way.

Peluffo has traced a pattern in the reception of the novel. Initial reactions were either high praise or condemnation. For example, Juan de Arona called Matto "ignorant," a "creator of ridiculous figures" ("autora de mamarrachos"), and a *marimacho,* that is, a masculine or butch woman.[101] Mariátegui does not mention Matto when he discusses *indigenista* literature in *Seven Interpretive Essays.* Other critics expressed hostility toward women writers, as when a detractor calls Matto "a literary seamstress." [102] Matto's critical fortunes looked up in 1934 when the woman critic Concha Meléndez included a chapter on *Aves sin nido* in her *La novela indianista en Hispanoamérica, 1832–1889* (The Indian-theme novel in Spanish America, 1832–1889). [103]

Current-day feminists may see Matto's statements about women as hesitant and incomplete. As Marta A. Umanzor puts it, "The reader has the feeling that [*Aves sin nido*] leaves the central situation concerning women's liberation unresolved, even when the author points out the problem of the social and political exploitation of women." [104] Yet Matto's fiction provides a valuable sample of early Spanish American feminism.

*T*he late-nineteenth-century taste for realism marks not only the most widely read texts of the period but also writing that finds few readers beyond its country of origin and foreign specialists. An example is the Argentine Generation of 1880. The most-noted members of this generation are prominent citizens, often with careers in public service, who write as a sideline. Although they are involved in public life and social activities, the writers from this group are prolific. They often compose short texts for particular occasions or as brief magazine and newspaper pieces. At times they seem to be calling attention to the lightweight character of their writing by referring to it as chat or idle musings. Despite their fondness for striking a casual pose as writers, the intellectuals of this generation on occasion produce narrative works of some substance, favoring a generally realistic manner of presentation. The most prominent writers associated with the Generation of 1880 include Miguel Cané (1851–1905), Eduardo Wilde (1844–1913), Lucio Vicente López (1848–1894), and Lucio V. Mansilla (1831–1913). Though Mansilla is grouped with the Generation of 1880 and indeed wrote during the 1880s, his best-remembered work is the 1870 *Una excursión a los indios ranqueles* (*An Expedition to the Ranquel Indians*), a lengthy and surprisingly thoughtful text that includes ethnographic descriptions and reflections on the relations between the Amerindian and European components of national culture. An Argentine writer whose novels are today more read than those of his contemporaries, Eugenio Cambaceres (1843–1888) is chronologically of the same generation but differs markedly in his outlook on society and approach to writing. Cambaceres will be discussed in the next chapter along with other Spanish American practitioners of naturalism.

The 1880 writers have an ultra-Establishment image in Argentina, where their works are still part of school readings. It is true that a number of them were from well-positioned families and moved in elite circles. The most prestigious private clubs appear named and described in their newspaper columns and fiction. The well-known and often polemical Argentine critic David Viñas has particularly singled out the Generation of 1880 as representatives of a self-satisfied ruling class.[105] Given their advantageous placement in Argentine society, one might expect these writers to exhibit a complacent outlook on the prevailing social arrangement. While they are undeniably smug at moments, their works also express a sense of dissatisfaction.

An example of this disaffected vision is *La gran aldea* (The big village), an 1884 novel by López that is often read in Argentina, though it has not made much of an impact outside the country. López was born in Uruguay in 1848 into a family of Argentine exiles from the Rosas regime. He made his career in Buenos Aires, where he died in a duel in 1894. While his most celebrated novel has a plot, which follows the life of the alienated narrator-protagonist, readers tend to remember it most for its descriptions of Buenos Aires, the big village of the title. The protagonist, Julio, views the city as it evolves from the 1860s to the early 1880s. Julio might seem to enjoy an insider's perspective on the city; for example, he gains entry to the exclusive Club del Progreso. Yet he is a perennial outsider whose outlook on Buenos Aires becomes increasingly critical. In its earlier incarnation, Buenos Aires appears to him staid, straitlaced, and hypocritically nationalistic. The ideal is to appear to be from an old-line family, and there is a general contempt for intellectual activity and innovation. As the title hints, the city resembles a small town where the principal citizens all know and pass judgment on one another. As Buenos Aires becomes more cosmopolitan and capitalistic, consumerism and pleasure-seeking replace the stodginess of the 1860s. Society has loosened up, allowing greater autonomy for individual action, but the narrator sees this liberty being squandered in a frivolous way. Neither in the priggish 1860s nor the decadent 1880s do learning and critical thought receive the respect that the narrator would like them to enjoy.

Research on the Generation of 1880 almost inevitably focuses attention on these writers' roles in Argentine society, since they were in a position to exercise considerable influence at the time that the country was undergoing rapid modernization. In recent years, though, one may discern a critical effort to move beyond the monolithic image of the Generation of 1880 as representatives of the national Establishment and its ideology. David William Foster, in his 1990 *The Argentine Generation of*

1880: Ideology and Cultural Texts, draws attention to the neglected element of literary art in the writing of this generation. Foster points out that some of their texts, particularly *La gran aldea,* take the form of well-composed narrative fiction.[106]

*B*y the late years of the nineteenth century, swifter changes were under way in Spanish American narrative. Throughout the Spanish American countries, writers and the literary public began to demand greater innovation. Romanticism had been a force since early in the century. By now there was a widespread call to discard romantic conventions, although in practice they often proved difficult to weed out. The literary nationalism that had been such a dominant theme in nineteenth-century Spanish American narrative was also losing the interest of readers. Realism had not been on the scene as long as romanticism and the literature of nation-building, but it, too, was due for renovation. As the century moves toward its close, two tendencies in particular claim the attention of readers: naturalism, which of course has many links to the already established realism, and the movement known as *modernismo.*

| 𝒩ATURALISM AND *MODERNISMO*

*D*uring the last years of the nineteenth century, literary life changed at a swifter pace. Writers initiated literary innovations and took up new influences more rapidly than in the early years of the century. With faster communications and travel, trends moved swiftly between regions and nations. This chapter looks at two tendencies that began in the 1880s, were well entrenched by the 1890s, and continued into the twentieth century, though the discussion here runs only to the end of the nineteenth. Naturalism, of course, began in France when novelists sought to move beyond realism. Naturalist writers were to assume the role of scientific observers of society; fictional narrative would be the laboratory in which they carried out their studies. Spanish-language novelists and short-story writers transformed it to suit their own societies, and Spanish American naturalism is not identical to the European version. Even in a modified form, though, naturalism made only limited inroads into Spanish American narrative. *Modernismo,* in contrast, is widely hailed as the first literary movement to begin among Spanish American writers. While it is especially linked to poetry, *modernismo* also appears in Spanish American prose narrative.

Spanish-language intellectuals were aware of, and sometimes upset by, French naturalism. As exemplified by the celebrated French novelist Emile Zola (1840–1902), naturalism was associated with a deterministic outlook, in which nature and nurture were perceived as controlling human behavior. This view was at odds with Catholic doctrine, where concepts of good and evil were predicated on the assumption that human beings enjoyed free will. Readers in Spanish-speaking countries were more likely to employ theological criteria in assessing literature than were European audiences. Aside from the problem of free will, Spanish-language readers objected more strenuously than French ones to the way in which naturalism broke with decorum. Naturalist novels are known for their tendency to show humankind at its worst and to include scabrous and revolting scenes, which authors sought to present in a nonjudgmental way. Readers in Spanish-speaking countries often expected literature to offer ethical guidance. Spanish American authors who used elements of naturalism had to adapt the European movement for their reading public.

Almost as soon as naturalism emerged in France, Spanish-language writers became involved with the questions it raised. In 1880 Zola published his often-cited "Le roman expérimental" ("The Experimental Novel"), a manifesto for the literary naturalism that he had already been expounding and practicing during the 1870s. Zola had been influenced by the biological sciences, and one of his ideas was that novelists could go about their work scientifically, inquiring into the ills that afflicted society.

This position statement was soon being debated in Spain and Spanish America. The central problem was whether the new trend should be discouraged in the Spanish-speaking world, or whether naturalism could be made suitable for countries where, among other differences, Catholicism was more pervasive than in France. During the winter of 1882–1883, the countess Emilia Pardo Bazán (1851–1921), the respected yet controversial Spanish novelist, published a series of essays on the topic. Her reflections, which first appeared in periodical form and then in a much-reprinted pamphlet, were entitled *La cuestión palpitante* (The burning issue). The title alludes to the debate over the spread of French naturalism. Both in this often-cited essay and in her own narrative, Pardo Bazán accepts the naturalist idea of making the novel a study of society. She suggests ways of transforming naturalism to make it compatible with progressive Catholicism. In the portrayal of fictional characters, she seeks recognition of the spiritual and ethical capabilities that set human beings apart from the other species.

Enrique Laguerre has examined the changes that naturalism underwent as it entered Spanish and Spanish American writing. He notes that there was much alarm over the arrival of French naturalism, which was seen as undermining morality. Pardo Bazán's essay served to reassure progressive writers and readers that naturalism could be a beneficial force. It also gave the trend a great boost. According to Laguerre, "*The burning issue* brought about extraordinary sales of naturalist novels."[1]

In this critic's analysis, most Spanish and Spanish American writers who utilized elements of naturalism favored the softened form of the movement that Pardo Bazán had recommended, so Spanish-language naturalism is less crude and brutal than the French phenomenon. In addition, with their often-noted propensity for combining literary tendencies, Spanish-language writers often employed only certain characteristics of naturalism in works that also exhibited features of realism, romanticism, and other tendencies. Laguerre points out that, if one includes texts in which naturalism is only one of a mixture of elements, many Spanish-language novels can be included under the category. In the course of his discussion, he names a number of novels from Spain and Spanish American nations that to some degree demonstrate the existence of naturalism in the literature of these countries.[2]

Despite this diffuse presence of naturalism, only a few Spanish American novels and short stories stand out as distinctly in the naturalist mode. This discussion focuses on outstanding examples published during the nineteenth century. One should remember, though, that naturalism continues to exercise its influence well into the twentieth.

*D*uring the 1880s, naturalism found a limited place in Spanish American writing. Readers in the Southern Cone countries of Argentina, Uruguay, and Chile seem to have been especially fascinated with this tendency. Paul Groussac, born in France in 1848, became an important participant in Argentine literary life and at his death in 1929 was director of the National Library. He was in contact with naturalist literary circles in France and drew upon this tendency in his Spanish-language novels, including the 1884 *Fruto vedado* (Forbidden fruit), a novel of adultery whose sexual frankness alarmed many contemporaries.

Probably the novel most often cited as exemplifying Spanish American naturalism is the 1885 *Sin rumbo* (Adrift) by the Argentine Eugenio Cambaceres (1843–1889). Myron Lichtblau points out that Cambaceres softens in some ways the French model of naturalism.[3] Still, *Sin rumbo* contains scenes of unusual brutality and violence. The final scenes retain to this day the ability to upset readers.

The author of *Sin rumbo* is associated with the Argentine Generation of 1880, discussed in the previous chapter. Cambaceres's life fits the characteristic pattern of writers associated with this group. He was from a wealthy family, completed a law degree, and pursued a career in politics. In public life he upheld the liberal ideology of the time, favoring growth and modernization, and was best known as the sponsor of a bill establishing separation of church and state. However, as a writer he is not so typical of this group. While the writers of the Generation of 1880 tended to exhibit genteel restraint, Cambaceres was more given to breaking taboos.

Cambaceres, whose father was a French immigrant to Argentina, spent periods in Paris. According to Nélida Salvador, "In this way he came into direct contact, at their high point, with French realism and naturalism, whose esthetic orientation proves evident in most of his creative production."[4] He appears to have taken up the concept, typical of French naturalism, that the work of the novelist was to carry out an almost scientific study of the workings of humankind. In this spirit, the author added to the original title of *Sin rumbo* the subtitle *estudio,* which does not appear in reissues. At the same time that he looked to European models, Cambaceres drew upon Argentine sources for his thematic material. This writer's wealth came from sheep ranching, and he spent a fair amount of time on his land.[5] In his most celebrated novel some chapters take place on the protagonist's sheep ranch, which is described in detail. The novel's disturbing opening scene depicts workers roughly shearing a flock of wretched but resigned sheep. The shearing is done with so little care that the sheep are left with great slash wounds in their hides, and one receives a puncture in the abdomen.

As the title indicates, Andrés, the main character of *Sin rumbo,* lacks any mooring and presents a study in disaffection. The brief, fast-paced novel follows him during the last three years of his life, which ends in a gruesome suicide. The third-person narrator keeps Andrés in close-up throughout the novel, revealing his thoughts and feelings. The other characters remain distant and opaque, as they are to the protagonist. As Noé Jitrik comments, "Andrés is made to stand out so much over the other elements and characters that he goes beyond the mere notion of a protagonist; he occupies the entire narrative structure, which pales in comparison; he dominates the total economy of the story."[6]

While providing readers with an intimate look at this jaded character, the narrator does not necessarily share Andrés's outlook and at times makes patent the unfairness of this character's misanthropic judgments. Throughout the first two-thirds of the novel, the protagonist is hardly likable. At the turning point in the narrative, Andrés rather suddenly reveals a previously hidden human side as he seeks out something that had been missing in his life, an attachment to another human being. This bond humanizes the protagonist and temporarily draws him out of his thoughts of suicide. Though he inspires more sympathy in the final chapters of the novel, Andrés continues to be a figure of extreme fragility. A good deal of the discussion of the novel has always been devoted to diagnosing and explaining the boredom, despair, and lack of connection that eventually destroy Andrés.

Some clues to Andrés's problem emerge from the novel's use of both rural and urban settings. The protagonist first appears on his ranch, then wintering in the city, then back in the country. Andrés, like many landed Argentines, divides his time between his agricultural holdings and Buenos Aires. In the two environments Andrés reveals different aspects of his affliction.

In the country Andrés incarnates the rootless Argentine, a figure who often appears in fiction and essays. He is from the landowning class, but the novel emphasizes his indifference to and ignorance of the Argentine countryside and the people who dwell on it. Though Andrés spends at least half of each year living on his ranch, he exercises little leadership there and only fitfully pays attention to its workings. The foreman and his trusty old hands are the ones who really understand the operation and keep it going during the master's frequent periods of distraction. The person who owns the land at times seems like a city slicker on his own estate. When his underlings update him on developments on the ranch, Andrés grows even more bored and irritable than usual. At moments, he disregards common sense about rural living and brings about the apparent death of one of his loyal peons when he insists on crossing a flooded creek on horseback. Accustomed to imported comforts, he is unable to sleep on country linens: "The sheets, some sheets of thick, hard linen, made a disagreeable impression on his skin, accustomed as it was to batiste." [7]

Dependent as Andrés is on the country folk to operate his ranch, he treats them with a disturbing lack of respect. The novel presents many painful, and probably quite realistic, examples of the coarsely imperious way in which the ranch owner addresses the workers. He is uninhibited in using the term *chino,* a pejorative term for country people that contains a reminder of their indigenous ancestry. Andrés never gives a second thought to impregnating the daughter of one of his most loyal and trusting peons and simply leaving her when it is time for him to winter in Buenos Aires. The workers who were raised on the family ranch obey Andrés as the entitled heir, however erratically or insultingly he behaves. A hired hand, though, does not accept the owner's ways, and a minor subplot has to do with his opposition to Andrés.

In the early scenes on the ranch, Cambaceres makes the detached Andrés a negative example of the Argentine landed gentleman. The author is not making a sentimental plea for a return to the soil. There is no suggestion that Andrés should become a work-roughened, hands-on type of rancher, though clearly he should be more conscientious. What Cam-

baceres would like is for the nation's landowning elite to provide responsible leadership for the livestock-growing areas. *Sin rumbo* does not
idealize Argentine peasants, rural labor, or folk culture. Even so, the narrator shows that Andrés's workers are not the annoying primitives that
he perceives them to be. Though the narrator accords scant attention to
the peasants, he depicts them in a relatively sympathetic manner, especially the young woman who has the misfortune to attract the owner's
eye. The novel realistically stresses the rough conditions under which
rural workers live.

Indicative of the novel's vision are the passages in which the narrator
pauses to admire the Argentine plains. He encourages readers to appreciate the almost empty landscape of the pampas: "the infinite swath of
the pampas, a green reflection of the blue sky, helpless, alone, naked,
splendid, drawing its beauty, like a woman, from its very nakedness."[8]
There is no indication that Andrés, absorbed in his own pleasures and
miseries, is aware of the majesty of the lands around him.

As the person who should take charge of these industrious laborers
and admirable scenery, Andrés is remiss. By traditional aristocratic
standards, he is not exhibiting noblesse oblige toward his peasants. By
the liberal criteria typical of Cambaceres, Andrés is doing nothing to
bring about national prosperity and progress. At moments he nearly
drags himself and his sheep-raising operation into financial disaster.

The subsequent thirteen chapters, set in Buenos Aires, show Andrés
still dissatisfied after escaping the tedium of rural life. Dismissing his rustic conquest from his mind, he begins an affair with the prima donna of
a touring Italian opera company. Unlike the simple ranch girl, whom Andrés unceremoniously grabs and tosses onto a nearby bed, the opera star
is an expensive and demanding conquest. In pursuit of her favors, Andrés buys her flowers and jewels and takes her to a sumptuously decorated retreat that he maintains for such occasions. But this accomplished
and relatively sophisticated mistress, passionate, elegant, "majestic, with
that artificial majesty of the queens of the theater,"[9] quickly bores the
protagonist, too. Soon every aspect of the opera star comes to annoy Andrés, from the diva mannerisms that initially attracted him down to her
gait, posture, and left-handedness.

As the narrator describes Andrés's thoughts, it becomes increasingly
clear that the protagonist harbors scorn toward all women. While it is
fair to call him a misogynist, he is not seen treating any man with respect. The narrator says that Andrés associates only with a select few
kindred souls: "An intractable snob, he let no one in who was not of

his school." [10] These soul mates remain unknown, and what the narrator actually shows is Andrés arriving at his men's club and avoiding all interaction.

Just after taking Andrés to an extreme of isolation, the narrative brings him back into contact with a fellow human being. He takes an intense interest in the child that, he realizes, must by now have resulted from his rural mistress's pregnancy. The previously aimless Andrés now throws himself into purposeful action. He rushes back to his ranch, where he discovers that the country girl has died after producing a daughter. The ranch owner proclaims the child to be his, gives her the feminine version of his own name, and sets up a home for her.

The final part of the novel begins with Andrés now transformed into a devoted, if neurotically apprehensive and overindulgent, father. This new era in his life lasts only two years, ending with the daughter's death from diphtheria and Andrés's suicide. Cambaceres crams both these episodes with unnerving details. In the first, a country doctor unsuccessfully attempts to save the toddler by performing a tracheotomy. The distraught father insists on staying in the room, although he almost has a breakdown over "the horrible spectacle. The unfortunate child seemed to him like a lamb with its throat cut." [11] Even more gruesome is the novel's closing scene, in which Andrés disembowels himself in front of his daughter's corpse. Andrés reaches into his abdomen, which he has just slit open, and yanks out his intestines: "A torrent of blood and excrement leapt out; it soiled his face, his clothes, it splattered his daughter's cadaver on the bed, while he, gasping, writhed on the floor." [12]

The scene of Andrés's suicide may be naturalistic in providing unpleasant details. At the same time, this account of self-disembowelment is so lurid as to go beyond naturalism. It would be fair to see in this episode the persistence of romanticism, with its penchant for the portrayal of extreme experiences and out-of-control situations.

Upon its appearance, *Sin rumbo* was admired by more liberal readers but denounced by the Catholic right. It was common knowledge that Cambaceres was an agnostic, and as a legislator he had worked to limit the powers of the Catholic church in Argentina. Conservative critics found it especially easy to associate the shocking features of his work with the moral dangers of godlessness. *Sin rumbo* was singled out, not only for the poor example set by its protagonist, but also for erotic scenes that, while they would scarcely raise eyebrows today, at the time struck many as pornographic.

Sin rumbo is of interest in part as an Argentine example of the fascination, often found in late-nineteenth-century literature, with world-weariness and decadence. Andrés resembles other jaded protagonists of contemporary literature in wallowing in ennui amid sumptuous surroundings. During the waning years of the nineteenth century, French intellectuals discovered the writings of the noted German philosopher Arthur Schopenhauer (1788–1860). Soon there was an international vogue among the literary public for the pessimistic vision of this thinker, whose writings were often blamed for spreading despair and nihilism. The narrator of *Sin rumbo* reports that Andrés is devoted to the writings of Schopenhauer and of other philosophers, such as Friedrich Nietzsche (1844–1900), unlikely to lift his spirits.

The most celebrated example of decadent literature, centered on disaffected protagonists, is the 1884 novel *À rebours* (translated into English as *Against the Grain*) by the French novelist Joris-Karl Huysmans (real name, Charles Marie Georges Huysmans; 1848–1907). *À rebours* is often mentioned in discussions of *Sin rumbo,* and the two novels do have in common the boredom and wealth of their protagonists. Nonetheless, *Sin rumbo* is in other ways unlike the French novel. Among other differences, considerable portions of Cambaceres's novel take place on a sheep ranch, and one of its themes is the responsibility of the Argentine landowning elite to strengthen the nation. Huysmans shows no concern over France's agricultural sector. Aída Apter Cragnolino observes that Huysmans's lead character is a languid young man unable to take action, while Andrés is a robust individual whose energies are misspent rather than lacking. Cragnolino also notes that *Against the Grain* manifests an attitude of aggression toward nature, whereas "in *Sin rumbo* it is a creative environment, Andrés's means of liberty and regeneration." [13]

Noé Jitrik observes a link between certain features of the plot of *Sin rumbo* and Cambaceres's political vision. Jitrik notices that, throughout the novel, Cambaceres shows an unappealing exterior hiding a beautiful interior. The love nest that Andrés maintains for his mistresses appears to be an unimposing structure in a run-down neighborhood, but the interior is lavishly decorated. Andrés, too, appears inconsiderate and ill-humored until his obsession with his daughter reveals his inner wealth of feeling. In Jitrik's analysis, this emphasis on the private virtues of the individual, along with the fact that *Sin rumbo* has only one fully portrayed character, corresponds to Cambaceres's individualistic approach to social problems. Like most members of the progressive circles of the 1880s, Cambaceres does not look for solutions to come from his countrymen making common cause but from especially gifted members of the elite. [14]

Sin rumbo continues to be read, although, as Jitrik observes, it is read by students of literature rather than by the general public.[15] It is partly of continuing interest as one of the limited number of Spanish American narratives that can reasonably be called naturalistic. In addition, *Sin rumbo* is a gripping novel. George D. Schade identifies stylistic features and aspects of the novel's narrative construction that generate dynamism and vitality. He notes that while most novels of the late nineteenth century unroll at a leisurely pace, *Sin rumbo* is highly compressed, moving the story swiftly along through brief, intense chapters that, according to Schade, follow a symmetrical pattern.[16] This critic concludes that "the naturalistic subject matter, which [Cambaceres] handles with the greatest sureness and success in *Sin rumbo,* would not be enough to account for its renown, were it not also for the economy and the art of its structure. The novel possesses an admirable narrative concentration that merits the term *classic.*"[17]

*T*he Caribbean writer most often viewed as a practitioner of Spanish American naturalism is the Puerto Rican physician, journalist, politician, and literary writer Manuel Zeno Gandía (1855–1930). Though he wrote poetry, essays, and narrative fiction, he is most often remembered for his novels. His best-known and most naturalistic novel is *La charca: crónicas de un mundo enfermo* (the two English translations are entitled *La Charca* and *The Pond*), published in Ponce, Puerto Rico, in 1894. The subtitle, which translates as "chronicles of an ailing world," was one that Zeno Gandía gave to all four novels that he published between 1894 and 1925. *La charca* is a novel of rural life set in the coffee-producing mountains of Puerto Rico. The narrator often pauses to provide admiring descriptions of the highland scenery, although it is the backdrop for a human story full of misery and degradation. The novel has two sets of characters, distinguished by social class. Most of the characters are wretchedly poor, illiterate *jíbaros* (peasants), while just three are ruling-class men who have benefited from an excellent education. The novel's main plot is set among the impoverished characters, who become involved in a botched burglary scheme and its aftermath. In contrast to the peasant characters, who throw themselves into the riskiest actions with scarcely a thought, the representatives of the island's elite seldom appear engaged in activity. Instead, the narrator shows them conversing and taking meals together and reveals their thoughts. *La charca*'s three educated characters, a socially aware landowner, a priest, and a doctor, are friends and debating partners who discuss the fundamental nature of the problem afflicting the island and, especially, the population of *jíbaros*. Their conversations focus more on the correct diagnosis of the illness than on the most effective means of combating it. The landowner tends to ponder the island's political situation (still a Spanish colony at the time) and to mull over the various explanations, including a biological basis for human behavior, that social scientists have given for the deplorable condition of a considerable portion of Puerto Rico's population. The priest insists that the spiritual condition of the islanders must be considered first, while the physician's participation in their debates reflects his background in the health sciences.

Of the peasant characters, the one that the novel most spotlights is a sweet young woman named Silvina. Throughout the novel, she struggles unsuccessfully against exploitation by her mother and husband. She is by nature good-hearted and would like to live ethically, but her sordid environment never allows her to do so. She is forced to participate in criminal activity and degrading sexual relations. *La charca* gives special importance to this woman who seeks to rise above her surroundings. Silvina is the first character to appear in the novel, which ends just after she dies by plunging, apparently during a seizure, from a height.

Of the better-educated characters, the landowner Juan del Salto is the one upon whom the novel concentrates. Apart from his conversations with the priest and the doctor, del Salto devotes his spare moments to searching his soul and brooding over the plight of his island. His ruminations, relayed in detail by the omniscient narrator, fill pages of *La charca*. As Laguerre points out, Zeno Gandía made a habit of including in each of the novels in this series at least one character who could function as a "spokesperson" for the author's views.[18] Del Salto is an especially well read and articulate example. In Laguerre's analysis, these "spokesperson-characters" are one of the weaknesses of Zeno Gandía's fiction: "They talk too much and, at the same time, they lack the initiative to act . . . [through them] the author thunders against the criminal silence surrounding the illiterate, hungry peasants, but what effective action do his spokespeople take to avoid such abuses? They simply talk and then let themselves drop away."[19]

A reader of *La charca* may well wonder why del Salto, who in conversation expresses such dismay over the sad state of the *jíbaros*, makes no real effort to improve the status of the peasants working on his own lands. Del Salto tries to be a good landowner; he supervises his estate closely, knows all the peasants personally, and seeks to prevent the overseer from beating the laborers. Yet he speaks to his workers as if they were children who would behave irresponsibly if he were not there to reprove them. Though he is familiar with advanced social ideas, his speech and actions toward members of the peasantry seem little different from those of a traditional benevolent landed squire who regards the *jíbaros* on his land as part of his estate and a lowly part of his family.

There are a number of recent editions of *La charca,* but it was not republished for some time after its first edition in 1894. One may reasonably speculate that readers, especially in Puerto Rico, were upset by the novel's portrayal of the mountain peasants.[20] Drunkenness, crime, and generally unthinking behavior appear to be the norm among this population. At the same time, the novel attributes to the *jíbaros* an underlying strength of character that occasionally expresses itself, as in a scene in which seven peasants leap into raging floodwaters to save a child. Some of the peasants attempt to live in an orderly way despite their poverty. The implication is that these mountain people are by no means inherently depraved, though many have been made so by their wretchedly poor and unhealthy existence.

Throughout the novel the narrator directs readers' attention to the streams and rivulets coursing chaotically down the mountain slopes. Clearly the meandering turbulence of the creeks parallels the disorganized lives of the novel's peasant characters. Aníbal González, while noting this evident metaphor, also sees a philosophical basis for the narrator's preoccupation with water flowing downhill. While Zola drew upon the biological sciences, "instead, the physical science on which Zeno bases his picture of Puerto Rican life is the one on which Lucretius also based his work: the older discipline of hydraulics, a branch of physics that deals with liquids and their flow . . . Zeno often describes his characters as 'atoms' or 'particles' caught in a whirlpool of socioeconomic circumstances they cannot control."[21] In the judgment of this critic, *La charca* is an outstandingly sophisticated novel in great measure because of "its aquatic metaphors and its recourse to hydraulic physics (with all it implies in terms of the role of chance in the narrative)."[22]

Since *La charca* first appeared, readers have become accustomed to the harshness of naturalist novels, and the novel is unlikely to shock. It is now respected as a landmark work of Puerto Rican literature and certainly the first Puerto Rican novel to win widespread notice. In addition to its place in literary history, *La charca* possesses considerable esthetic complexity. Readers also turn to the novel to trace the ways in which Zeno Gandía formulated his ideas about Puerto Rico and its subordinate relations with more powerful nations. Zeno Gandía was one of the most prominent of the island's public figures during a period when Puerto Rico lost the opportunity to become politically independent. *La charca* was composed prior to the 1898 U.S. takeover of Puerto Rico, after which Zeno Gandía became an advocate for the island's independence. He was part of the delegation that, at the height of the 1898 crisis, went to Washington to make the case for granting Puerto Rico political autonomy. The 1894 novel shows the author already troubled by Puerto Rico's disadvantaged situation.

Throughout the 1890s, new writers continued to publish fiction that drew upon naturalism to varying degrees. In Uruguay Javier de Viana (1868–1926) attracted notice during the late nineteenth and early twentieth centuries with his stories of the rough lives of rural people. Later readers may be disturbed by his portrayal of *mestizo* ranch workers as brutal and wily.

Naturalism was still a force when the nineteenth century came to an end. Some distinguished practitioners of Spanish American naturalism, or of realism with some naturalistic elements, made their major impact early in the twentieth century. For this reason Baldomero Lillo (Chile, 1867–1923), whose disturbing stories of miners' lives appeared in the early 1900s, is beyond the scope of this survey. The 1903 Mexican novel *Santa* by Federico Gamboa (1864–1939), noted in the previous chapter's discussion of realism, also exhibits some features of naturalism, along with Christianity and romanticism. The early twentieth century was the period of flourishing of other writers influenced by naturalism, such as the Uruguayan Carlos Reyles (1868–1938).

*M*odernismo was the last important literary movement to appear in nineteenth-century Spanish America. As is often pointed out, it was the first literary tendency to arise in Spanish America, from which it spread to Spain. While *modernismo* is original in this sense, it also has many links with contemporary European writing. As is often noted, *modernistas* were attentive readers of French symbolist and Parnassian poetry and made a creative synthesis of these two tendencies. Spanning the period from the 1880s through the 1910s, although it began to lose force after about 1910, *modernismo* exercised a pervasive influence on Spanish American culture, comparable to that of romanticism earlier in the nineteenth century. While this survey examines only narratives published in the 1800s, it should be kept in mind that *modernismo* continues well into the twentieth century.

Over the years, critics have struggled to define *modernismo*. Here I provide not any absolute definition but rather a working characterization whose purpose is to enable readers to recognize *modernista* writing when they encounter it. In line with the topic of this book, the emphasis is on *modernismo* as it manifested itself in narrative prose. A logical first question is why writers felt compelled to move away from the existing tendencies, which were chiefly romanticism, realism, a limited amount of naturalism, *costumbrismo,* and mixtures of the above.

One of the most frequent complaints about the literary language of romanticism, whether in poetry, theater, or prose, is that precision and polish are sometimes lacking. Romantic writers place highest importance on the expression of feeling and often seek to convey the effect of spontaneity in their work. A tradeoff is involved, since it is difficult for a writer to create the effect of artless outpourings and at the same time cultivate a polished literary language. Romantic writing, intended to disguise the artful nature of literature, at times appears careless. After romanticism had held sway for several decades, the pendulum began to swing back toward a more deliberate, painstaking ideal of writing. Younger writers who had grown up during the romantic period were eager to make greater use of the repertory of techniques and devices available in literary Spanish. They were willing to allow the artifice inherent in literature to be visible. It was no longer so important to appear natural and simple.

The fundamental goal, though, was not to make literary Spanish sound outstandingly artificial but to make it more beautiful and melodious. There was some feeling that romantic and realist authors had failed to take full advantage of the rhythmic qualities of Spanish. The next wave of writers accorded special importance to this issue, whether in poetic meter or the less regular rhythms of prose. Even before the emergence of *modernismo* as such, writers were already devoting more attention to the crafting of their style.

Whether romantic, realistic, or a bit of both, the fictional narratives that enjoyed success during the middle to late nineteenth century generally had strongly marked plots. Romantic novels and short stories are well known for their dramatic twists of fate, dark secrets, astonishing revelations, and bizarre coincidences. Characters unwittingly fall in love with their half siblings, make enormous sacrifices out of hopeless devotion, narrowly escape catastrophes, and pour out long-buried secrets on their deathbeds. As Spanish American fiction shifts away from romanticism and incorporates more features of realism, great importance is still given to impressive plotting. An example is the 1862 *Martín Rivas* by Alberto Blest Gana, a predominantly realist novel with an elegantly designed plot involving interlocking amorous triangles, as discussed in Chapter 4.

As *modernismo* begins to take shape, it becomes less important for narratives to be driven along by an event-filled plot. One experimental subgenre that *modernistas* particularly favored was a type of writing that crossed the genre boundaries between poetry and prose forms. Known variously as poetic prose, artistic prose, or the prose poem, this experimental writing usually took the form of a stretch of beautifully worked and memorable prose describing a scene or evoking an intense moment. Indeed, all of *modernista* prose was affected by the principle that the language of essays and fiction should be as painstakingly crafted as that of verse. Even when *modernistas* composed novels and short stories, the narration of events was not the all-important task it had earlier been, and very little happens in some works of *modernista* fiction. José Olivio Jiménez and Antonio R. de la Campa, seeking to characterize the typical *modernista* short story, give as its primary identifying trait "an extreme attenuation of the plotline, which comes to be almost a mere pretext for setting out the personal intuitions of the author concerning the true theme that underlies the weak plot." [23]

Modernista writing is sometimes called objective, especially by contemporaries. While "objective" is not the best term to apply to any creative writing, one can see why this descriptive term would occur to readers accustomed to literary romanticism. In comparison with the passionate romantics, the *modernistas* assigned a lesser value to feelings and a greater one to information received through the senses. Elaborate, often highly innovative descriptive passages are common in *modernista* narratives. *Modernistas* went beyond the visualization of scenes to refer to other sensory stimuli, including melodious sounds, aromas, tactile phenomena, and unusual sensations from within the body. In this, they drew influences equally from Parnassianism and symbolism, two movements that in their native France had seemed incompatible. *Modernista* writing is also objective in that physical objects figure prominently in it, especially beautiful, luxurious, and rare ones such as exotic urns and other imported items of decor, remarkable gems, and sumptuous interior furnishings.

As the *modernista* tendency gained strength, it acquired more distinctive characteristics. The consolidation of this movement was in great part the work of Rubén Darío (1867–1916), the Nicaraguan-born poet and prose writer who became an international figure and the foremost representative of *modernismo*, which he is generally credited with naming. *Modernismo* eventually became a diverse and wide-ranging phenomenon. It is a broader concept than just the particular stylistic, structural, and linguistic features that mark texts as belonging to *modernismo*. The movement includes as well mystical beliefs about the transforming powers of literary language, a medium that a visionary poet could employ to see the hidden connections between all things in the universe.

With some notable exceptions, *modernista* writing is not as overt in its social commentary as Spanish American literature of earlier in the century. Though their statements about social problems are subtle and oblique, *modernista* writers nonetheless question the values of the society around them. Recent critics have investigated the ways in which *modernismo* constitutes a critique of the changes that Latin American nations were undergoing between 1870 and the First World War. Accelerated technical and economic development and stronger financial ties to U.S. and western European economies were creating what *modernistas* saw as a more mercantile outlook. In the critical perception of some *modernistas,* growth, foreign investment, and international trade were flourishing at the expense of spiritual and artistic values. Along with many other observers, *modernistas* expressed anxiety that Latin American nations would be at a disadvantage in their relations with the United States, which in the 1890s was coming to the fore as a powerful nation with strong interests in the region. These concerns grew more pronounced after the Spanish-American War of 1898 and the U.S. acquisition of the Canal Zone in 1903.

This chapter, though, covers only the first stirrings and the early years of *modernismo,* when it was beginning to coalesce into an organized movement. I am also limiting my coverage to narrative prose. While the *modernistas* produced outstanding examples of the prose poem and of the *crónica* (a brief vignette or commentary, usually first published in a newspaper or magazine), such texts are not fundamentally narrative in nature and therefore fall outside the scope of this study.

*M*odernismo produces a good deal of prose writing, but only a few novels emerge from this movement. Some of the most innovative *modernista* prose is scarcely narrative at all, but rather paints a scene or evokes an intense mood. Even when *modernista* authors compose short stories and novels, they generally rely less on plot than the previous generation of writers did. There is an effort to move away from the type of novel, whether romantic, realistic, or a fusion of the two, in which readers are drawn along by a desire to learn the outcome of hair-raising adventures or to discover the arcane secrets that the protagonists have been harboring. Writers rely less on such time-honored plot devices as characters who fall in love, only to learn that they are half siblings, or long-lost letters that turn up and reveal family secrets. Greater prominence is given to description and to the effort to capture a state of mind.

The *modernista* movement comes on the scene gradually, and no one can identify with certainty its first practitioner. The Cuban writer and independence fighter José (Julián) Martí (y Pérez) (1853–1895) is the best known of the early authors who compose texts in the *modernista* manner. His oeuvre includes a novel, the 1885 *Lucía Jerez,* which Martí published in installments in the New York serial *El Latino-Americano* under the title *Amistad funesta* (Ill-fated friendship). Martí used the female pseudonym Adelaida Ral; the true authorship of the novel came to light only in 1911.[24] The author appears to have had no great esteem for this work, which on first reading can certainly seem to be something of a potboiler.[25] Later readers have had to make a deliberate effort to perceive and appreciate its complexities.

Like many *modernista* narratives, *Lucía Jerez* has a fairly minimal plot. The title character, a socialite who is perennially tormented by obsessive jealousy, becomes the friend of a gorgeous young woman with a guilelessly pure heart. It is soon obvious that trouble lies ahead, and indeed the novel ends with the jealous woman fatally shooting the great beauty. On the way to this outcome, the novel offers numerous descriptions, especially of elegantly dressed women socializing against impressive backgrounds. In some cases, the setting stands out for its artificial, arranged character. For example, Lucía commits her crime at a sophisticated party, painstakingly decorated and illuminated by then-novel electric bulbs concealed among baskets of roses. While the novel makes these highly manipulated and staged environments appear fascinating, it also accords a respectful treatment to the other extreme, nature scarcely marked by human intervention. When the characters are out in the countryside, the unadorned scenery of blue skies and open, uncluttered vistas seems to be the ideal setting. Flowers, both cultivated and naturally occurring varieties, appear frequently throughout the novel. The novel repeatedly turns the reader's attention to the blooms of a large, too carefully pruned magnolia tree in Lucía's yard. The flowers clearly harbor significance, since not only the third-person narrator but also the characters often devote time to their consideration.

Martí's only novel has never really fallen into obscurity, but only in the mid twentieth century did it begin to win critical appreciation. In the 1950s Enrique Anderson Imbert became the first well-known researcher to analyze *Lucía Jerez*. This scholar pointed to the novel as an example of Martí's innovation in developing a lyrical prose style.[26] Of subsequent critics, Manuel Pedro González has been one of the most influential defenders of *Lucía Jerez* as a substantial work, overseeing the 1969 Spanish edition and composing a lengthy critical introduction.[27] This critic heavily favors the "artistic novel" of *modernismo,* whose defining feature is its beautifully composed prose, over the romantic and realistic novels that predominated during most of the nineteenth century. In a drastic comparison González states: "Compare the style of this work with that of any of the many novels written in [Spanish] America and Spain during the nineteenth century and you will notice the esthetic abyss that separates it from them all and outdoes them all in poetic values."[28] While few critics today would express such low regard for the major novels of Spanish-language romanticism and realism, González is correct in seeing *Lucía Jerez* as the beginning of a very different approach to the writing of fiction.

Aníbal González updated the reading of *Lucía Jerez* in his 1987 study of the *modernista* novel.[29] He interprets Martí's novel as an allegory about writing itself. In this critic's reading, *Lucía Jerez* is part of the quest for the type of writing best suited to the expressive needs of Spanish American intellectuals. The tormented Lucía Jerez is, throughout the novel, strongly associated with metaphor. Lucía, with her love of the artificial, resembles the strikingly unusual, at times arcane metaphors devised by creative writers. The innocent beauty who provokes her jealousy is more like a simple metaphor that springs to mind so readily as to seem spontaneous. Following this analysis, "The murder of Leonor/Sol by Lucía marks the triumph, in the novel, of metaphor as a purely artificial, cultural entity."[30] Aníbal González considers *Lucía Jerez* a modern novel because of its inquiry into the nature of literary writing.[31]

The mixed-genre volume *Azul... (Azure;* first edition, 1888) by Darío is the most renowned *modernista* publication. This celebrated book contains poetry, poetic prose, and short stories. In this case it would be difficult to draw a line of demarcation between Darío's short stories as such and his poetic prose texts. One of this writer's great innovations was to spin out fictional texts without requiring the support of a substantial plot. Whether the resulting texts can be called short stories is of secondary importance.

Darío was also given to using short narratives to illustrate his beliefs about art. A number of his protagonists are artists who receive scant respect in a society focused on such bourgeois values as the acquisition and display of wealth. The stories repeatedly make the point that the ideal life is one devoted to esthetic, rather than materialistic, goals. Aníbal González observes that some of the texts in *Azul* . . . that are commonly referred to as short fiction are not primarily stories; they are "at most, allegories of esthetic theories." [32] Readers accustomed to thinking of *Azul* . . . as a *modernista* work may discover with surprise that it includes one short story, "El fardo" ("The Load"), executed in a realist manner tinged with naturalism. Evidently Darío, who was about twenty when he composed the pieces in *Azul* . . . , was still trying out different approaches and had not committed himself exclusively to *modernismo*.

Indisputably, the texts in prose that appear in *Azul* . . . display a high level of originality and experimentation. Even so, they contribute less to innovation in narrative as such than they do to the great renovation in Spanish-language literary prose that Darío and the other *modernistas* would carry out. The prose texts, including those that might be classified as short stories, insistently draw attention to their own elegantly wrought, melodious language.

A story added to the second (1890) edition of *Azul* . . . , "La muerte de la imperatriz de la China" ("The Death of the Empress of China"), hints at the fascination with bizarre psychological twists that would characterize many subsequent *modernista* stories. Again the protagonist is an artist (a sculptor), but the story does not play up his suffering in a society indifferent to esthetic concerns. Instead, it tells the story of a man who falls in love with a porcelain statue. Though the story features a narrator with a chatty, light-hearted manner, it promotes a serious tenet of Darío's program, a belief in the supreme power of art. The sculpted bust exerts a stronger hold on the sculptor's imagination and affections than does his flesh-and-blood wife.

Over the course of his lengthy career, Darío composed a number of short stories, usually for publication in magazines and newspapers. Innovating within the tradition established by Edgar Allan Poe, he often favored strange mental states and paranormal phenomena as subject matter for his stories. One should keep in mind, though, that Darío did not make his mark as a fiction writer or a storyteller. He is renowned as a poet and as a writer of harmonious, artistic prose that often appeals strongly to the senses.

The most widely acclaimed novel produced under the impetus of *modernismo* is the novel *De sobremesa* (After-dinner conversation) by the Colombian José Asunción Silva (1865–1896). *De sobremesa* has a complicated history, both as a manuscript and as a book. The original version of the novel was probably begun in the late 1880s. It was among the manuscripts that Silva lost in the 1895 wreck of *L'Amérique,* the ship he was taking back from Europe. Silva's friend Hernando Villa, concerned over the writer's state of mind, thought a project might revive his spirits. Villa asked Silva to describe the lost texts, then urged him to regenerate one of them. According to an often-circulated story, the author asked Villa to choose the project that he deemed worthiest of reconstructing, and his friend chose the novel. In 1896 Silva completed a new version of the lost novel but committed suicide that year.

The novel was not published in its entirety until 1925. Between 1896 and 1925, and even after the complete novel had appeared in print, excerpts from *De sobremesa* were published. These are passages in which the novel's protagonist expounds his views, but when published out of context, they appear to be essays in Silva's own voice.[33] As Betty Tyree Osiek observes, this practice resulted in Silva's imaginative writing being "used to prove different ideas that the author could not possibly have meant."[34] Osiek represents the widespread belief that Silva's family delayed the publication of the novel in complete form, feeling that it might damage the Silva name with its "shock value."[35]

The title *De sobremesa* refers to conversation carried on at the table after a meal. It is a leisure-class custom, for those who can linger without attending to business or chores. José Fernández, the protagonist of *De sobremesa,* is a wealthy, refined esthete who appears to live chiefly on his fortune. He only occasionally refers, with evident boredom, to some financial transaction or diplomatic charge that he has had to carry out. The rest of his time, his attention goes to the appreciation of paintings, of which he is a connoisseur, his inner state of being, and the quest for an elusive feminine ideal. As the novel opens, Fernández has attained some success as a poet. In recent years, though, he has not been focused enough to write poetry, instead becoming a dilettante who makes superficial headway in various areas. He has been dabbling in radical politics, cultivating rare hothouse blooms, and studying Arabic for his sideline as an amateur archeologist. He is devising a plan whereby he would become the benevolent dictator of Colombia and force it to prosper. This project, laid out at some length in his diary, sounds both fascistic and hare-brained. In between these more or less intellectual pursuits, Fernández has been devoting considerable energy to his erotic exploits.

The after-dinner exchange, narrated in the third person, occupies relatively little space in the novel. Its purpose is to frame Fernández's intimate journal, which is transcribed into the novel as the fictitious author reads it aloud. Fernández has invited over some of his kindred spirits. The narrator provides a detailed description of the sumptuous interior of Fernández's home. The implication is that the décor attests not only to the owner's wealth but also to his fascination with beautiful things. The conversation leads to a request for Fernández to read aloud a journal that he composed during his recent European stay. One of the listeners gives some tantalizing clues as to the contents of the manuscript. For example, it should reveal the meaning of an emblem, a butterfly hovering over three leaves, that Fernández has adopted lately.

Fernández is easy to recognize as a typically uncommitted, decadent character. He is a clearer instance of this literary phenomenon than Andrés, the erratic hero of Cambaceres's *Sin rumbo,* since the latter at moments takes an interest in his sheep ranch and attempts to be a devoted father. Fernández wanders about western Europe in a state of dissatisfaction, distracting himself by successfully pursuing a number of women. By preference, he seeks out high-strung, worldly, sexually skilled women who are accustomed to staying in grand hotels. Some are aristocratic libertines; others are demimondaines. Toward the end of his diary, Fernández becomes addicted to the thrill of poaching other men's spouses, in one case cuckolding a friend who has asked him to keep his wife entertained. He takes to bed an international variety of married beauties, including the daughter of an American robber baron and a German baroness who identifies him with Nietzsche's concept of the superman. While Fernández only occasionally pays outright for sex, he attracts women by displaying his wealth and taste, so his sizable fortune is a factor in his erotic success. These easy conquests leave him with a sense of revulsion and a feeling that sexually active women are a menace to his well-being. Critics of the novel have often remarked on Fernández's tortuous, contradictory relations with his mistresses. Aníbal González notes that "Fernández fancies himself a Don Juan, although he also claims to have been emotionally victimized by women."[36] As later events reveal, Fernández categorizes women, following the tradition of machismo, as either whores or sexless saints.

Relying on opium to relieve his world-weariness, Fernández outwardly fits the profile of a wealthy, bored South American, traveling through Europe in search of esthetic stimulation and sensual pleasures. Inwardly, though, he desires more transcendental fulfillment. Though Fernández is an advanced thinker in some regards, he still harbors the long-standing Catholic ideal of the asexual, selfless woman. In the dining hall of a hotel in Geneva, longing to rise above his dissipated existence, he catches sight of Helena, a fifteen-year-old girl who fulfills his criteria for female perfection. This pale, mysterious creature, with long, slender hands, her hair a proliferation of tendrils, is the exact type of unearthly beauty idealized by the Pre-Raphaelite Brotherhood. It should be remembered that Pre-Raphaelite painting was admired in *modernista* circles for its deliberate artifice, self-consciousness, and rejection of realism. Fernández notices that Helena is registering in his mind more as an abstraction than as a woman: "A strange idea crossed my mind. That name, Helena, did not evoke in me any image of a woman that would go with it . . . I dreamed of Princess Helen in Tennyson's idyll."[37] As González observes, "Helena is nothing more than a vision, an object of contemplation, or, concretely, a painting."[38]

This ethereal being is accompanied by her father, an ascetic, melancholy man who also appears more spirit than flesh. Helena has little in common with the sexually knowledgeable women whom Fernández customarily pursues. Though the two never speak to one another, going no further than exchanging glances, he is certain that she is pure and innocent. He describes her in worshipful terms. When the young beauty looks his way, "That gaze poured over my spirit the peace that descends upon the heart of a Christian after making a confession and receiving absolution; a deep, humble peace, filled with gratitude for the divine compassion that I read in her eyes."[39] Helena leaves behind an object, which Fernández retrieves: a cameo decorated with a butterfly above three leaves. Finding no opportunity to return it to her, Fernández preserves the brooch as a relic and adopts the figure upon it as his personal emblem.

To describe Helena and evoke her exceptional presence, Fernández alludes to paintings that he admires. These references are one of many clues that, for Fernández, women, exercising attraction through their appearance, are associated with art and the spell that it casts through representation. Indeed, Fernández's quest for Helena leads not to her person but first to the cameo and then to a Pre-Raphaelite painting that could easily be her portrait, though it is that of her mother. Researching the portrait, Fernández learns that his beloved is related to Lizzie Siddal, the celebrated muse of the Pre-Raphaelite painter and poet Dante Gabriel Rossetti (1828–1882). While many of the paintings to which Fernández alludes in his journal exist in the real world, this portrait is apparently a fiction.[40]

From Fernández's perspective, possession of the painting is in several respects more satisfactory than it would be to find Helena herself. Since he adores her as a figure of chastity, it would be counterproductive to add her to his growing list of conquests. Another problem becomes evident when Fernández consults a neurologist with a philosophical bent. The physician urges him to locate Helena, marry her, and lead a well-regulated existence. This suggestion revolts Fernández. Although he seeks an alternative to living in dissipation, he does not want any part of bourgeois normality. Besides, a member of one's household cannot remain an ideal. Fernández recalls his reaction at the doctor's words: "My god, I, Helena's husband! Helena, my wife! The intimacy of daily contact, the details of married life, that vision deformed by motherhood."[41]

Helena is connected to the other pure woman in Fernández's life, the pious grandmother who dotes on her wayward descendant. Shortly before Helena appears, this matriarch has died. Fernández transcribes into his diary a letter from home that contains an account of his grandmother's last hours, spent in what sounds like delirious prayer. At first she pleads with God to save Fernández from perdition. A revelation relieves her anxiety, and she utters this mysterious sentence: "Blessed be the sign of the cross made by the hand of the virgin and the bouquet of roses that fall in her night like a sign of salvation!"[42] Fernández believes the prophecy to be fulfilled when a silhouetted figure appears on the balcony of Helena's room, makes the sign of the cross, and casts down to him a bouquet of white roses.

Other links connect Helena to several European countries. She appears in Geneva, having just come from Nice, France. Fernández overhears Helena and her father conversing in Italian and gathers that they have been roaming the Continent. In addition, Helena has a British connection as a relation of Rossetti's celebrated model. Helena's affiliations with securely established European nations add to the mystique in which Fernández envelops her. Peter Elmore observes that Fernández, a South American whom the French view as a nouveau riche upstart, is in love with "the quintessence of European spirituality." This critic suggests that the love of an ultra-European lady is a symptom of the *modernistas*' enchantment with the high status of certain foreign countries.[43]

At the end of Fernández's diary, he reports coming across Helena's tombstone. Although the discovery throws him into a fresh crisis, he realizes that he cannot mourn Helena as he would a woman. He tells her, "Perhaps you have never existed and you are only a luminous dream of my spirit."[44] The conjecture that Helena has been Fernández's dream or projection is plausible, since throughout the diary Helena's personality and character are assigned to her by her admirer rather than manifested by her behavior. Very little information about her has come from sources other than Fernández himself.

Readers have long given thought to what Fernández represents. This character has often been conflated with Silva himself. An example is the earlier-noted practice of publishing the fictional character's reflections as if they were the author's own essays. Yet some obvious factors distinguish the character from his creator. Fernández has accomplished nothing substantial over the past seven years, while Silva was a productive writer. The fictional esthete is fabulously wealthy and only on rare occasions needs to turn his mind to financial concerns. During the years he wrote his novel, Silva was involved in an unsuccessful struggle to keep his family's business afloat. But more significant than these biographical considerations are the many indications that Silva is offering a critical look at an intellectually gifted Colombian gentleman who squanders his potential. A major clue is the incoherence with which Fernández expounds his scheme to rule the country and force it to develop according to his ideas.

It seems unlikely that Fernández is a stand-in for either Silva or any other particular individual. More plausible is the idea that, through the characterization of Fernández, Silva is presenting a critical examination of a more general category of people, their potential strengths and their current shortcomings. Aníbal González pursues this notion, viewing *De sobremesa* as one of several late-nineteenth-century narratives that show the difficult emergence of modern intellectuals on the Spanish American cultural scene. Certainly Latin American countries had many well-read, up-to-date people who were concerned with ideas. In this critic's analysis, these individuals did not become modern intellectuals but rather men of action, such as the independence leaders and the leaders of the subsequent task of nation-building, or men and women of letters. (Careers in public service were reserved for men, while women had made some headway in the field of literature.) A wider-ranging intellectual life had not yet coalesced around common goals and issues to be thrashed out in a public discussion. There was a widespread sense that the life of the mind did not yet have a mission in the Latin American nations. González finds most significant "the 'self-portrait' . . . that Silva produces in his novel, of a Spanish American writer on the eve of his transformation into an intellectual."[45]

In González's analysis, the narrative thread of *De sobremesa* shows a composite figure of the thinking Latin American, well versed in the latest cultural trends, but in uneasy search of an intellectual agenda. As the novel opens, Fernández has spent years roaming from place to place, darting from one woman's bed to the next, dabbling in various scholarly disciplines and spiritualistic endeavors, and developing his grandiose political plan. For González, this restless dilettantism represents "the ceaseless groping of turn-of-the century writers . . . in search of an ideology, a cause, a transcendent principle." [46] After catching sight of his ideal, Fernández abandons his political project "to devote himself to the cult of Helena, which is, of course, the cult of fiction, of Art (with a capital *A*)." [47] This change in Fernández corresponds to a tendency under way among real-world Latin American thinkers and creative people, who were beginning to look to art as the force that would transform society and human life. One of the central tenets of *modernismo* is an exceptional belief in the powers of artistic creation.

De sobremesa is a valuable repository of ideas that were fashionable in the closing years of the nineteenth century. Fernández is ceaselessly up to the minute, and his dilettantism has been in the current hot areas. He studies archeology and ancient religions just as astonishing discoveries in Egypt and elsewhere are fascinating the public worldwide. His references to literary and philosophical works provide readers today with a list of what one read in the 1890s to keep current, from Nietzsche to theosophical writings to the diary of Marie Bashkirtseff.

Especially revealing of 1890s thought are the lengthy visits that Fernández has with two neurologists whom he respects. Fernández seeks medical attention because of collapses, often following stints of wild living, that can leave him incapacitated for days. His interchanges with the two thoughtful neurologists often resemble leisurely conversations more than they do medical consultations. As Peter Elmore remarks, "In this novel doctors are not there to cure, but to offer the narrator clues" to the mysteries that tantalize him. [48]

The two neurologists represent divergent contemporary notions of what constitutes health. One of the physicians, an Englishman, takes a holistic outlook and advocates moderation in all things, stability, and rational good sense. The other, named Charvet in the novel, is most likely a literary version of Jean Martin Charcot (1825–1893), the founder of clinical neurology who mentored Sigmund Freud and Georges Gilles de la Tourette. The English doctor, Rivington, prides himself on taking a humanistic and philosophical approach to his patients, and knows a fair amount about art and literature. Though he is sympathetically portrayed, his value-laden approach at times weakens his rapport with Fernández. The patient suspects that the doctor wants to rid him not only of his illness but also of his exceptionality, making him stodgier and more bourgeois. Rivington's recommendation that Fernández transform Helena into his wife and the mother of his children shows that he is not fully attuned to the notion of Helena as an ideal. Fernández does not care to be demystified but rather to be vigorous enough to pursue his mystique. Yet, in other ways, this same physician wins Fernández's gratitude and trust. It is he who supplies the portrait of Helena's mother.

Benigno Trigo has examined the sources of Rivington's concepts of health. In his analysis, Rivington is applying the theory of consciousness developed by Max Nordau (1849–1923), the German physician and essayist who exercised considerable influence in the late nineteenth and early twentieth centuries.[49] As Trigo points out, in the view of both the real-world Nordau and the fictional Rivington, human beings are constantly in danger of going out of balance and must focus their energy on self-governance and the maintenance of normality. Such thinkers "turn the state of well-being and normality into an ideal state that must be maintained at all costs."[50] Trigo suggests that Rivington may be asking too great a sacrifice from Fernández to achieve such a well-managed, regulated condition. If Fernández were to follow all of this physician's advice, he would lose his distinctive characteristics and his most intense pleasures.

Charvet also expresses concern over Fernández's irregular life, which certainly appears to be undermining his health. Yet he is more respectful of his patient's need to be extraordinary and original. Although he is also knowledgeable about art and contemporary thought, his approach to medicine is more value-free and clinical. The French doctor comprehends that, while Fernández seeks to avoid actual illness, he does not desire to be normal. This doctor avoids any attempt to make his patient average. While Charvet does not seek to impose his beliefs on Fernández, there is relatively little he can do for him. When Fernández inquires about the name of his syndrome, Charvet, much to his credit, confesses that he has no diagnostic category in which to place it. (His real-world model, Charcot, is remembered for recognizing, defining, and labeling a number of neurological syndromes that are today almost common knowledge. The novel suggests that the fictional Charvet is an excellent diagnostician, but also aware of the limits of diagnosis.)

Less-than-clever physicians also make an appearance in the novel, providing a comic note and satirizing some of the shortcomings of modern medicine. In Paris, with New Year's approaching, Fernández becomes unable to do more than lie in bed moaning. He suddenly discovers his room swarming with physicians that his servant has summoned. The physicians are baffled by Fernández's symptoms, but their professional pride compels them to make an authoritative-sounding pronouncement. Their spokesman gives Fernández a pompous speech, reciting the catalogue of neurological diagnostic labels. The late nineteenth century was the period when clinical neurology was struggling to become established, with a resultant proliferation of diagnoses. Fernández takes amusement in the doctor, who speaks "in an especially self-satisfied way of the recently invented diseases, of *railway brain* and *railway spine,* of all the morbid fears."[51] Despite these physicians' display of up-to-date terminology, the only treatment that they can think of is the time-honored purgative, "as if a horse were involved."[52]

It is not easy to make a single evaluation of the esthetic value of *De sobremesa.* Idiosyncratic in its narrative organization, the novel from some perspectives seems less than optimally composed. At the same time, it is absorbingly complex, particularly in its intricate weave of allusions and references. Whatever readers' judgment on its unity of composition, *De sobremesa* is of great worth for its exemplification of the *modernista* outlook and for the information it contains about the intellectual world of an up-to-date South American gentleman of the 1890s.

In thinking about *modernismo* in prose fiction, one should remember that the movement continued to exercise an influence for some years into the twentieth century. As well as the above-discussed works by Martí and Silva, the *modernista* novel includes works that Manuel Díaz Rodríguez (Venezuela, 1887–1927) published in the earliest years of the then-new century, starting with *Ídolos rotos* (Broken idols) in 1901. Leopoldo Lugones (Argentina, 1874–1938) brought out what may well be the single most impressive collection of *modernista* short stories, *Las fuerzas extrañas* (*Strange Forces*) in 1906. In 1908 another Argentine writer, Enrique Larreta (1875–1961) published one of the most widely read *modernista* novels, *La gloria de don Ramiro* (The glory of Don Ramiro). Horacio Quiroga (Uruguay-Argentina, 1878–1937), one of the masters of the Spanish American short story, began his career as a *modernista* poet and, though he changed his esthetic before composing his celebrated short stories, *modernista* elements are evident in these works. *Modernista* traits continue to appear in novels and short stories published farther into the twentieth century. One of the best-known novels to draw substantially on *modernismo* is *Alsino* by the Chilean writer Pedro Prado (1886–1952); this work was first published in 1920. The *modernista* spirit of experimentation, especially in literary language, never ceases to exert an influence.

CONCLUSION
Then and Now

This survey comes to an end in 1900, although many of the tendencies characterized in the sections on the late nineteenth century are still going full force as the nineteenth century ends. In conclusion, I would like to consider briefly the relations between, on the one hand, early Spanish American narrative and, on the other, scholarship, creative writing, and general public knowledge in the twentieth and twenty-first centuries.

The narrative accounts of the events of the Spanish conquest have certainly fared well in recent times. From the second half of the twentieth century onward, there has been a sharp rise in the attention paid to these early writings, both in scholarly circles and among nonspecialists. The cultural programs designed to commemorate the five hundredth anniversary of Columbus's landing undeniably stimulated both scholarly research into and public interest in the conquest and colonization era.

But the 1992 commemoration of the "Encounter of Two Cultures" does not account for all the research and creative undertakings that look back to the conquest and the documents that recorded it. Well before 1992, the period of the conquest had already been drawing fresh attention, in large measure as a result of the advent of colonial and postcolonial studies.

One indication of this fascination with the "chronicles of the Indies" is the number of new editions of works that narrate the conquest and its aftermath. Some are critical editions with extensive scholarly annotations while others are intended for a broader readership. Not only have new Spanish-language editions been appearing, but also English-language publishers have brought out some worthy translations. An excellent example of the latter is the English version that Frances M. López-Morillas made of Alvar Núñez Cabeza de Vaca's *Naufragios.* This English edition, *Castaways: The Narrative of Alvar Núñez Cabeza de Vaca,* is cited in Chapter 1 of this study. In addition, filmmakers have revisited the conquest on a number of occasions. Well-known examples include *Aguirre, or the Wrath of God,* the 1972 film directed by Werner

Herzog, and the 1992 *Cabeza de Vaca,* a Spanish-Mexican production directed by Nicolás Echeverría.

The perspective and expression of the Amerindian communities, whether before, during, or following the conquest, are increasingly being taken into account. To explore the records left by indigenous peoples, researchers have had to expand their concept of what constitutes writing. Scholars are finding it necessary to acquire and utilize knowledge of indigenous languages and of a wide variety of notational and representational systems, including some that have a considerable pictorial element. Research in this area brings the insights of archeology, cultural anthropology, and art history to bear on literary studies. The bibliography to this volume lists several examples of innovative recent research on the narrative of the period of the conquest and the Spanish colonial regime.

Another sign of the renewed concern with these accounts is the revisiting of the conquest in recent historical novels by Spanish American writers. Since the 1970s, the production of new works that critically re-examine Spanish American history has become a very marked phenomenon. It is the topic of such studies as *Latin America's New Historical Novel* (1993) by Seymour Menton. In a number of these cases, the new historical novels are imaginative rewritings of early accounts by conquistadors, missionary priests, and others involved in the conquest and subsequent colonization effort. The Argentine novelist Abel Posse (b. 1936) draws extensively on records of the conquest in the writing of his three novels collectively known as the Columbus trilogy. The first of these, *Daimón* (1978), re-elaborates the story of Lope de Aguirre. The figure of this conquistador-explorer, remembered both for his grandiose delusions and for his rebellion against Spanish colonial officials, raises questions about imperialism, authority, and other perennial issues. Posse's 1983 *Los perros del paraíso* (*The Dogs of Paradise*) revisits the story of Columbus, while his *El largo atardecer del caminante* (The long dusk of the traveler, 1992) is a new, imaginative reworking of Cabeza de Vaca's account of his wanderings. In Posse's case, the motive for a fresh exploration of the era of the conquest is very often an undisguised desire to comment indirectly on the issues of the author's own time.

Fresh attention has also centered on the more settled colonial era that followed the major campaigns of conquest. An increase in scholarly activity is indicated by, among other signs, the 1992 founding of the *Colonial Latin American Review.* Among nonspecialists there has been enormous fascination with Sor Juana Inés de la Cruz. The circumstances of her life and her celebrated letter of self-defense, discussed in Chapter 2, have attracted greater notice than Sor Juana's baroque poetry and drama. The 1982 appearance of the book-length essay *Sor Juana or, The Traps of Faith,* by the distinguished Mexican thinker Octavio Paz, greatly stimulated the public's enthusiasm for everything related to Sor Juana. So did the new feminist readings of Sor Juana discussed in Chapter 2. Since the late years of the twentieth century, the focus of attention has broadened somewhat to include other women writers of the colonial era. This development is especially noteworthy if one remembers that, until recent years, few readers could name colonial women writers other than Sor Juana. Students of Spanish American literature are still discovering, with amazement, how many women wrote during the period of Spanish colonial rule.

The phenomenon of the baroque presents scholars with an apparently inexhaustible research topic. While all aspects of baroque studies continue to flourish, the *barroco de Indias* (baroque of the Indies), writing in this style carried out in the Spanish American colonies, has particularly attracted critics. One often-stated hypothesis is that the baroque writing of Spain's American lands contains encoded or implied resistance, whether to colonial rule or toward authority generally. A great proportion of studies of the literary baroque focuses on writing in verse, whether poetry or drama, probably because of the higher frequency with which baroque stylistic features occur in verse genres. Manifestations of the baroque in prose narrative have not come in for as much attention. Baroque prose may attract more notice as students of the baroque seek new research topics.

When one examines the literary and cultural currents of the nineteenth century, it becomes clear that many of the tendencies of that era are still making themselves felt. The nationalistic concerns that often dominated nineteenth-century Spanish American writing have scarcely died out over the years. The global interconnections of current-day life have not prevented nationalism from being an unavoidable force in society and politics. As well as being a enduring factor in real-world politics, nationalism is attracting growing attention from scholars. Renewed concern with this phenomenon leads researchers back to the nineteenth-century fiction of Spanish America, as witness the impact made by Doris Sommer's 1991 *Foundational Fictions: The National Romances of Latin America.*

Researchers are not concerned with nineteenth-century Spanish American narrative simply as raw material from which to extract evidence of the beliefs and attitudes of contemporary intellectuals. The fiction of this era, and particularly the novels that commanded such attention among readers of the period, have come in for new appreciation as artistic works whose structural and linguistic features deserve closer analysis. An example of this concern for the narrative construction of nineteenth-century fiction is John S. Brushwood's 1981 *Genteel Barbarism: Experiments in Analysis of Nineteenth-Century Spanish-American Novels.*

It was during the nineteenth century that significant numbers of women began participating publicly in Spanish American literary life. Over the past few decades, researchers have discovered many more women writers from the nineteenth century than had initially been expected. No doubt many more remain to be encountered.

Two literary tendencies of the latter nineteenth century, realism and *modernismo,* continue to exercise an influence. The realist strain in Spanish American fiction has been continuous, although during some periods literary realism has been eclipsed by narrative composed in a more highly inventive and imaginative manner. *Modernismo* as such played itself out early in the twentieth century, but its indirect effects continue to the present day. The *modernista* preoccupation with creating innovations in literary language reemerges in such later movements as the Spanish American vanguard movements and the "Boom" novel of the 1960s. In addition, *modernismo* is strongly associated with the effort to develop a distinctively Spanish American mode of literary expression. This drive has certainly never lost its impetus.

Spanish American writing of the twentieth and twenty-first centuries is often studied as a topic unto itself. Undeniably, a great deal of worthy literature has appeared since 1900, more than enough to provide the subject matter for a course or a panoramic study. Few would like to see less attention paid to the literature of more recent centuries. Yet the reading of post-1900 Spanish American literature is considerably enriched by a basic knowledge of colonial and nineteenth-century authors, works, and tendencies. It is my hope that the current study will not only help acquaint readers with Spanish American narrative up to 1900 but also strengthen their understanding of more recent writing by Spanish American authors.

ᕽNOTES

Introduction and Background

1. Martín Lienhard, *La voz y su huella: escritura y conflicto étnico-social en América Latina 1492–1988,* 3rd rev. ed. (Lima: Editorial Horizonte, 1992), 45.

2. Ibid., 46.

3. Walter D. Mignolo, *The Darker Side of the Renaissance: Literacy, Territoriality, and Colonization* (Ann Arbor: University of Michigan Press, 1995), 77.

4. Lienhard, *La voz y su huella,* 47.

5. Ibid., 46.

6. Jeffrey Quilter and Gary Urton, eds., *Narrative Threads: Accounting and Recounting in Andean Khipu* (Austin: University of Texas Press, 2002).

7. Mignolo, *The Darker Side of the Renaissance,* 77.

8. Lienhard, *La voz y su huella,* 31.

9. Ibid., 55.

10. Miguel León-Portilla, ed., *The Broken Spears: The Aztec Account of the Conquest of Mexico,* rev. ed., trans. Angel María Garibay and Lysander Kemp (Boston: Beacon, 1992).

11. Beatriz Pastor, *The Armature of Conquest: Spanish Accounts of the Discovery of America, 1492–1589,* trans. Lydia Longstreth Hunt (Stanford: Stanford University Press, 1992). Spanish edition, *Discursos narrativos de la conquista: Mitificación y emergencia,* rev. ed. (Hanover, N.H.: Ediciones del Norte, 1988).

12. Dennis Tedlock, *Popol Vuh: The Mayan Book of the Dawn of Life, With Commentary Based on the Ancient Knowledge of the Modern Quiche Maya,* rev. ed. (New York: Simon and Schuster, 1996), 28.

13. Ibid., 29–30.

14. Ibid., 30.

1. Narrative Accounts of the Encounter and Conquest

1. Margarita Zamora, *Reading Columbus* (Berkeley: University of California Press, 1993), 39.

2. Ibid., 72.

3. Pastor, *The Armature of Conquest,* 28.

4. Ibid., 36.

5. Zamora, "'If Cohonaboa learns to speak...': Amerindian Voice in the Discourse of Discovery," *Colonial Latin American Review* 8, no. 2 (1999): 192–193.

6. Ibid., 191–205.

7. Pastor, *The Armature of Conquest*, 44.

8. Christopher Columbus, *The Log of Christopher Columbus*, trans. Robert H. Fuson (Southampton, Eng.: Ashford Press, 1987), 77.

9. Ibid.

10. Ibid., 79.

11. Ibid., 107.

12. Ibid., 120.

13. Lienhard, *La voz y su huella*, 49.

14. Zamora, "'If Cohonaboa learns to speak...,'" 92–93.

15. Pastor, *The Armature of Conquest*, 46, typifies the modern reader's horror at Columbus's use of *head* to state the number of women captives.

16. Sandra Messinger Cypess, *La Malinche in Mexican Literature: From History to Myth* (Austin: University of Texas Press, 1991).

17. Hernán Cortés, *Letters from Mexico*, ed. and trans. Anthony Padgen (New Haven: Yale University Press, 1986), 73.

18. Ibid., 74.

19. Ibid., 51–52.

20. Ibid., 73.

21. Ibid., 84.

22. Ibid., 85–86.

23. Ibid., 86–87.

24. Ibid., 88.

25. Ibid., 166.

26. Ibid., 132.

27. Fernando de Alva Ixtlilxochitl, in León-Portilla, ed., *The Broken Spears*, 90. To read this passage in context, see Alva Ixtlilxochitl, "Relación de venida de los españoles y principio de la ley evangélica," in Bernardino de Sahagún, *Historia general de las cosas de Nueva España*, ed. Angel María Garibay K. (Mexico City: Porrúa, 1956), 1:194.

28. Códice Ramírez (anonymous), in Hernando Alvarado Tezozomoc, *Crónica mexicana* (Mexico City: Porrúa, 1980), 144–145. For an English translation of the critical passage in this account, see Pastor, *The Armature of Conquest*, 71.

29. Bernardino de Sahagún, *Conquest of New Spain, 1585 Revision*, trans. Howard F. Cline and S. L. Cline (Salt Lake City: University of Utah Press, 1989), 84. This volume later seems to be correcting the Aztec account by including a speech by Cortés to the Aztec nobles in which he justifies the Spanish troops' actions, denies Spanish responsibility for Moctezuma's death, and states, "You threw stones at him in such a fashion that you wounded him; he died from the stoning he received from you" (107).

30. Ibid., 85.

31. Pastor, *The Armature of Conquest,* 68.

32. Ibid., 69.

33. Ibid.

34. Zamora, "'If Cohonaboa learns to speak . . . ,'" 93.

35. Alvar Núñez Cabeza de Vaca, *Castaways: The Narrative of Alvar Núñez Cabeza de Vaca,* trans. Frances M. López-Morillas, ed. Enrique Pupo-Walker (Berkeley: University of California Press, 1993), 14.

36. Ibid., 7.

37. Ibid., 42.

38. Ibid., 49.

39. Ibid.

40. Ibid., 72.

41. Ibid., 110.

42. Bernal Díaz del Castillo, "Preface by the Author," in his *Discovery and Conquest of Mexico,* trans. A. P. Maudslay (New York: Grove Press, 1958), xxxiii.

43. Joaquín Ramírez Cabañas, "Introducción," in Díaz del Castillo, *Historia verdadera de la conquista de la Nueva España* (Mexico City: Porrúa, 1960), 17.

44. Díaz, *Discovery and Conquest of Mexico,* 138.

45. Ibid., 67.

46. Ibid., 135.

47. Ibid., 178.

48. Ibid., 179.

49. Ibid., 294.

50. Ibid., 310.

51. Cabeza de Vaca, *Castaways,* 126.

52. Sahagún, *Conquest of New Spain,* 31.

53. Ibid., 43.

54. Ibid., 64.

2. The Seventeenth and Eighteenth Centuries

1. Garcilaso de la Vega, El Inca, "Preface to the Reader," in his *Royal Commentaries of the Incas and General History of Peru,* trans. Harold V. Livermore, foreword Arnold J. Toynbee (Austin: University of Texas Press, 1966), 4.

2. Ibid., 62.

3. Ibid., 50.

4. Ibid.

5. Ibid., 331–332.

6. Alberto Escobar, "Lenguaje e historia en los *Comentarios reales,*" in César Toro Montalvo, ed., *Los garcilasistas: antología* (Lima: Universidad Inca Garcilaso de La Vega/Consejo Nacional de Ciencia y Tecnología, 1989), 298–321.

7. See, for example, José Antonio Mazzotti, *Coros mestizos del Inca Garcilaso: resonancias andinas* (Mexico City: Fondo de Cultura Económica, 1996).

Mazzotti examines the elements of Andean oral tradition that figure in the written works of the Inca Garcilaso. He emphasizes that he is not seeking to isolate the features that the Inca Garcilaso derived from his background as a participant in this oral culture; rather he is concerned with showing how the Inca made a dynamic synthesis of these traits and the other tradition he had mastered, that of European philosophy and belles lettres.

8. Garcilaso, *Royal Commentaries,* 574.

9. Ibid.

10. Ibid., 230–231.

11. Ibid., 232.

12. Ibid., 70.

13. Ibid.

14. Ibid., 30.

15. Ibid., 36.

16. Ibid., 37.

17. Ibid., 87.

18. Ibid., 86.

19. Ibid., 17.

20. Ibid., 607.

21. Garcilaso, "Prólogo," in his *Historia general del Perú* (Córdoba: Viuda de Andrés de Barrera, 1616), n.p. Facsimile edition in Benson Latin American Collection, University of Texas at Austin.

22. Garcilaso, addendum to dedication, in his *Historia general del Perú,* n.p.

23. Rolena Adorno, *Cronista y príncipe: la obra de don Felipe Guaman Poma de Ayala* (Lima: Pontificia Universidad Católica del Perú, 1989), 86.

24. For a summary of the travels of the manuscript, see ibid., 51.

25. Ibid., 24.

26. Ibid., 87.

27. With reference to this assertion, Adorno, ibid., observes, "This legend and others similar to it were very widespread in the colonial era" (15).

28. Dario Achury Valenzuela explores the possible meanings of the title in "De la palabra 'carnero' y su polisemia," a section of his foreword to Juan Rodríguez Freyle, *El carnero* (Caracas: Ayacucho, 1979), l–lvi.

29. David William Foster, "Notes Toward Reading Juan Rodríguez Freyle's *El carnero:* The Image of the Narrator," *Revista de Estudios Colombianos* 1 (1986): 3.

30. Ibid., 4.

31. Ibid., 11. The entire study runs 1–15.

32. Ibid., 15.

33. Ibid., 8.

34. Georgina Sabat-Rivers, "A Feminist Rereading of Sor Juana's *Dream,*" in Stephanie Merrim, ed., *Feminist Perspectives on Sor Juana Inés de la Cruz* (Detroit: Wayne State University Press, 1991), 143.

35. Sor Juana Inés de la Cruz, *A Woman of Genius: The Intellectual Autobiog-*

raphy of Sor Juana Inés de la Cruz, trans. Margaret Sayers Peden (Salisbury, Conn.: Lime Rock Press, 1982).

36. Sor Juana Inés de la Cruz, "The Reply to Sor Philotea," in *A Sor Juana Anthology,* ed. and trans. Alan Trueblood, foreword by Octavio Paz (Cambridge: Harvard University Press, 1988), 205–245.

37. Sor Juana Inés de la Cruz, "The Poet's Answer to the Most Illustrious Sor Filotea de la Cruz," in *The Answer=La respuesta,* ed. and trans. Electa Arenal and Amanda Powell (New York: Feminist Press at the City University of New York, 1994), 38–105, annotations 106–143.

38. Asunción Lavrín, "Unlike Sor Juana? The Model Nun in the Religious Literature of Colonial Mexico," in Merrim, ed., *Feminist Perspectives,* 77.

39. Electa Arenal and Stacey Schlau, eds., *Untold Sisters: Hispanic Nuns in Their Own Works,* trans. Amanda Powell (Albuquerque: University of New Mexico Press, 1989); Elisa Sampson Vera Tudela, *Colonial Angels: Narratives of Gender and Spirituality in Mexico, 1580–1750* (Austin: University of Texas Press, 2000).

40. Jean Franco, *Plotting Women: Gender and Representation in Mexico* (New York: Columbia University Press, 1989), xii.

41. This is the topic of the first chapter of Franco's *Plotting Women,* "Writers in Spite of Themselves: The Mystical Nuns of Seventeenth-Century Mexico," 3–22.

42. Ibid., 4.

43. Ibid., 21.

44. Octavio Paz, *Sor Juana or, The Traps of Faith,* trans. Margaret Sayers Peden (Cambridge: Belknap Press of Harvard University Press, 1988), 198.

45. Ibid., 392.

46. Georgina Sabat de Rivers, *En busca de Sor Juana* (Mexico City: Universidad Nacional Autónoma de México, 1998), 34. (This scholar styles her name Sabat-Rivers when publishing in English and Sabat de Rivers in her Spanish-language publications.)

47. Arenal and Powell, in their introduction to Sor Juana, *The Answer,* report that "St. Francis de Sales had used the same pseudonym to write to nuns" (13).

48. Manuel Fernández de Santa Cruz, "Admonishment: The Letter of Sor Philotea de la Cruz," in Sor Juana Inés de la Cruz, *A Sor Juana Anthology,* 200.

49. Georgina Sabat-Rivers, "Sor Juana Inés de la Cruz," in Carlos A. Solé and Maria Isabel Abreu, eds., *Latin American Writers* (New York: Scribner's, 1989), 1:89.

50. Paz, *Sor Juana.* See especially Chapter 25, "An Ill-Fated Letter," 389–410, and Chapter 26, "The Response," 411–424.

51. Ibid., 403.

52. Ibid. Paz explains that "the Bishop writes a prologue hidden behind a female pseudonym; ridicule and insult for Aguiar y Seijas."

53. Ibid., 410.

54. Ibid., 403.

55. Sor Juana, "The Reply to Sor Philotea," 205.

56. Ibid., 206.

57. Josefina Ludmer, "Tricks of the Weak," in Merrim, ed., *Feminist Perspectives,* 87.

58. Ibid., 88.

59. Ibid., 89.

60. Sor Juana, "The Reply to Sor Philotea," 212.

61. Ibid.

62. Dorothy Schons, "Some Obscure Points in the Life of Sor Juana," in Merrim, ed., *Feminist Perspectives,* 40.

63. Ibid., 45.

64. Ibid., 212.

65. Ibid., 45.

66. Ibid., 206.

67. Ibid., 212.

68. Ibid., 217.

69. Ibid., 218-219.

70. Ibid., 218.

71. Sor Juana, *Autodefensa espiritual de Sor Juana,* ed. Aureliano Tapia Méndez (Monterrey, Nuevo León, Mexico: Universidad de Nuevo León, 1981).

72. Sor Juana, "Letter from Sister Juana Inés de la Cruz Written to the R[everend] F[ather] M[aster] Antonio Núñez de Miranda of the Society of Jesus," in Paz, *Sor Juana,* 495-502.

73. Merrim, "Toward a Feminist Reading of Sor Juana Inés de la Cruz: Past, Present, and Future Directions in Sor Juana Criticism," in her *Feminist Perspectives,* 28.

74. Sor Juana, "Letter from Sister Juana Inés," 502.

75. Sabat-Rivers, "A Feminist Rereading," 142-161.

76. Ibid., 146.

77. Georgina Sabat de Rivers, *Estudios de literatura hispanoamericana: Sor Juana Inés de la Cruz y otros poetas barrocos de la colonia* (Barcelona: PPU, 1992).

78. Alejo Carpentier, "Problemática de la actual novela latinoamericana," in his *Tientos y diferencias* (1966; reprint, Havana: Unión de Escritores y Artistas de Cuba, 1974), 32.

79. Concolorcorvo, *El Lazarillo: A Guide for Inexperienced Travelers between Buenos Aires and Lima, 1773,* trans. Walter D. Kline (Bloomington: Indiana University Press, 1965), 205-206.

80. Ibid., 245.

3. The Struggle for Nationhood and the Rise of Fiction

1. John S. Brushwood, *Genteel Barbarism: Experiments in Analysis of Nineteenth-Century Spanish-American Novels* (Lincoln: University of Nebraska Press, 1981), 3.

2. Francine Masiello, *Between Civilization and Barbarism: Women, Nation, and Literary Culture in Modern Argentina* (Lincoln: University of Nebraska Press, 1992), 3.

3. Doris Sommer, *Foundational Fictions: The National Romances of Latin America* (Berkeley: University of California Press, 1991), 7.

4. Nancy Vogeley, *Lizardi and the Birth of the Novel in Spanish America* (Gainesville: University Press of Florida, 2001), 19.

5. Jorge Ruedas de la Serna, ed., *La misión del escritor: ensayos mexicanos del siglo XIX* (Mexico City: Universidad Nacional Autónoma de México, 1996). Especially deserving of attention is Ruedas de la Serna's explanation of his key phrase in his prefatory "Presentación," 7–13.

6. Celia Miranda Cárabes, "Estudio preliminar," in Cárabes, ed., *La novela corta en el primer romanticismo mexicano* (Mexico City: Universidad Nacional Autónoma de México, 1985), 18.

7. José Luis Martínez, "Fernández de Lizardi y los orígenes de la novela en México," *La expresión nacional* (Mexico City: Universidad Nacional Autónoma de México, 1993), 83.

8. Jefferson Rea Spell, "José Joaquín Fernández de Lizardi," *Bridging the Gap: Articles on Mexican Literature*, ed. L.M.S. (Mexico City: Editorial Libros de México, 1971), 103. Spell's detailed account of the episode covers 103–105.

9. Ibid., 125.

10. Ibid.

11. Jacobo Chencinski, "Estudio preliminar," in José Joaquín Fernández de Lizardi, *Obras* (Mexico City: Universidad Nacional Autónoma de México, 1963), 1:50.

12. Ibid., 1:49.

13. The relations between *The Itching Parrot* and the best-noted Spanish picaresque novels are examined by Sonia Marta Mora in the first five chapters (pages 43–250) of her *De la sujeción colonial a la patria criolla: El Periquillo Sarniento y los orígenes de la novela en Hispanoamérica* (Heredia, Costa Rica: EUNA, 1995).

14. José Joaquín Fernández de Lizardi, *El Periquillo Sarniento* (Madrid: Editora Nacional, 1976), 2:860. These translations are mine. The existing English version, *The Itching Parrot*, ed. Katherine Anne Porter, trans. Eugene Pressly (Garden City, N.Y.: Doubleday, Doran, 1942), is incomplete.

15. Ibid., 1:73.

16. Ibid., 1:204.

17. Spell in "The Historical and Social Background of *El Periquillo Sarniento*," *Bridging the Gap*, 195, identifies the site of Pedro's retreat as a historical Mexico City monastery, since demolished. In this article (171–196), Spell demonstrates that many of the educational and religious institutions mentioned in *The Itching Parrot* correspond to historically existing schools, churches, and religious houses.

18. Vogeley, *Lizardi and the Birth of the Novel*, 114.

19. Fernández de Lizardi, *El Periquillo Sarniento*, 1:56.

20. Ibid., 1:57.

21. Ibid., 1:60.

22. Vogeley, *Lizardi and the Birth of the Novel*, 183.

23. Two often-reprinted examples are José Joaquín de Olmedo, *La victoria de Junín: Canto a Bolívar* (The victory at Junin: song to Bolívar) from 1825, the year following the decisive battles over the Spanish royalists, and Andrés Bello, *La agricultura de la Zona Tórrida* (The agriculture of the Torrid Zone), 1826.

24. Esteban Echeverría, *The Slaughter House*, ed. and trans. Angel Flores (New York, 1959).

25. Esteban Echeverría, "El matadero," in Juan María Gutiérrez, ed., *Revista del Río de la Plata* 1 (1871): 556–562. After Gutiérrez debuted "The slaughtering ground," it appeared in the edition of Echeverría's complete works (1870–1874).

26. Leonor Fleming, "Introducción," in Esteban Echeverría, *El matadero. La cautiva* (Madrid: Cátedra, 1986), 70.

27. Noé Jitrik, *Esteban Echeverría* (Buenos Aires: Centro Editor de América Latina, 1967), 32.

28. Fleming, "Introducción," 70.

29. Echeverría, *La cautiva. El matadero* (Buenos Aires: Kapelusz, 1963), 81.

30. Ibid., 86.

31. Ibid., 82.

32. Ibid., 83.

33. Ibid.

34. Ibid., 93.

35. Fleming, "Introducción," 74.

36. Ibid., 74–75.

37. Noé Jitrik, "Forma y significación en 'El matadero,' de Echeverría," in his *El fuego de la especie: ensayos sobre seis escritores argentinos* (Buenos Aires: Siglo XXI, 1971), 92.

38. Ibid., 93.

39. Enrique Anderson Imbert, *Genio y figura de Sarmiento* (Buenos Aires: Editorial Universitaria de Buenos Aires, 1967), 26.

40. Noé Jitrik, *Muerte y resurrección del Facundo* (Buenos Aires: Centro Editor de América Latina, 1983), 10.

41. Diana Sorensen Goodrich, *Facundo and the Construction of Argentine Culture* (Austin: University of Texas Press, 1992), 2.

42. Jitrik, *Muerte*, 13.

43. Ibid., 15.

44. Goodrich, *Facundo*, 2.

45. Jitrik, *Muerte*, 123.

46. For example, the scholarly concern with nationalism in Spanish American writing is evident in the essays collected in Tulio Halperin Donghi, ed., *Sarmiento, Author of a Nation* (Berkeley: University of California Press, 1994).

47. Brushwood, *Genteel Barbarism*, 4.

48. For a summary of research into this novel's dates of composition, see José Servera, "Introducción," in Gertrudis Gómez de Avellaneda, *Sab* (Madrid: Cátedra, 1999), 46.

49. Nara Araujo, "Raza y género en Sab," *Casa de las Américas* 33, no. 190 (Jan.–Mar. 1993): 44.

50. Quoted in Jerome Branche, "Ennobling Savagery? Sentimentalism and the Subaltern in *Sab*," *Afro-Hispanic Review* 17 (Fall 1998): 16.

51. Gertudis Gómez de Avellaneda y Arteaga, *Sab*, ed. and trans. Nina M. Scott (Austin: University of Texas Press, 1993), 140.

52. Branche, "Ennobling Savagery?" 16.

53. Gómez de Avellaneda, *Sab*, 108.

54. Hugh A. Harter, *Gertrudis Gómez de Avellaneda* (Boston: Twayne, 1981), 129.

55. Gómez de Avellaneda, *Sab*, 130.

56. Ibid.

57. Susan Kirkpatrick, "Gómez de Avellaneda's *Sab:* Gendering the Liberal Romantic Subject," in Noël Valis and Carol Maier, eds., *In the Feminine Mode: Essays on Hispanic Women Writers* (Lewisburg, Pa.: Bucknell University Press, 1990), 120.

58. Branche, "Ennobling Savagery?" objects to "the (uneven) slave-wife analogy" (14). In the course of his analysis, Branche identifies as a major inconsistency in *Sab* the novel's sparse references to women slaves: "In Avellaneda's story no text of sisterhood or sympathy emerges to vindicate the enslaved Black women in their hapless condition" (ibid.).

59. Gómez de Avellaneda, *Sab*, 144–145.

60. Ibid., 39.

61. Ibid., 57.

62. Ibid.

63. Sommer, "Sab C'est Moi," in her *Foundational Fictions*, 117. Originally in Spanish under the same title in *Hispamérica* 16, no. 48 (1987): 26.

64. Sommer, "Sab C'est Moi," 28.

65. Kirkpatrick, "Gómez de Avellaneda's *Sab*," 120.

66. Ivan A. Schulman reviews the evidence of the dates of composition of Manzano's autobiography and hazards an educated guess in his introduction to Juan Francisco Manzano, *The Autobiography of a Slave*, modernized Spanish version by Schulman, English trans. Evelyn Picon Garfield (Detroit: Wayne State University Press, 1996), 12–16. Schulman states that "we can conclude that . . . [Manzano] began to write it in June of 1835. We might further speculate that he did not finish the second part until 1839" (16). He notes several competing dates of birth for Manzano but does not decide between them; he accepts 1836 as the year in which Manzano became a free man.

67. William Luis, *Literary Bondage: Slavery in Cuban Narrative* (Austin: University of Texas Press, 1990), 92–98, reviews the English version of 1840.

68. Ibid., 99.

69. Juan Francisco Manzano, *Autobiografía, cartas y versos de Juan Fco. Manzano,* ed. and introduction José L. Franco (Havana: Municipio de la Habana, Administración del Alcalde, 1937); made available in 1970 through Kraus Reprints (Nendeln), bound with *Poesías completas de Plácido* by another well-known African-Cuban poet, "Plácido" (real name, Gabriel de la Concepcion Valdés).

70. Luis, *Literary Bondage,* 99.

71. Manzano, *Autobiography,* 95.

72. Robert Richmond Ellis, "Reading through the Veil of Juan Francisco Manzano: From Homoerotic Violence to the Dream of a Homoracial Bond," *PMLA* 113 (1998): 422-435.

73. Ibid., 422.

74. Ibid., 431.

75. Ibid.

76. Sylvia Molloy, "From Serf to Self: The Autobiography of Juan Francisco Manzano," in her *At Face Value: Autobiographical Writing in Spanish America* (Cambridge: Cambridge University Press, 1991), 43.

77. Ibid., 54.

78. Manzano, *Autobiography,* 103-104.

79. Molloy, "From Serf to Self," 42.

80. Ibid., 36-54.

81. Sonia Labrador-Rodríguez, "La intelectualidad negra en Cuba en el siglo XIX: el caso de Manzano," *Revista Iberoamericana* 62, no. 174 (Jan.-Mar. 1996): 16.

82. Manzano, *Autobiography,* 55.

83. Luis, *Literary Bondage,* 94.

84. Labrador-Rodríguez, "La intelectualidad negra en Cuba en el siglo XIX," 20.

85. A useful and wide-ranging work on Spanish American writers of African heritage is Richard L. Jackson, *Black Writers and the Hispanic Canon* (New York and London: Twayne Publishers/Prentice Hall International, 1997).

86. Marvin A. Lewis, *Afro-Argentine Discourse: Another Dimension of the Black Diaspora* (Columbia: University of Missouri Press, 1996).

4. The Mid-Nineteenth Century

1. Michael Winkler, "Realism," in Alex Preminger and T. V. F. Brogan, eds., Frank J. Warnke, O. B. Hardison Jr., and Earl Miner, assoc. eds., *New Princeton Encyclopedia of Poetry and Poetics* (Princeton: Princeton University Press, 1993), 1016.

2. John S. Brushwood, *Mexico in Its Novel: A Nation's Search for Identity* (Austin: University of Texas Press, 1966), 114.

3. Brushwood, *Genteel Barbarism,* 42. In his chapter "The Focus of Action:

José Mármol's *Amalia*" (39–62), Brushwood demonstrates that, though conventionally melodramatic, *Amalia* is complex enough to sustain a detailed analysis.

4. Jorge Ruedas de la Serna, "La novela corta de la Academia de Letrán," in Cárabes, ed., *La novela corta*, 58.

5. José Mármol, *Amalia* (Mexico City: Porrúa, 1971), 398.

6. Juan Carlos Ghiano, "Prólogo," in ibid., xvi.

7. José Mármol, "A los suscritores de *La Semana*," *La Semana* 2, no. 40 (9 February 1852), 390. Reproduced in Beatriz Curia, "Introducción," in José Mármol, *Amalia*, ed. Curia (Mendoza, Argentina: Facultad de Filosofía y Letras, Universidad Nacional de Cuyo, 1989), 8.

8. Curia, "Introducción," 9.

9. Ibid.

10. Mármol, *Amalia*, 101.

11. Ibid., 191–192.

12. Ibid., 18.

13. Ibid., 161.

14. Ibid., 133.

15. Trinidad Pérez, "Prólogo," in José Mármol, *Amalia* (Havana: Casa de las Américas, 1976), xxxviii.

16. David Viñas, "Mármol: los dos ojos del romanticismo," in his *Literatura argentina y realidad política* (Buenos Aires: Jorge Alvarez, 1964), 133.

17. Ibid.

18. Doris Sommer, "*Amalia:* Valor at Heart and Home," in her *Foundational Fictions*, 111.

19. Hebe Beatriz Molina, "Introducción," in her *La narrativa dialógica de Juana Manuela Gorriti* (Mendoza, Argentina: Editorial de la Facultad de Filosofía y Letras de la Universidad Nacional de Cuyo, 1999), 12–13.

20. For a detailed account of the circumstances that led to the Gorriti family's exile, see María Laura de Arriba, "República, erotismo y escritura. Una mujer, muchas mujeres," in Amelia Royo, ed., *Juanamanuela, mucho papel: algunas lecturas críticas de textos de Juana Manuela Gorriti* (Salta, Argentina: Ediciones del Robledal, 1999), 82–84.

21. Molina, "Introducción," 13.

22. Masiello, *Between Civilization and Barbarism*, 46.

23. Cristina Iglesias, "Prólogo," in Iglesias, ed., *El ajuar de la patria: ensayos críticos sobre Juana Manuela Gorriti* (Buenos Aires: Feminaria, 1993), 9.

24. Francine Masiello, "Disfraz y delincuencia en la obra de Juana Manuela Gorriti," in Iglesias, ed., *El ajuar de la patria*, 63.

25. Mary G. Berg, "Juana Manuela Gorriti," in Diane E. Marting, ed., *Spanish American Women Writers: A Bio-Biographical Source Book* (Westport, Conn.: Greenwood Press, 1990), 231.

26. Ibid., 230.

27. Iglesias, "Prólogo," 8.

28. Amelia Royo, "Siglo XIX: escrituras de la historia del salón a la cocina," in Royo, ed., *Juanamanuela, mucho papel,* 161.

29. Ibid., 162.

30. Ibid., 163.

31. Juana Manuela Gorriti, "El Lucero del Manantial," in her *Sueños y realidades* (Buenos Aires: Biblioteca de la Nación, 1907), 1:294.

32. Ibid., 1:312.

33. Gorriti, "La quena," in her *Sueños y realidades,* 1:29.

34. Ibid.

35. Elena Altuna, "Alianzas imposibles: la tematización del mundo indígena en Juana Manuela Gorriti y las Veladas Literarias," in Royo, ed., *Juanamanuela, mucho papel,* 27–51.

36. Altuna discusses Gorriti's promotion of the *yaraví* in ibid., 44–47.

37. Ibid., 50.

38. Ibid., 43.

39. Martha Mercader, *Juanamanuela, mucha mujer* (Buenos Aires: Sudamericana, 1980).

40. De Arriba, "República, erotismo y escritura," 87.

41. For a characterization of the salons over which Gorriti presided in these two cities, see Graciela Batticuore, *El taller de la escritora: veladas literarias de Juana Manuela Gorriti, Lima–Buenos Aires (1876/7–1892)* (Rosario, Argentina: Beatriz Viterbo Editora, 1999).

42. De Arriba, "República, erotismo y escritura," 87.

43. Jorge Ruedas de la Serna, "La novela corta de la Academia de Letrán," in Cárabes, ed., *La novela corta,* 57.

44. Lucía Guerra Cunningham, "Visión marginal de la historia en la narrativa de Juana Manuela Gorriti," *Ideologies and Literature* 2, no. 2 (Fall 1987): 67.

45. Ibid., 66–67.

46. Ibid., 67.

47. Masiello, "Disfraz y delincuencia," 64; Guerra Cunningham, "Visión marginal de la historia," 67.

48. Masiello, "Disfraz y delincuencia," 64.

49. Masiello, *Between Civilization and Barbarism,* 2.

50. Those interested in discovering more nineteenth-century women journalists from Argentina may see Francine Masiello, ed., *La mujer y el espacio público: el periodismo femenino en la Argentina del siglo XIX* (Buenos Aires: Feminaria Editora, 1994), and Bonnie Frederick, *Wily Modesty: Argentine Women Writers, 1860–1910* (Tempe: Arizona State University Center for Latin American Studies Press, 1998).

51. Alberto Blest Gana, *Martín Rivas,* trans. Tess O'Dwyer (New York: Oxford University Press, 2000), 15.

52. Ibid., 360.

53. Ibid., 388.

54. Ibid., 389.

55. Jorge Román-Lagunas, foreword to Blest Gana, *Martín Rivas* (Santiago de Chile: Nascimento, 1975), 15.

56. Alone, quoted in Jaime Concha, introduction to Blest Gana, *Martín Rivas*, Oxford University Press edition, xxviii.

57. Concha, ibid.

58. Throughout his introduction, xiii–l, Concha argues that *Martín Rivas* betrays the inadequacies of Blest Gana's supposedly progressive social vision. See also this critic's "Prólogo," in Alberto Blest Gana, *Martín Rivas* (Caracas: Ayacucho, 1995), ix–xxxix.

59. Juan Durán-Luzio, "Significación contextual de *Martín Rivas*, de Alberto Blest Gana," *Revista de Crítica Literaria Latinoamericana* 13, no. 26 (1987): 43–54.

60. Ibid.

61. Hernán Poblete Varas, *Alberto Blest Gana y su obra* (Santiago: Pehuén, 1995), 108.

62. Ibid., 108–109.

63. Ibid., 108.

64. Blest Gana, *Martín Rivas*, Oxford University Press edition, 352.

65. Ibid., 5.

66. Ibid., 168.

67. George D. Schade, "Alberto Blest Gana," in Carlos A. Solé and Maria Isabel Andreu, *Latin American Writers* (New York: Scribner's, 1989), 1:206.

68. Román-Lagunas, foreword to Blest Gana, *Martín Rivas*, 14.

69. Because there are so many editions of this extremely popular novel, here I cite chapter numbers rather than page numbers.

70. Sylvia Molloy, "Paraíso perdido y economía terrenal en *María*," *Sin Nombre* 14, no. 3 (1984): 47.

71. Ibid., 46–47.

72. Doris Sommer, "*María*'s Disease: A National Romance (Con)Founded," in her *Foundational Fictions*, 172–203.

73. Ibid., 188.

74. Molloy, "Paraíso perdido," 39.

75. Brushwood, *Genteel Barbarism*, 86.

76. Donald McGrady, *Jorge Isaacs* (Boston: Twayne, 1971), 123. McGrady cites an 1879 critique by Mariano A. Pelliza, published in Buenos Aires.

77. Rodolfo A. Borello, "Sociedad y paternalismo en *María*," *Cuadernos Hispanoamericanos* 562 (April 1997): 72.

78. Raymond Leslie Williams, *The Colombian Novel, 1844–1987* (Austin: University of Texas Press, 1991), 156.

79. Ibid., 151–160.

80. Ibid., 157.

81. Borello, "Sociedad y paternalismo en *María*," 72.

82. Molloy, "Paraíso perdido," 51.

83. Margo Glantz, "De la erótica inclinación a enredarse en cabellos," in her *De la amorosa inclinación a enredarse en cabellos* (Mexico City: Ediciones Océano, 1984), 34.

84. Williams, *The Colombian Novel*, 155.

85. Ibid., 159.

86. Juan León Mera, *Cumandá, o un drama entre salvajes* (Bogotá: Editorial El Conejo, 1986), 46.

87. Ibid.

88. Ibid., 109.

89. Ibid., 110.

90. Ibid., 156.

91. Sommer, "Starting from Scratch: Late Beginnings and Early (T)races," in her *Foundational Fictions*, 240.

92. Francisco E. Aguirre V., "Juan León Mera: política y literatura," in Manuel Corrales Pascual, ed., *Cumandá: contribución a un centenario* (Quito: Ediciones de la Universidad Católica, 1979), 31.

93. Antonio Benítez Rojo, "Nineteenth-Century Spanish American Novel," in Roberto González Echevarría and Enrique Pupo-Walker, eds., *Cambridge History of Latin American Literature* (Cambridge: Cambridge University Press, 1996), 1:460.

94. Mera, *Cumandá*, 15.

95. Aguirre V., "Juan León Mera," 25.

96. Manuel Corrales Pascual, "*Cumandá* y las raíces del relato indigenista ecuatoriano," in Corrales Pascual, ed., *Cumandá: contribución a un centenario*, 134.

97. Aguirre V., "Juan León Mera," 17–24.

98. Ibid., 24–31.

99. Corrales Pascual, "*Cumandá* y las raíces del relato indigenista ecuatoriano," 119–135.

100. According to Corrales Pascual, ibid., "The general opinion is that literary indigenismo begins with *Plata y bronce* [Silver and bronze] (1927), by Fernando Chaves" (119).

101. Ibid., 129.

102. Benítez Rojo, "Nineteenth-Century Spanish American Novel," 467.

103. Doris Sommer, "From Romance to Novel: Populism as the Rhetoric of Frustrated Love," in her *One Master for Another: Populism as Patriarchal Rhetoric in Dominican Novels* (Lanham, Md.: University Press of America, 1983), 16. Sommer presents her central thesis that *Enriquillo* is best understood as a romance in the subsection of this chapter entitled "The National Romance," 14–17. She then analyzes the work in detail in the next chapter, "The Other Enriquillo."

104. Sommer, "From Romance to Novel," 15.
105. Sommer, "The Other Enriquillo," 68.

5. **Late-Nineteenth-Century Narratives of Social
Commentary and National Self-Reflection**

1. Raimundo Lazo, "*Cecilia Valdés:* estudio crítico" in Imeldo Alvarez, ed., *Acerca de Cirilo Villaverde* (Havana: Letras Cubanas, 1982), 233–273.

2. Cirilo Villaverde, *Cecilia Valdés, o la Loma del Angel* (New York: Imprenta de El Espejo, 1882).

3. Reynaldo González, "A White Problem: Reinterpreting Cecilia Valdés," in Pedro Pérez Sarduy and Jean Stubbs, eds., *AfroCuba: An Anthology of Cuban Writing on Race, Politics, and Culture* (London: Latin American Bureau, 1993), 205.

4. Cirilo Villaverde, *Cecilia Valdés o La Loma del Angel,* ed. Jean Lamore (Madrid: Cátedra, 1992), 100, 100–101. All subsequent quotations are taken from this edition.

5. Ibid., 328, 517–518, 593.

6. Ibid., 100.

7. Ibid., 101.

8. Ibid., 414.

9. Lazo, "*Cecilia Valdés:* estudio crítico," 266.

10. Villaverde, *Cecilia Valdés,* 413.

11. Ibid., 171.

12. Lazo, "*Cecilia Valdés:* estudio crítico," 245.

13. Antonio Benítez-Rojo, "The Nineteenth-Century Spanish American Novel," in González Echevarría and Pupo-Walker, eds., *Cambridge History of Latin American Literature,* 1:483.

14. Sommer, *Foundational Fictions,* 127, states: "Hardly anyone in *Cecilia Valdés* escapes the charge of racism, not the mulatta or her white lover, and certainly not the white narrator."

15. Matías Montes Huidobro, "Cuba," in David William Foster, ed., *Handbook of Latin American Literature,* rev. ed. (New York: Garland, 1992), 239.

16. Ibid.

17. María Teresa Aedo, "*Cecilia Valdés:* Diosas, vírgenes y madres en la identidad mestiza de Cuba," *Acta Literaria* 20 (1995): 5–6.

18. Ibid., 16.

19. Villaverde, *Cecilia Valdés,* 232.

20. Ibid.

21. Ibid., 233.

22. Ibid.

23. Ibid., 397.

24. Ibid., 415.

25. Ibid., 302.

26. Ibid., 424.

27. Ibid., 272.

28. Ibid., 273.

29. Ibid., 471–472.

30. Anselmo Suárez y Romero, *Francisco: El ingenio o las delicias del campo* (New York: Imprenta y Librería de N. Ponce de León, 1880).

31. Sommer, *Foundational Fictions*, 126.

32. Luis, *Literary Bondage*, 44.

33. Luis, ibid., 53, summarizes the reactions of contemporaries, both Cuban and foreign, to Suárez y Romero's novel.

34. Eduardo Castañeda, foreword to Anselmo Suárez y Romero, *Francisco: El ingenio o las delicias del campo* (Havana: Publicaciones del Ministerio de Educación, Dirección de Cultura, 1947), 14.

35. Luis, *Literary Bondage*, 57.

36. Mario Cabrera Saqui, "Vida, pasión y gloria de Anselmo Suárez y Romero," in Suárez y Romero, *Francisco*, Publicaciones del Ministerio de Educación edition, 22.

37. Jorge Ruedas de la Serna, "Presentación," in Ruedas de la Serna, ed., *La misión del escritor*, 7–8.

38. Ibid., 9.

39. See, for example, the feminist reading of *El Zarco* in the chapter by Margarita Vargas, "Romanticism," trans. David E. Johnson, in David William Foster, ed., *Mexican Literature: A History* (Austin: University of Texas Press, 1994), 97–99. Vargas observes that, through this novel, Altamirano is warning Mexican women to remain at home and be obedient family members.

40. José Luis Martínez, "Inclán," *La expresión nacional*, 296.

41. Manuel Sol, "Estudio preliminar," in Ignacio M. Altamirano, *El Zarco* (Xalapa: Universidad Veracruzana, 2000), 28.

42. Stephen M. Bell, "Mexico," in Foster, ed., *Handbook of Latin American Literature*, 386.

43. Castro Leal, "Prólogo," in José López Portillo y Rojas, *La parcela* (Mexico City: Porrúa, 1973), ix.

44. Altamirano, endnote to *Clemencia*, in his *Clemencia y La Navidad en las montañas* (Mexico City: Porrúa, 1966), 214.

45. Altamirano, *Clemencia*, 12.

46. Ibid., 214.

47. Carlos Monsiváis, "*El Zarco*: los falsos y los verdaderos héroes románticos," in Altamirano, *El Zarco* (Mexico City: Océano, 1986), 12.

48. Altamirano, *Clemencia*, 225.

49. Ibid., 225.

50. Ibid., 293.

51. Monsiváis, "*El Zarco*: los falsos y los verdaderos héroes románticos," 13–14.

52. Altamirano, *El Zarco*, 34.

53. Ibid.

54. Josefina Zoraida Vásquez, "Prólogo," in Manuel Payno, *Los bandidos de Río Frío* (Mexico City: Promexa Editores, 1979), xii. Vásquez notes that Payno and some of the other participants in these evening gatherings, "filled with literary nationalism," later published a multi-authored collection of essays promoting the use of literature as a mean of nation-building.

55. Antonio Castro Leal, "Prólogo," in Payno, *Los bandidos de Río Frío* (Mexico City: Porrúa, 1964), vii. Brushwood discusses this issue in his *Mexico in Its Novel*. From reading Payno's *El fistol del diablo*, Brushwood surmises that this writer was concentrating on each installment "without much concern for what had gone before or what had gone later" (73). In Brushwood's analysis, serial publication in some cases led to such piecemeal writing, but not invariably: "The serialized novel can overcome many of the difficulties imposed by the manner of publication" (74).

56. Margo Glantz, "Huérfanos y bandidos: *Los bandidos de Río Frío*," in Glantz, ed., *Del fistol a la linterna: Homenaje a José Tomás Cuéllar y Manuel Payno, en el centenario de su muerte, 1994* (Mexico City: Universidad Nacional Autónoma de México, 1997), 221–239.

57. Ibid., 222.

58. Ibid., 223.

59. Ibid.

60. Carlos Monsiváis, "Manuel Payno: México, novela de folletín," in Glantz, ed., *Del fistol a la linterna*, 232–252.

61. Ibid., 251–252.

62. Ibid., 252.

63. Martínez, "Cuéllar," *La expresión nacional*, 304.

64. Glantz, introduction to José Tomás de Cuéllar, *The Magic Lantern: Having a Ball and Christmas Eve*, trans. Margaret Carson (New York: Oxford University Press, 2000), xxvi.

65. For a good indication of why current-day readers have taken an interest in this nineteenth-century moralist, see Glantz's above-cited introduction in its entirety, xi–xxxv.

66. Cuéllar, title page for *Christmas Eve, The Magic Lantern*, 119.

67. Joaquina Navarro, *La novela realista mexicana* (Mexico City: Editorial Amatl/Universidad Autónoma de Tlaxcala, 1992), 159.

68. Ibid., 161.

69. Mario Martín-Flores, "Nineteenth-Century Prose Fiction," trans. David William Foster, in Foster, ed., *Mexican Literature*, 1994, 116.

70. Brushwood, *Mexico in Its Novel*, 133.

71. Enrique Pupo-Walker, "The Brief Narrative: 1835–1915," in González-Echevarría and Pupo-Walker, eds., *Cambridge History of Latin American Literature*, 1:494.

72. Aníbal González, "Journalism versus Genealogy: Ricardo Palma's *Tradi-*

ciones peruanas," in his *Journalism and the Development of Spanish American Narrative* (New York: Cambridge University Press, 1993), 64.

73. José Carlos Mariátegui, "Literature on Trial," in his *Seven Interpretive Essays on Peruvian Reality,* trans. Marjorie Urquidi (Austin: University of Texas Press, 1971), 196.

74. Sebastián Salazar Bondy, "La extraviada nostalgia," in his *Lima la horrible* (Mexico City: Era, 1964), 13.

75. Ibid.

76. Raúl Porras Barrenechea, "Palma romántico," in *Tres ensayos sobre Ricardo Palma* (Lima: Librería Mejía Baca, 1954), 26.

77. Ibid., 27–28.

78. Ibid., 27.

79. Juan Durán Luzio, "Ricardo Palma, cronista de una sociedad barroca," *Revista Iberoamericana* 53, no. 140 (July–September 1987): 581.

80. Ibid., 585.

81. Ibid., 587.

82. González, "Journalism versus Genealogy," 81.

83. Ibid.

84. Ana Peluffo, "El poder de las lágrimas: sentimentalismo, género y nación en *Aves sin nido* de Clorinda Matto de Turner," in Mabel Moraña, ed., *Indigenismo hacia el fin del milenio. Homenaje a Antonio Cornejo-Polar* (Pittsburgh: Biblioteca de América, 1998), 119.

85. Luis Mario Schneider, "Clorinda Matto de Turner," introduction to Matto, *Aves sin nido* (New York: Las Américas, 1968), xx–xi, cites as earlier *indigenista* novels *El padre Horán* (1848) by Narciso Aréstegui and *La trinidad del indio o costumbres del interior* (1885) by José T. Itolarres (pseudonym of José Torres y Lara).

86. Mary G. Berg, "Writing for Her Life: The Essays of Clorinda Matto de Turner," in Doris Meyer, ed., *Reinterpreting the Spanish American Essay: Women Writers of the Nineteenth and Twentieth Centuries* (Austin: University of Texas Press, 1995), 80.

87. Ibid., 81.

88. Schneider, "Clorinda Matto de Turner," xxii–xiii, identifies correspondences between González Prada's famous speech and Matto's novel.

89. Clorinda Matto de Turner, "Preface," in her *Birds without a Nest: A Story of Indian Life and Priestly Oppression,* trans. J.G.H., emended by Naomi Lindstrom (Austin: University of Texas Press, 1996), 1–2.

90. Matto de Turner, *Birds without a Nest,* 133.

91. Ibid., 100.

92. Peluffo, "El poder de las lágrimas," 127–128.

93. Ibid., 128.

94. María del Pilar Sinués de Marco, *El ángel del hogar; estudios morales acerca de la mujer,* quoted in Matto de Turner, *Birds without a Nest,* 140.

95. Cornejo Polar, "Prólogo," *Aves sin nido* (Havana: Casa de las Américas, 1974), xvii–xviii.

96. Peluffo, "El poder de las lágrimas," 121.

97. Brushwood, *Genteel Barbarism*, 147.

98. Antonio Cornejo Polar, *Literatura y sociedad en el Perú: la novela indigenista* (Lima: Lasontay, 1980), 39–40.

99. Matto de Turner, "Preface," 1.

100. Cornejo Polar, *Literatura y sociedad en el Perú*, 40.

101. Peluffo, "El poder de las lágrimas," 119.

102. Ibid., 119. Peluffo does not attribute this remark to a particular individual.

103. Concha Meléndez, "*Aves sin nido,* por Clorinda Matto de Turner," in her *La novela indianista en Hispanoamérica, 1832–1889* (1934; reprint, Rio Piedras, P.R.: University of Puerto Rico, 1961), 177–84.

104. Marta A. Umanzor, "El discurso de la mujer en el mundo artístico de Clorinda Matto de Turner," in *La voz de la mujer en la literatura hispanoamericana fin-de-siglo,* ed. Luis Jiménez (San Jose, Costa Rica: Universidad de Costa Rica, 1999), 74.

105. For examples of David Viñas's outlook on the Generation of 1880, see especially his *Literatura argentina y realidad política: apogeo de la oligarquía,* rev. ed. (Buenos Aires: Siglo Veinte, 1975).

106. David William Foster, *The Argentine Generation of 1880: Ideology and Cultural Texts* (Columbia: University of Missouri Press, 1990). See, in particular, Foster's analysis of *La gran aldea* in Chapter 3, "Writing the Tensions of Transition," 92–104.

6. Naturalism and *Modernismo*

1. Enrique Laguerre, "Prólogo," in Manuel Zeno Gandía, *La charca* (Caracas: Ayacucho, 1978), xxiv.

2. Ibid., xxiv–xxvi.

3. Myron Lichtblau, "A Century After: Eugenio Cambaceres' *Sin rumbo* (1885–1985)," in *Louisiana Conference on Hispanic Languages and Literatures,* ed. *LA CHISPA '85* (New Orleans: Louisiana Conference on Hispanic Languages and Literatures/Tulane University, 1985), 213–218, points out that Cambaceres's beautiful descriptions of the pampas and other features represent a departure from naturalism. Aída Apter Cragnolino, "Naturalismo y decadencia en *Sin rumbo,*" *Revista de Crítica Literaria Latinoamericana* 13, no. 26 (1987): 55–65, argues that *Sin rumbo* is both a naturalistic and a decadent novel.

4. Nélida Salvador, "Eugenio Cambaceres," in Pedro Orgambide and Roberto Yahni, eds., *Enciclopedia de la literatura argentina* (Buenos Aires: Sudamericana, 1970), 112.

5. Ibid., 111.

6. Noé Jitrik, "Cambaceres: adentro y afuera," in his *Ensayos y estudios de literatura argentina* (Buenos Aires: Galerna, 1970), 37.

7. Eugenio Cambaceres, *Sin rumbo* (Buenos Aires: Editorial Minerva, 1924), 41.

8. Ibid., 15.

9. Ibid., 55.

10. Ibid., 95.

11. Ibid., 163.

12. Ibid., 166.

13. Apter Cragnolino, "Naturalismo y decadencia en *Sin rumbo*," 61.

14. Jitrik, "Cambaceres: adentro y afuera," 35-54.

15. Ibid., 35.

16. George D. Schade, "El arte narrativo en *Sin rumbo*," *Revista Iberoamericana* 44, nos. 102-103 (1978): 17-29.

17. Ibid., 28.

18. Laguerre, "Prólogo," xxxix.

19. Ibid.

20. With reference to the delay in republishing *La charca*, Laguerre, ibid., xxxviii, points out that until the appearance of this novel, the traditional image of the *jíbaro* had been quaint and colorful; Zeno Gandía's naturalistic portrait no doubt disturbed many readers.

21. Aníbal González Pérez, "Manuel Zeno Gandía," in Solé and Abreu, eds., *Latin American Writers*, 2:324.

22. Ibid.

23. José Olivio Jiménez and Antonio R. de la Campa, "Introducción," *Antología crítica de la prosa modernista hispanoamericana* (New York: Eliseo Torres, 1976), 29.

24. Manuel Pedro González, "Prefacio a la edición española de 'Lucía Jerez,'" in José Martí, *Lucía Jerez* (Madrid: Gredos, 1969), 33-39, details the circumstances of the work's composition. González concludes that Martí wrote the novel largely "because he was in real need of the $44.00 miserable dollars that the manuscript would bring him" (38).

25. González, ibid., identifies Martí as the author of a derisive preface written for a planned edition of his own novel in book form. Although that edition did not materialize, Martí's preface for it, in the Cuban author's difficult-to-read handwriting, was preserved among his papers. González reproduces the preface (36-38).

26. Enrique Anderson Imbert, "La prosa poética de José Martí," in his *Estudios sobre escritores de América* (Buenos Aires: Raigal, 1954), 125-165.

27. González, "Prefacio a la edición española de 'Lucía Jerez,'" 9-58.

28. Ibid., 47.

29. Aníbal González, "Guerra florida: el intelectual y las metáforas en *Lucía Jerez*," in his *La novela modernista hispanoamericana* (Madrid: Gredos, 1987), 53-81.

30. Ibid., 78.

31. Ibid., 79.

32. Aníbal González, "Modernist Prose," in González Echeverría and Pupo-Walker, eds., *Cambridge History of Latin American Literature*, 2:83. As examples of short stories that are "at most, allegories of esthetic theories," González names "El pájaro azul" ("The Bluebird") and "El rey burgués" ("The Bourgeois King"), both from *Azul* . . . .

33. The information on the publication history of *De sobremesa* comes from Betty Tyree Osiek, *José Asunción Silva* (Boston: Twayne, 1978), 94–95.

34. Ibid., 94.

35. Ibid., 94–95.

36. González, "Modernist Prose," 2:103.

37. José Asunción Silva, *De sobremesa* (Bogotá: Ediciones Sol y Luna, 1965), 88.

38. González, *La novela modernista hispanoamericana*, 96.

39. Silva, *De sobremesa*, 85.

40. González, *La novela modernista hispanoamericana*, 98, reports that "This painting, so far as is known, never existed in reality (although there are several from which Silva might have drawn inspiration)."

41. Silva, *De sobremesa*, 105–106.

42. Ibid., 51.

43. Peter Elmore, "Bienes suntuarios: el problema de la obra de arte en *De sobremesa*, de José Asunción Silva," *Revista de Crítica Literaria Latinoamericana* 22, nos. 43–44 (1996): 207.

44. Silva, *De sobremesa*, 218.

45. González, *La novela modernista hispanoamericana*, 106.

46. Ibid., 111.

47. Ibid.

48. Elmore, "Bienes suntuarios," 208.

49. Benigno Trigo, *Subjects of Crisis: Race and Gender as Disease in Latin America* (Hanover: Wesleyan University Press, 2000), 115–118.

50. Ibid., 118.

51. Silva, *De sobremesa*, 140.

52. Ibid., 141.

Selected Bibliography

The following selected bibliography lists works of research and criticism of Spanish American writing, 1492–1900. Works of primary literature appear only if they include substantial critical introductions. I have made a particular effort to include research by Spanish American scholars that is available in English translation. Important studies originally composed in English also have a place here. In other cases, I have included worthy examples of research that has not yet been translated, hoping that it will find its way into English.

Adorno, Rolena. *Cronista y príncipe: la obra de don Felipe Guaman Poma de Ayala.* Lima: Pontificia Universidad Católica del Perú, 1989.
———. *Guaman Poma: Writing and Resistance in Colonial Peru.* Austin: University of Texas Press/Institute of Latin American Studies, 1986.
Alvarez, Imeldo, ed. *Acerca de Cirilo Villaverde.* Havana: Letras Cubanas, 1982.
Arenal, Electa, and Stacey Schlau, eds. *Untold Sisters: Hispanic Nuns in Their Own Works.* Trans. Amanda Powell. Albuquerque: University of New Mexico Press, 1989.
Benítez-Rojo, Antonio. "The Nineteenth-Century Spanish American Novel." In *Discovery to Modernism.* Vol. 1 of *Cambridge History of Latin American Literature,* ed. Roberto González Echevarría and Enrique Pupo-Walker, 417–489. Cambridge: Cambridge University Press, 1996.
Brushwood, John S. *Genteel Barbarism: Experiments in Analysis of Nineteenth-Century Spanish-American Novels.* Lincoln: University of Nebraska Press, 1981.
———. *Mexico in Its Novel: A Nation's Search for Identity.* Austin: University of Texas Press, 1966.
Concha, Jaime. Foreword to *Martín Rivas,* by Alberto Blest Gana, xiii–l. Trans. Tess O'Dwyer. New York: Oxford University Press, 2000.
Corrales Pascual, Manuel, ed. *Cumandá, 1879–1979: contribución a un centenario.* Quito: Ediciones de la Universidad Católica, 1979.
Cypess, Sandra Messinger. *La Malinche in Mexican Literature: From History to Myth.* Austin: University of Texas Press, 1991.
Foster, David William. *The Argentine Generation of 1880: Ideology and Cultural Texts.* Columbia: University of Missouri Press, 1990.

Foster, David William, ed. *Handbook of Latin American Literature*. Rev. ed. New York: Garland, 1992.

———, ed. *Mexican Literature: A History*. Austin: University of Texas Press, 1994.

Franco, Jean. *Plotting Women: Gender and Representation in Mexico*. New York: Columbia University Press, 1981.

Frederick, Bonnie. *Wily Modesty: Argentine Women Writers, 1860–1910*. Tempe: Arizona State University Center for Latin American Studies Press, 1998.

González, Aníbal. "Journalism versus Genealogy: Ricardo Palma's *Tradiciones peruanas*." In his *Journalism and the Development of Spanish American Narrative*, 62–82. New York: Cambridge University Press, 1993.

———. *La novela modernista hispanoamericana*. Madrid: Gredos, 1987.

———. "Modernist Prose." In *The Twentieth Century*. Vol. 2 of *Cambridge History of Latin American Literature*, ed. Roberto González Echeverría and Enrique Pupo-Walker, 69–113. Cambridge: Cambridge University Press, 1966.

Goodrich, Diana Sorensen. *Facundo and the Construction of Argentine Culture*. Austin: University of Texas Press, 1992.

Halperin Donghi, Tulio, ed. *Sarmiento, Author of a Nation*. Berkeley: University of California Press, 1994.

Harter, Hugh A. *Gertrudis Gómez de Avellaneda*. Boston: Twayne, 1981.

Iglesias, Cristina, ed. *El ajuar de la patria: ensayos críticos sobre Juana Manuela Gorriti*. Buenos Aires: Feminaria, 1993.

Jitrik, Noé. *Ensayos y estudios de literatura argentina*. Buenos Aires: Galerna, 1970.

———. *Esteban Echeverría*. Buenos Aires: Centro Editor de América Latina, 1967.

———. *Muerte y resurrección del Facundo*. Buenos Aires: Centro Editor de América Latina, 1983.

León-Portilla, Miguel, ed. *The Broken Spears: The Aztec Account of the Conquest of Mexico*. Rev. ed. Trans. Angel María Garibay and Lysander Kemp. Boston: Beacon Press, 1992.

Lienhard, Martín. *La voz y su huella: escritura y conflicto étnico-social en América Latina 1492–1988*. 3rd rev. ed. Lima: Editorial Horizonte, 1992.

Luis, William. *Literary Bondage: Slavery in Cuban Narrative*. Austin: University of Texas Press, 1990.

Manzano, Juan Francisco. *The Autobiography of a Slave*. Critical introduction and modernized Spanish version by Ivan A. Schulman. Trans. Evelyn Picon Garfield. Detroit: Wayne State University Press, 1996.

Marting, Diane E., ed. *Spanish American Women Writers: A Bio-Biographical Source Book*. Westport, Conn.: Greenwood Press, 1990.

Masiello, Francine. *Between Civilization and Barbarism: Women, Nation, and Literary Culture in Modern Argentina*. Lincoln: University of Nebraska Press, 1992.

McGrady, Donald. *Jorge Isaacs.* Boston: Twayne, 1971.

Merrim, Stephanie, ed. *Feminist Perspectives on Sor Juana Inés de la Cruz.* Detroit: Wayne State University Press, 1991.

Mignolo, Walter D. *The Darker Side of the Renaissance: Literacy, Territoriality, and Colonization.* Ann Arbor: University of Michigan Press, 1995.

Núñez Cabeza de Vaca, Alvar. *Castaways: The Narrative of Alvar Núñez Cabeza de Vaca.* Trans. Frances M. López-Morillas. Ed. Enrique Pupo-Walker. Berkeley: University of California Press, 1993.

Pastor Bodmer, Beatriz. *The Armature of Conquest: Spanish Accounts of the Discovery of America, 1492–1589.* Trans. Lydia Longstreth Hunt. Stanford: Stanford University Press, 1992.

Paz, Octavio. *Sor Juana or, The Traps of Faith.* Trans. Margaret Sayers Peden. Cambridge: Belknap Press of Harvard University Press, 1988.

Pupo-Walker, Enrique. "The Brief Narrative in Spanish America: 1835–1915." In *Discovery to Modernism.* Vol. 1 of *Cambridge History of Latin American Literature,* ed. Roberto González Echevarría and Pupo-Walker, 490–535. Cambridge: Cambridge University Press, 1996.

Sabat de Rivers, Georgina. *En busca de Sor Juana.* Mexico City: Universidad Nacional Autónoma de México, 1998. (This scholar publishes in English as Sabat-Rivers.)

Sabat-Rivers, Georgina. "Sor Juana Inés de la Cruz." In *Latin American Writers,* ed. Carlos A. Solé and Maria Isabel Abreu, 1:85–105. New York: Scribner's, 1989.

Schele, Linda, and David Freidel. *A Forest of Kings: The Untold Story of the Ancient Maya.* New York: Morrow, 1990.

Sommer, Doris. *Foundational Fictions: The National Romances of Latin America.* Berkeley: University of California Press, 1991.

Spell, Jefferson Rea. *Bridging the Gap: Articles on Mexican Literature.* Mexico City: Editorial Libros de México, 1971.

Trigo, Benigno. *Subjects of Crisis: Race and Gender as Disease in Latin America.* Hanover, N.H.: Wesleyan University Press/University Press of New England, 2000.

Viñas, David. *Literatura argentina y realidad política: apogeo de la oligarquía.* Rev. ed. Buenos Aires: Siglo Veinte, 1975.

Williams, Raymond Leslie. *The Colombian Novel, 1844–1987.* Austin: University of Texas Press, 1991.

Zamora, Margarita. *Reading Columbus.* Berkeley: University of California Press, 1993.

_I_NDEX